Army Wives on the American Frontier

Army Wives on the American Frontier

LIVING BY THE BUGLES

Anne Bruner Eales

JOHNSON BOOKS
Boulder

Published in the United States by Johnson Books, a division of Johnson Publishing Company, 1880 South 57th Court, Boulder, Colorado 80301.

9 8 7 6 5 4 3 2 1

Cover design: Debra B. Topping
Cover photo: Major Anson Mills (seated on the left), his wife, Nannie (the woman on the right), their two children, and friends enjoy a picnic on the Gila River near Fort Thomas, Arizona, mid-1880s. (Courtesy National Archives and Records Administration, 111 SC 83730)

Library of Congress Cataloging-in-Publication Data
Eales, Anne Bruner.
    Army wives on the American frontier: Living by the bugles / by Anne Bruner Eales.
        p.   cm.
    Includes bibliographical references (p.   ) and index.
    ISBN 1-55566-166-1 (pbk.: alk. paper).
    1. Women pioneers—West (U.S.)—Biography. 2. Army spouses—West (U.S.)—Biography. 3. United States. Army—Military life—History—19th century. 4. Frontier and pioneer life—West (U.S.)
5. West (U.S.)—Biography. I. Title
F596.E25 1996   96-31900
978—dc20   CIP

Printed in the United States by
Johnson Printing
1880 South 57th Court
Boulder, Colorado 80301

 Printed on recycled paper with soy ink

Contents

*This book is dedicated to the
military wife,
whether the frontier her husband explores
is in the air, on the land, or at sea*

Preface

WHEN HE FOUND OUT that I was writing a book, my five-year-old grandson, William Stewart Eales, asked me if it was a "Once upon a time . . ." kind of story. After some thought, I told him that it was, because the army wives who lived the adventures described in this book come from another time and another way of thinking. In an age of equality and women's rights, it is difficult to relate to "ladies" who were raised in the restrictive chrysallis of nineteenth-century traditions and Victorian viewpoints. Most of the military wives included in this story were on the frontier between the end of the Civil War, in 1865, and the beginning of the Spanish-American War, in 1898. It was an era of western expansionism in a class-structured America that had, by modern standards, a twisted form of political correctness that amplified cultural and racial divisions.

Many officers' wives were from wealthy and influential families who had provided them superior educations, extremely comfortable surroundings, and the assurance that they were better than everybody else. Arrival on the frontier was not only a blow to their physical well-being, it also was an assault on their self-esteem. Military wives discovered that the harshness, danger, and new experiences of life in the West challenged eastern concepts of womanhood, civilization, and class in the interests of adaptation and survival. As with their husbands, a strong sense of duty kept these women living with newspaper tablecloths, toadstool carpets, and plaster ceilings that collapsed just as they were serving dinner to seventeen people.

The ladies whose ideas and lifestyles are described in this book were only a small segment of the women who lived in the trans-Mississippi West. The focus is on officers' wives because, more than any other segment of western culture, they had the education and opportunity to produce extensive letters, journals, and memoirs. Some of the women evoke sympathy and even admiration while others reflect an image of self-centeredness and superiority. Their viewpoints are of a life lived on officers' row; laundresses who scraped their knuckles on a scrubbing board would undoubtedly have written a much different story. Even those women who shared a similar perspective related different versions of the same event, as when Seventh Cavalry wives received word of George Armstrong Custer's defeat at the Little Big Horn.

This book is not a historian's view of life within the frontier army—the words and imagery are from almost fifty military wives who lived it. Three of the women are predominant: Katherine Garrett Gibson, Martha Dunham Summerhayes, and the most famous army wife of the period, Elizabeth Bacon Custer. The books by Summerhayes, Custer, and Katherine Gibson Fougera, based on her mother's memoirs, are eloquent, and readers who search them out will be more than rewarded for the effort.

These wives all had a unique opportunity to study the frontier because the military constantly relocated not only men and their families but also entire fortifications in response to the changing demographics of settlement in the West. One family moved nineteen times in twenty years. Camps became forts and territories became states, making it sometimes difficult to pinpoint the exact location of a specific wife. For example, Camp McDowell became Fort McDowell, and wives referred to Fort Robinson in both Wyoming Territory and the state of Nebraska. There was a Fort McKenny in Texas and a Fort McKinney in Wyoming. Oklahoma was known as Indian Territory during the 1870s; within a year of the land run on April 22, 1889, part of it became Oklahoma Territory. Army wives living in the area during these two decades referred to it by both names. In an effort to avoid adding to this confusion, I have chosen, as much as possible, to use the geographic locations wives listed in their writings.

Another bewildering element of the nineteenth-century army was the question of rank. Those officers who had won advanced brevet (temporary or honorary) rank during the Civil War found themselves demoted when peace arrived. Thus, Brevet Maj. Gen. George Armstrong Custer became Lieutenant Colonel Custer during his service with the Seventh Cavalry on the frontier. However, as a courtesy, people continued to call him "General." As an army bride, Frances Roe wrote to her family that the first lieutenant in her husband's company was called "Major," and the captain was referred to as "General." Lieutenants were simply "Mister." When Mrs. Roe, still used to civilian titles, called the general/captain Mr. Phillips, the officer's son giggled at her mistake, for which, Frances felt, the child should have been sent to bed at once.

Although resounding from over one hundred years ago, some of these stories of army life will seem familiar to today's military wife. The frontiers and the nature of warfare are different, but women of the twentieth century still wait for their men to return after months and even years away from home. While husbands fight in the desert sands or try to keep others from doing so in European mountains, army wives pursue careers, take children to have broken bones set, attend classes on how to keep the family car running, and learn about fuses, hot-water heaters, and self-propelled lawnmowers that aren't.

"Be all that you can be!" has been a popular recruiting slogan for the U.S. Army during recent years. The words suggest a potential for personal development within the military system, encouraging listeners to believe that life in the army offers opportunities for growth, self-fulfillment, and pride. While the slogan wasn't created for the military wife, it certainly applies. The challenges overcome, the experiences gained, and the memories shared truly have made military wives, whatever their service or century, "all that they could be."

Acknowledgments

ON THE SHELF of my bedroom closet are two large boxes, taking up space that I urgently need for sweaters and out-of-season shoes. The boxes are stuffed with reference notes, photographs, maps, drafts of manuscripts, and the final master's thesis they were all used to produce. If it were not for the people I am about to list, that is all this book would ever have been—an academic endeavor on a closet shelf.

Primary credit for its existence must go to Robert M. Kvasnicka, an esteemed colleague and valued friend. For three years I was fortunate enough to share an office at the National Archives with this noted authority on records relating to Native American history. His knowledge of the West and his expertise as an editor inspired me to ask him to review both the thesis and this book. He was kind enough to commend the thesis to Herman Viola of the Smithsonian Institution, who in turn recommended it to Felix Lowe, former director of the Smithsonian Press. If it were not for the assistance, support, and encouragement of these three talented and dynamic men, this book would still be in the box.

The man who figuratively opened the closet door was Stephen Topping, editorial director at Johnson Books. Although I have been a writer and editor for many years, I soon discovered that producing a book is a lot harder than coming up with a thousand words for a journal article. When I was most insecure and discouraged, Steve's interest, advice, and sense of humor over the telephone invariably made me change my mind about setting fire to the manuscript. During the final stages, Mira Perrizo, the managing editor at Johnson, set deadlines when I badly needed them and always used the greatest patience and tact when suggesting where the book could be made just a little bit better. Thanks to those wonderful new friends, I now have a file cabinet and bookcase full of items—in addition to the files on the closet shelf.

In gathering the research material for the text, I had extensive help from Jeffery Hartley of the National Archives library staff. His ability was matched by his good humor as he repeatedly searched data bases for obscure books and articles I requested.

Frederick Pernell and Mary Ilario at the Still Picture Branch of the National Archives were of great assistance to me in procuring many of the photographs that are used in this book. Peter J. Blodgett, of The Huntington Library, and family friend, James Noel, provided valuable help in obtaining photographs of various army wives. I am extremely grateful to Robert Barthelmess of Miles City, Montana, for permission to use photographs from the outstanding collection by his grandfather, Christian Barthelmess, and to John B. Riggs of the same city for his assistance in obtaining copies of the Barthelmess pictures.

Dr. Richard J. Sommers, Michael J. Winey, and Randy W. Hackenburg of the U.S. Army Military History Institute at Carlisle Barracks, Pennsylvania, generously shared their vast knowledge of the valuable textual, photographic, and cartographic holdings at MHI.

Cheryl McCain, an enthusiastic graduate student at the University of Oklahoma with an interest in history, provided much-appreciated help in reviewing series and locating photographs at the university's Western History Collections. Her efforts contributed especially to the chapter entitled "Cholera and Creosote."

Dr. Sharon Gibbs Thibodeau, my supervisor and director of the Archival Publications and Accessions Control Staff at the National Archives, has been extremely supportive during my preparation of both thesis and book.

Archivists, curators, historians, librarians, and reference specialists at several establishments responded promptly and extremely capably to my pleas for information. They include John H. Akers, Arizona Department of Library, Archives and Public Records; Rebecca Ballenger and Carie Weddle, Western History Collections, University of Oklahoma; Nathen E. Bender and Marjorie David, Merrill G. Burlingame Special Collections, The Libraries, Montana State University; Ann E. Billesbach, Nebraska State Historical Society; Rhonda Brown, State Historical Society of North Dakota; Paul West Chavoya and Ann Nelson, Division of Parks & Cultural Resources, Wyoming Department of Commerce; Cate M. Fitzmaurice, New Mexico Highlands

University; Park Ranger Steven R. Fullmer, Fort Laramie National Historic Site, Wyoming; David Kessler, Manuscripts Division, Bancroft Library, University of California, Berkeley; John Manguso, Fort Sam Houston Museum, Texas; Patricia Middleton, Beinecke Rare Book and Manuscript Library, Yale University; Chris Morgan, Fort Gibson Military Park, Oklahoma; Robert Munson, Fort Verde State Park, Arizona; David Preisler, University Libraries Archives and Manuscripts, Arizona State University; Claudia Rivers, Special Collections, University of Texas at El Paso; Judith A. Sibley, United States Military Academy Library, West Point, New York; Peter L. Steere, University Library Special Collections, University of Arizona; Park Ranger Mary Williams, Fort Davis National Historic Site, Texas; and Stefanie A. Wittenbach, General Libraries, University of Texas at Austin.

Drs. Jane Turner Censer, Peter Henriques, and Joseph Harsh of the History Department at George Mason University in Fairfax, Virginia, are mentors and friends who worked intensively with me on production of the thesis that formed the basis for this publication.

Good friends Sharon Brickman and Dee Dorminey read the text, offering insightful suggestions and additions. They even proved more proficient than my computer at correcting my unique way of spelling.

Finally, I have had the strongest support of all at home, in this as in every endeavor I undertake. My daughter, Laura, cooked and managed the house while I researched, read, and wrote. My oldest son, Stewart, had his phone bill increase from listening to passages read to him over the phone; my youngest son, Mark, carried books back and forth to the library. My husband, Lonnie, spent hours in the Pentagon library, days taking notes at Carlisle Barracks, and weeks preparing the map for this volume. He has listened to the entire text read through at least three times and made suggestions that have proven invaluable.

To Lonnie I wish to express the greatest thanks of all, for making me an army wife who knows what it means to live on the frontier, do without, and have my mind opened to new people and different ideas. Whether they have echoed across the parade ground at Yongsan Military Compound in Seoul, Korea, or reverberated through Drake-Edwards Kaserne at Frankfurt, Germany, we, too, have heard the bugles call.

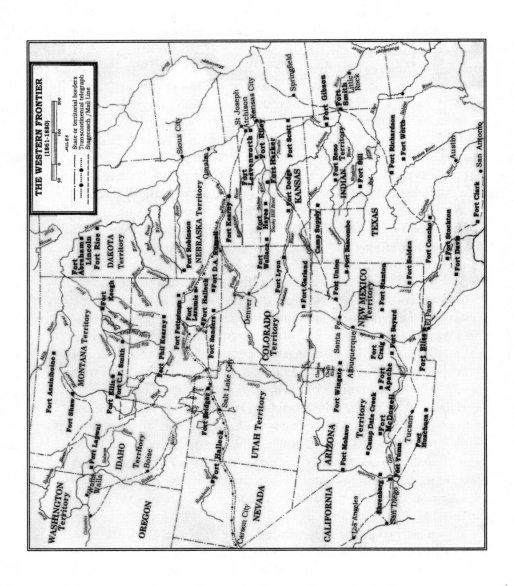

The Girl I Left Behind Me

FOR TWO DAYS the size of Alice Blackwood Baldwin's world had been approximately ten feet long by four feet wide. Wrapped in fur robes and blankets, with hay piled around her legs and feet to keep them warm, this army bride from Michigan had seen virtually nothing except the inside of the military ambulance transporting her and her husband, Lt. Frank Baldwin, to their new home at Fort Harker, Kansas. Her only opening to the outside world was a porthole-sized gap in the front canvas that allowed the enlisted man who was driving to see the mules; the back opening was cinched tight against a snowstorm. Even if both ends of the canvas had been completely open, however, Alice could not have seen very far. A white curtain of snow blurred the view ahead and rapidly concealed the trail behind. What was passed was lost; the future hidden by the swirling snow.

Army officers' wives such as Alice Baldwin found that more than the countryside blurred with each mile they traveled toward the American frontier. The demands of a lonely, harsh, and often dangerous existence in the West would gradually obscure many of the Victorian viewpoints and traditions learned in an increasingly remote civilization. Most army wives came from affluent backgrounds and were educated but, like the trail, their eastern lifestyles of comfort and gentility would also fade into the distance. Although they were not immediately aware of it, the frontier would change not only their lives but also their view of life.

In their movement west, the women left behind a stereotyped and confining Victorian gender role that had identified them as social appendages to their husbands. In the nation's early years, families had worked together, sharing common values and viewpoints, to make

1

farms or cottage industries successful. However, industrialization, immigration, and gradual urbanization in the nineteenth century had brought rapid changes, unsettling and transforming the pattern of American life. Children moved west or left the farm for factories in cities, where they were exposed to a jumble of new ideas, religions, cultures, and temptations. Fathers, too, left home, pursuing wealth and success in a marketplace they considered unfit for the "gentler sex." Uneasy about the implications of these changes for society, traditionalists decided that the family needed a "gyroscope," a moral stabilizer to keep husband and children from whirling out of control. If there was to be order in the home and, hence, in society, "ladies" would have to be that unchanging core in the midst of confusion. In their "cult of domesticity," people of the upper class were taught that wives existed to create for their husbands and children a secure and peaceful haven from the shifting world around them.

Contemporary literature championed the view that it was the "foremost responsibility of a new wife . . . to provide for her husband . . . the single spot of rest which a man has upon this earth for the cultivation of his noblest sensibilities."[1] Authors suggested that if a wife did not provide this supportive environment at home, her husband might begin to drink too much or pursue other "interests."

Wives and mothers were to "indoctrinate" their children with moral and religious precepts such as sobriety, self-control, and self-improvement through the "gentler emotions" while fathers instructed offspring in the "more important" qualities of logic and reasoning. To men of the period, this was only proper. Husbands considered their wives morally superior but also thought women were physically and probably mentally inferior. A husband loved his wife and cherished her central role as the moral mainspring of the family, expecting her to reciprocate by being properly submissive to his intellectual superiority and rationality. Although state governments increasingly gave women a voice in their own affairs during the nineteenth century, control of a woman's person and property often passed directly from her father to her husband. An army wife didn't even get to "own" her own name. She was called "Mrs. General Custer" or "Mrs. Colonel Grierson," reflecting her husband's status and authority rather than her own value as an individual.

Victorian ladies in the East "lived in a kind of earthly limbo . . . modesty and decorum were the order of the day."[2] They were trained to do good, be good, and look good, with the proper deportment, clothes, and coiffures. At the onset of puberty, the free-spirited Frances Elizabeth Willard complained, "This is my birthday and the date of my martyrdom. Mother insists that at last I must have my hair 'done up woman-fashion.' My 'back' hair is twisted up like a corkscrew; I carry eighteen hairpins; my head aches miserably; my feet are entangled in the skirt of my hateful new gown. I can never jump over a fence again so long as I live."[3]

Young women like Willard were taught that a wife's appearance and activities were a status symbol for her husband. Her pale complexion meant that she didn't have to work outside. Her restrictive corset and heavy petticoats proclaimed that her husband provided her with servants. (Bending to scrub floors or wash clothes was impossible in whalebone stays.) Dressed in a manner that projected an image of status and affluence, women were then expected to fulfill the duties of their station in a constant round of ritual visits or social calls on family members and friends. The ladies would visit and leave their cards at up to sixteen houses a day; one woman called it a "dabbling" lifestyle. Implicit in this obligatory social activity was the presence at home of servants to do the cooking and cleaning, seamstresses to do the sewing, and nurses (nannies) to care for the children. Eastern men of the upper class believed that for a man to uphold his place in society and proclaim his worth to the world, the demeanor of his Victorian wife had to be demure, deferential, and domestic.

This was especially true of military families in the East. Overlaid on the restrictive civilian culture was an array of army rituals and practices that had to be rigidly obeyed for social acceptance and professional advancement. A civilian wife was strictly segregated from her husband's career; in the military, however, where rank and seniority ruled, officers' wives could exercise a profound influence on their husbands' professional standing through the use of their connections and social skills. When Col. Benjamin Grierson was passed over for promotion to brigadier general in 1887, a visiting congressman told him that "it was the Washington, New York, and West Point social influence which promoted General (Wesley) Merritt . . .

and we can scarcely estimate the power of women and social influence in Washington."[4] In 1875, when Mrs. George Crook wanted her husband transferred from Arizona to a staff assignment in the East, she whispered her plea in the ear of President Ulysses S. Grant as the two strolled arm-in-arm during a White House reception. A similar exchange between Martha Dunham Summerhayes and President Grover Cleveland won her husband, John (Jack), promotion to captain and reassignment from the Eighth Infantry to the Army Quartermaster Corps. During the Civil War, Elizabeth (Libbie) Bacon Custer charmed senators, congressmen, and senior military officers into supporting the career of her husband, the "boy general," George Armstrong ("Autie") Custer. Gen. Philip Sheridan was so taken with her that he sent her a present from Appomattox Court House, Virginia, on April 10, 1865—the table Lt. Gen. Ulysses S. Grant had used to write the conditions of surrender for Gen. Robert E. Lee. Her charm and powerful connections not only furthered Custer's reputation in life; Libbie convinced friends to help her glorify him in death. The army leadership measured success for such women and their husbands by their political skill and social acceptability in an image-oriented, ceremonial environment.

If an officer, his wife, and their children exemplified the proper army (and Victorian) family, the potential for promotion for men who served on a headquarters staff was far greater than the opportunities available to men serving in "the other army," the line officers on the frontier. For this reason, officers in the East were especially sensitive and demanding about the behavior of their wives. Men trained to command others and accustomed to unquestioning obedience from their subordinates often applied that authoritarian approach to their family life. At least one excessively organized army colonel codified his wife's responsibilities through the following guidelines he established for her as a young bride:

1. You will see that meals are served on time.
2. You will not come to the table in a wrapper [robe].
3. You will smile at breakfast.
4. If possible, you will serve meat four times a week.

5. You will not move the furniture without my permission.
6. You will present the household accounts to me by the fifth of each month.
7. You will examine my uniforms every Tuesday and, if they need repair, you will take the necessary action.
8. You will do no work in the evenings. You will entertain me.
9. You will not touch my desk.
10. You will remember you are not in command of anything except the cook.[5]

Although nineteenth century women submissively accepted such dictates from their husbands, a very low Richter-scale rumbling of discontent did exist. Elizabeth Cady Stanton and Lucretia Mott spoke out at the Seneca Falls Convention for women's rights in 1848, but it was a minuscule movement. Women who wanted to challenge their limited lifestyle did it increasingly through literature. Two of the three best-selling novels of the nineteenth century were written by women: Harriet Beecher Stowe's *Uncle Tom's Cabin* and August Jane Evans Wilson's *St. Elmo*. Nathaniel Hawthorne called the lady authors "d—d scribbling women."[6] Writers such as E.D.E.N. Southworth, Mary Jane Holmes, and Ann Sophia Stephens popularized the strong, rebellious, and sensual heroine who manipulated men. Holmes sold a total of two million books, and Southworth was the most popular female author of the nineteenth century, suggesting that their expressly anti-Victorian characters were appealing to their readers.[7]

Traditionalist men and women published extensively in response to this perceived threat to society and the status quo. Their "politically correct" periodicals, journals, and guides reminded ladies of their proper place in the precepts of "true womanhood." Julia Ward Howe, author of the "Battle Hymn of the Republic," believed that a woman would refuse "to return to her chimney corner life of the fifties" after the Civil War, but the vast majority of eastern ladies still considered equality a step down.[8] One woman commented that giving women the vote would mean that "Bridget and Dinah [Irish servants and former slaves] will have it . . . a charming picture of equality for Southern ladies to contemplate."[9] Thousands of women had joined the work force during the war, but "a Louisianian was appalled to find an antebellum school friend clerking in a New Orleans department store in the eighties, for she had once been 'a lady.' "[10]

Such were the stereotypes army wives carried with them as they began their journeys west, packed along with their calling cards, crinolines, and the chamois-skin face masks used to protect their complexions against the sun.

The trip itself was a journey to self-discovery and individualism. Future army wife Katherine (Katie) Garrett began such a transition from eastern lady to western woman when she left her home in Washington, D.C., in the spring of 1874 to visit her sister, Margaret (Mollie) Garrett McIntosh. Despite family objections, Mollie had married Lt. Donald McIntosh, a part-Indian officer assigned to the Seventh Cavalry in Dakota Territory. The very reason the girl was going west to visit them involved a serious question of Victorian etiquette. Following the death of Katie's father, the ladies of the family had all donned culturally mandated heavy crepe mourning veils. When Katie developed a severe cough soon afterward, the doctor recommended that she discard the veil. Worried about how "such an unprecedented laxity of mourning conventions" might appear to family and friends, it was decided that Katie didn't have to wear the veil, as long as she was out of sight west of the Mississippi.[11]

The entire family went to the station to see the girl off. Katie's mother admonished her not to forget her cod liver oil and "gentle breeding," her sister Sally warned against strangers, and her former slave nurse advised her to watch out for Indians. As the train pulled out, she waved good-bye to them with her black-bordered handkerchief and stuffed her mourning veil away in a bag. The man across the aisle introduced himself as Monsieur Bois, a Frenchman from New Orleans, but Katie, mindful of her sister's warning, merely nodded. After a night in a lower berth, she awoke early the next morning and reached in the dimly lit carriage for her clothes. She went to the washroom and was in the process of brushing her teeth when the porter called through the door that the French gentleman said she had his pants. When Katie assured the porter that she certainly didn't have the trousers, he went away, only to return twice more to plead with her to give him the pants, which had $500 in the pocket. Throwing what she thought was her duster around her shoulders and storming out of the washroom, Katie faced the Frenchman—with the wide linen trousers draped around her. In the darkness, she had pulled the pants off the rail by mistake, and she was now terrified that the man would have her arrested for trying to steal the money. Katie apologized profusely, and, being a gentleman, Monsieur Bois was required to forgive a lady. He even invited her to breakfast. Katie, with Sally far away, daringly accepted the invitation. In her own words, she was now "launched upon the road of high adventure."[12]

Katie first thought of herself as an observer "in an alien world," but soon came to realize that she was becoming a part of that world, "groping into the unknown."[13] Instead of waiting to be called to dinner by a servant, she learned to elbow her way to the food table when the train stopped for meals at an eating shack. To keep warm when sleet began to fall, the girl accepted a drink out of a flask belonging to the man sharing her seat. Lacking a cup, she had hesitated, but he had insisted, saying, "Go right ahead, sister. I ain't afeared to drink after you."[14] Never having imbibed anything stronger than blackberry cordial as medicine, she coughed, sneezed, and ended up tipsy from the experience. Katie was exposed to gambling as the passengers wagered on everything, especially their arrival time at the next station, and her modesty was probably challenged when men urinated out the train windows, as they often did on western trips. As her train careened across the screeching, swaying Mississippi River bridge, Katie may well have considered the fearful yet exciting passage as symbolic of the changes in her life since leaving Washington only a few days earlier.

The train trip had been a revelation to Katie as she traveled westward, alone but in relative comfort and security. In sharp contrast, Mollie's solitary journey from Fort Abraham Lincoln to meet her sister's train at Columbia, Dakota Territory, required her to risk the ever-present dangers posed by Indians, outlaws, and inclement weather. In the East, Mollie's nerves had gone "jittery at a discord struck on the piano or guitar."[15] In the West, Mollie carried a gun, and Katie watched in awe as her older sister negotiated with the prostitutes at a bar called "One Eye Jim's" to get the girls sandwiches and coffee. When a woman in a low-cut green gown left to arrange for the food, Katie commented, "This One Eye Jim's wife seems to be kindly disposed." Mollie responded scornfully, "She's nobody's wife—just one of—of those women." "But," Katie commented naively, "she's not wearing scarlet."[16]

Later, stopping at a ranch for the night, the wealthy sisters shared a bed that had a missing leg and was propped up with a pile of dirty and musty old newspapers. When dawn came, the formerly fastidious Mollie refused to wash in the frigid morning air. While Katie determinedly broke the ice on the water in the pitcher, she thought about the great changes in her sister but may not have realized the beginning of her own metamorphosis.

As Katie had discovered, it didn't take long in the new environment for western reality to overwhelm eastern norms. In the performance-oriented West, a woman's talents rather than the image she projected received respect and won acceptance in what was a rough and hazard-filled man's world. Experiences gained during long separations at isolated posts required army wives to cultivate ingenuity and self-reliance, redefining even some of the officers' expectations of the proper attitudes and actions for women. Military men assigned to duty on the frontier had to focus primarily on the fulfillment of their mission, and, after that, on their family's survival in a hostile environment. Any other "givens" would be tested in a crucible of dust and danger.

Army wives discovered that western culture valued women and promoted equality far more than that of the East. The Homestead Act of 1862 allowed single women as well as men the right to claim 160 acres of federal land. Many territorial and state land-grant colleges in the West admitted women from the day they opened or began to do so soon after. Initially the women in Missouri had to march to class in two lines protected by chaperones, and female students at the State Agricultural College of Kansas were required to study "ladies' courses," such as "Household Management and Economy" and "The Management of Children and Their Private Instruction." By 1880, however, course offerings had expanded, and women represented one-third of all college students in the United States, many of them at western universities.[17]

Once women were educated the West presented them unique equality in employment. In 1869, Wyoming Territory passed a law declaring that "in the employment of teachers no discrimination shall be made in the question of pay on account of sex when the persons are equally qualified." California passed a similar law in 1872.[18] The Census of 1890 showed that the West had 4 percent of the country's women, but had 17 percent of the nation's actresses, 11 percent of its female writers and scientists, 14 percent of the lady lawyers, 10 percent of its female journalists, and 5 percent of its women professors.[19]

In western areas women could also vote, become judges, serve on juries, and even be elected to public office. In 1861 Kansas became the first state to allow women to vote in a local election for public officials. Sixteen years later, the same state had the first woman mayor in the United States when Mrs. Susanna Medora Salter was chosen in Argonia, Kansas. The following year, 1878, Oskaloosa, Kansas, not only elected Mary Lowman mayor but chose women to fill all five town council seats as well.[20] Although the Nineteenth Amendment to the Constitution gave women the right to vote in 1920, all but four western states had already granted them that privilege: Wyoming, 1869; Colorado, 1893; Utah and Idaho, 1896; Washington, 1910; California, 1911; Oregon, Kansas, and Arizona, 1912; Nevada and Montana, 1914; and Oklahoma and South Dakota, 1918. New York was the only eastern state that allowed women to vote before the constitutional amendment.[21]

In 1893, historian Frederick Jackson Turner, who believed that the frontier had been continually expanding since the settlement of America, wrote, "Each frontier did indeed furnish a new field of opportunity, a gate of escape from the bondage of the past . . . and scorn of older society, impatient of its restraints and its ideas."[22] Although Turner's thesis was undoubtedly male-oriented, women who moved west found potential for development, not least of all their own. While the frontier did not always provide as many economic opportunities for women as it did for men, the West afforded a more flexible atmosphere and an expanded view of women's role in society and their place in the home.

A French author, Charles Varigny, who visited the frontier in the 1890s wrote that the West released a woman from the chains of civilization but that it was her own talent that won her equality.[23] Many army wives met the opportunity with flexibility and independence.

Being young, they were usually more openminded about new ideas and experiences; several were even eager for adventure. Ada Adams Vogdes was "so full of life, it just burst out all the time in all directions."[24] Before marriage to Autie Custer, Libbie Bacon had scorned a "humdrum life," longing for more than "domestic cares" and "kitchen drudgery."[25] Annie Roberts Yates had been raised in the jungles of South America, where her father was an engineer with the railroad. She spoke several languages and proved her willingness to take risks when she defied society and married her husband, George, a divorced man. Helen Brace taught elocution at Vassar College and had studied acting in Paris before marrying an army doctor, Col. James Kimball. She counted among her friends Mark Twain and Henry James. Teachers at Jessie Benton Frémont's school said that although she was "extremely intelligent, (she) lacks the docility of a model student . . . (and) has the objectionable manner of seeming to take our orders and assignments under consideration, to be accepted or disregarded by some standard of her own."[26] In what would have been the ultimate condemnation in eastern society, an army wife named Mrs. Brice was described as having "almost too much energy and smartness to appear like a perfect lady."[27]

Living at isolated posts where each garrison established its own guidelines for proper behavior and acceptance gave women a freedom of thought and action they could never have experienced in the more regimented East. Visiting Fort Sill, Indian Territory (Oklahoma), Emily V. Mason wrote to her sister, Katherine Mason Rowland, that a "woman who *belongs to the service*" was considered unable to do wrong.[28] As they left on patrol, husbands frequently advised their wives to "do the best you can" and, through talent, perseverance, and ingenuity, the wives' best was usually more than good enough. Margaret Carrington said that the eastern "triplet" of "I never could, I never would, and I never will" became obsolete in the West."[29]

In the East men were traditionally head of the house; in the West officers' wives increasingly filled that role de facto as husbands spent months at a time away from home, campaigning in the Indian wars. While the men were gone, wives collected their pay, made vital family decisions that could not wait, and occasionally even carried out certain quasi-official military functions in their husbands' absences. When Lt. William Barton Lane left Fort Fillmore, New Mexico, to go on an Indian scout he left his wife, Lydia Spencer Lane, in command of the sergeant and ten men who remained at the post. She thus had control of the public funds, and the sergeant reported to her each day.[30]

Army wives from affluent families had lived in large, lavishly furnished houses in the East, but on the frontier they worked to make homes out of dugouts, tents, or even a chicken coop. At first much of their furniture was constructed from packing boxes, barrels, and army blankets. Wives who had been unwilling to remove a dead mouse from a trap in the East encountered rattlesnakes on their mantels, tarantulas in their kitchens, and bats hanging from the blankets on their beds. Women went hungry as food shipments were delayed in Indian attacks; they were buried in avalanches in Montana and trapped in quicksand in Nebraska. Army wives gave birth in the back of unsprung wagons with only a stranger to help them and then protected those children with a bullwhip or a pistol. They brained wolves with skillets and shot buffalo while riding sidesaddle on a galloping horse.

Some women were even prepared to kill themselves and their children rather than be taken alive by Indians. Moving from Camp Apache to Camp McDowell, Arizona, in 1875, Lt. Jack Summerhayes, his wife Martha, and an escort of six men approached a possible Indian attack at Sanford's Pass. Martha wrote that she obediently lay down on the bottom of the army wagon with her 3-month-old son in her arms. "I took my Derringer out of the holster and cocked it. I looked at my little boy lying there helpless beside me . . . and wondered if I could follow out the instructions I had received: for Jack had said . . . You have your Derringer. . . . Don't let them get either of you alive."[31]

Faced with these living conditions and experiences, army wives gradually discovered that they had the courage and ability it took to survive in the West. A modern frontier and women's historian, the late Sandra Myers, believed that "the more independent and less restrained lives (the women) lived in the West made (them) more aware of their own assets and abilities and made them more willing to step outside the 'woman's place.'"[32] Many army wives on the frontier not only expanded their own sense of self-worth but also were able to re-examine their prejudices about the value and roles of others. Wives of officers and enlisted men, laundresses, prostitutes, Indians, Mexicans, and female servants, who were usually foreign or black, often constituted a small community of isolated women who interacted in ways that would not have been acceptable in the stratified East. Views of Indians gained from authors such as James Fennimore Cooper were tested as the women watched, met, and sometimes entertained Native Americans in their frontier homes. Wives whose husbands served as officers with the new black regiments established after the Civil War found themselves living and traveling with African Americans. Many of the women had never even spoken to a black man before.

Even basic moral values were altered by the western experience. Ada Vogdes's traditional sense of modesty had apparently become a victim of her daily contact with Indians. When she served lunch to the scantily clad Sioux chief Red Cloud at Fort Fetterman, Wyoming, in 1870, Ada wrote, "I thought . . . how strange it would seem to an Eastern person . . . to see me sit with this naked man, but it does not seem strange to me at all now."[33] As army wives were forced to prove "their own resilience in the face of harsh demands imposed on them by the frontier environment," historian Glenda Riley believes that "(there was) an erosion of societal prescriptions" of women's proper place or sphere.[34] In a snowstorm much like the one experienced by Alice Baldwin, one army wife-to-be and her mother donned cavalry trousers to ride mules through the storm. Women in trousers! In the East, men wore the pants in the family—in the frontier army, they were shared. As military wives adapted to their new life in the West and worked alongside men at "inappropriate" tasks, the prim and proper Victorian lady with her limited horizon gradually became "the girl I left behind me."

If You Have Courage, Stay

MILITARY LEADERS MAY have had an idealistic, chauvinistic view of the army wife, but many women had an equally unrealistic image of life as an army dependent. Few were prepared for the adjustments required by reassignment from a manicured eastern post such as West Point, New York, to a remote and primitive fort on the American frontier. Teresa Griffin Viele described West Point as "the *coleur de rose* of army life . . . bait for the unsophisticated."[1] Frances Anne (Fannie) Mullen was one who bit, acknowledging that her only experience with the military before marriage to Lt. Orsemus Boyd was "seeing, entirely at its best, beautiful West Point, which I considered a fair type of every army post; so when I married . . . I thought that however far we might travel such a home would always be found at our journey's end."[2]

Another young woman who exchanged dreams for dirt was Martha (Mattie) Dunham, from a wealthy family in Nantucket. A year in Europe as the guest of the family of a German army general left her "infatuated with uniforms" and the "stimulation" of military life. The general's wife, a veteran with fifty years of experience as a military wife, warned her that such a life was "glittering misery," but Mattie returned to the United States determined "to join the army" through marriage.[3] The glamorous round of teas, receptions, and embassy balls in Europe, however, left the new wife of Lt. Jack Summerhayes unprepared for what Mattie later acknowledged as the "unknown dangers in a far country."[4]

Military officers who had served in the West were well aware of the liabilities of life there. When a young lieutenant proposed to Capt. Randolph Marcy's daughter, the captain objected and described to her with blunt accuracy the life she could expect. "His pay would hardly give you a miserable living, with a house that a man in civilized society would actually be ashamed to keep a horse in."[5] The graphic descrip-tion was accurate but wasted, just as the German army wife's had been. Image won over substance; the couple married anyway.

In an April 1865 letter to her father, Judge Daniel Bacon, Libbie Custer delighted in reminding him how he had tried to frighten her out of marrying Autie Custer by telling her the life was "no better than gipsying [sic] . . . in a covered wagon on the trail." She claimed, "I think it is grand fun."[6] However, after a few years on the frontier, Libbie acknowledged that becoming an army wife had meant "a sud-den plunge into a life of vicissitude [sic] and danger."[7] Autie Custer recognized his wife's life of devotion and deprivation, describing her as "my dear little army crow—following me around everywhere."[8]

It was Libbie's turn to offer practical advice when Lt. Frank Gib-son offered, at a dance under a western moon, to make Katie Garrett an army bride. The girl wrote that thirty-two-year-old Libbie "did not paint army life in the gay colors of an artist's brush. On the con-trary, she spoke seriously and bared every phase of it, from the ne-cessity sometimes of associating with uncongenial people, down to living in drab stockade posts. . . . She stressed the insufficient pay . . . pointed out the months of loneliness . . . the lack of comforts, even the prospect of going hungry at times; she spoke of dangers . . . yet nothing mattered if you loved your man." Libbie advised Katie, "If you have courage, stay. If not, go."[9] Katie was brave enough for life on the frontier but was somewhat afraid of her family's reaction to the fast engagement and marriage. "Who cares?" retorted her sister Mollie defiantly. "They have led shallow, sheltered lives . . . you can't expect them to understand."[10]

While some women did return east and others would not travel to the frontier in the first place, most army wives took the advice of Maj. Gen. William T. Sherman to move west with their husbands. He predicted that garrison life would be pleasant, mistakenly assuring the women that they "need have no fears about the hostile Indi-ans."[11] The wives were not aware that when someone commented to Sherman that the West "was a fine country and all that it needed was plenty of water and good society," the frontier veteran replied, "That is all hell needs."[12] When Fanny Corbusier's husband was ordered west, she wrote about Arizona: "The Almighty made it last and didn't have much material left."[13] Sherman agreed, saying, "We had one war with Mexico to take Arizona, and we should have another to make her take it back."[14] The U.S. government officially declared that "New Mexico can boast of nothing on a very extensive scale; unless it be . . . worthlessness."[15] One correspondent to the *Army and Navy Journal* in 1869 described the area he was assigned to as "on the Grand River Coloroso, about 800 miles from its junction with the Styx and just 400 miles from a charming little village called Hades, rejoicing in a deliciously warm climate."[16]

Western life, even the trials of getting there, required a major realignment of priorities for women accustomed to comfortable surroundings and servants. An excellent example would have been Mary Custis Lee. Before her husband, Robert E. Lee, earned a place in history during the Civil War, he served as a colonel with a cavalry regiment in the dust and heat of Texas. Lee wrote his daughter, Agnes, about the Comanches, wolves, rattlesnakes, and a temperature of 112 degrees.[17] In fact, the candles in his tent melted in the heat. Although ill health had prevented Mrs. Lee from accompanying her husband to the West, one can easily imagine the jarring adaptation in lifestyle that would have been required had she left the lavish Lee-Custis Mansion in Arlington, Virginia, for an army tent or log hut on the Texas frontier.

The demands of frontier service sometimes preempted romance. Orsemus Boyd received his orders to San Francisco and on to Camp Halleck, Nevada, in October 1867, two days after his marriage in New York City to 19-year-old Fannie. The following January she traveled alone to join him, going by steamer to Panama, then across the humid, disease-infested isthmus by train, and on to San Francisco by ship. Friends there warned her not to try to cross the Sierra Nevadas in winter, but Fannie continued, braving blizzards, boredom, and ankle-deep mud. She spent five days and nights sitting upright on a stage so crowded that if one passenger shifted, others were forced to realign at the same time. Sleep was fleeting, and meals were even scarcer. Eating at irregular hours, she consumed green biscuits and meats "which disguised their natural flavors so completely" that Fannie wondered what animal of the prairie she was eating.[18] She had a short respite when she met her husband, but it took them four more days to cover the last 100 miles to Camp Halleck by ambulance and army wagon. The first night Fannie slept in the ambulance, on a seat whose back let down to form a shaky and cold bed; the second evening she was given a rough plank bunk in the corner of an 18-foot-square hut occupied by ten men. They arranged curtains around the bunk to give her some privacy. The final night of the trip, she had the only bed in a cabin she shared with fifteen men, who slept in rows, and six dogs, who didn't. On the last day of her weeks' long journey, it took the Boyds twelve hours to go eighteen miles through drifting snow in an open, springless wagon. Amazingly, Fannie described that day as "the first on which I felt discouraged . . . in tears (I) was lifted out and carried into . . . my home for the next year."[19] The trip cost $500, but the experience had been even more expensive. Fannie acknowledged at almost the end of the journey that she "no longer felt particularly young." Having celebrated her twentieth birthday on the road, the girl was still chagrined to hear a bystander ask her husband, "How did the old woman stand the trip?"[20]

Those cavalry wives who moved west with a military column began their maturing process the very first morning of the journey, when the bugler sounded reveille at 4:00 A.M. The women, who had clocks readily available in the East, soon learned that reveille and taps defined their military day. As they lived literally within the sound of bugles, the wives began to tell time by the trumpeter's clock. Emily Mason, daughter of Indian commissioner John Thomson Mason, wrote to her sister from Fort Gibson, "You see we go by garrison time—instead of naming the hours . . . it is 'breakfast call,' 'guard mount' . . . 'recall' . . . which have become to us as familiar as 9 o'clock—2 o'clock—etc."[21] Helen Kimball began "to tell time by guns and bugles" at Fort Clark, Texas. She decided that "to one who has lived by bugle calls, their notes, subtle and gripping, stir the memory for all time."[22] Wives found when they returned east that it was a major adjustment to live again governed by actual timepieces.

After breakfast at 5:00, the bugler played "boots and saddles," the signal to march, at 5:30. The trek continued for fifty minutes with a ten-minute rest every hour. There was a break for lunch at noon, the column camped before dinner call was sounded at 5:00 P.M., and taps was blown at 9:00. In extremely hot weather, reveille was sounded as early as 2:00 A.M., "boots and saddles" at 4:00, and the march ended at noon before the worst heat of the day. For affluent women used to late nights and morning chocolate in bed, reveille was a rude awakening.

When the bugle sounded the order to move, wives climbed into a variety of vehicles. One officer took his family west in a carriage, while another used a sled for a short time. However, the women usually rode in army ambulances or Dougherty wagons, which had two seats facing each other and a seat outside for the driver. As Fannie Boyd had discovered, the inside seats would let down into uncomfortable beds. The canvas sides and back of the ambulance could be rolled up; a curtain behind the driver's seat allowed the women some privacy. An officer could purchase a condemned ambulance at Fort Leavenworth, Kansas, and redesign the interior space to fit his family's special needs. Arrangements in Eveline Alexander's wagon, for example, included "a high rocking chair which was fastened by cleats to the bottom of the ambulance . . . [and] in front was my box of books. . . . Hanging from the top of the ambulance were 2 leather pockets, one of them containing my revolver, the other a field glass; a looking glass; my sewing basket; and a lantern also swayed to and fro."[23] For his wife, Elizabeth, Maj. Andrew Burt raised the sides and top of her ambulance so it was tall enough to stand in. He built a small door in the rear and a window in the front that controlled the circulation of air. For cold-weather travel, Burt installed a camp kettle turned upside down and embedded in mortar that served as a stove. A pipe carried the smoke out through a zinc-lined opening in the top of the canvas. After the birth of their child, the Burts added a champagne basket lined with cotton that served as a baby bed. It was suspended from the ceiling and made a natural cradle as it swung with the motion of the moving ambulance. In 1866, on a move from Jefferson Barracks to Fort Bridger, Utah, Elizabeth shared these close accommodations with her baby son; her youngest sister, Kate; Maggie, a former slave who was the family cook; their driver, Mason; and Betty, the family dog.

Four mules normally pulled each ambulance, but it took six to move the massive blue, unsprung army wagons that carried belongings, laundresses, and sometimes the wives and children of enlisted personnel. The teamsters driving the mules swore fluently, even in the presence of ladies—a new experience that Mattie Summerhayes said made shivers run up and down her spine.[24] One of these wagons was assigned to each company to carry tents, camp outfits, trunks, and all of the officers' household goods—a total of four thousand pounds.[25] This meant that the three officers (a captain and two lieutenants) had to be extremely selective in what they chose to carry on a move. Barrels held kitchen utensils packed in hay; treasured books, pictures, and china nestled in large chests; bedding and rugs were rolled and wrapped in waterproof material; and trunks held family clothing not needed on the trip. When the Seventh Cavalry was ordered to Dakota Territory, one wife packed her children's clothing in a trunk with a spring lock. When the lid slammed shut, accidentally locking the key inside, parts of various garments remained outside. As it was against regulations for the trunk to travel that way, a soldier with a hatchet hacked off the protruding sleeves and pant legs. When they got to Dakota, where clothing was scarce, the children had to wear the outfits that way. The mother was amazed that it created something of a fashion trend for local families. Another military wife might have been delighted to follow the style. All of her family's trunks had been soaked when the column crossed the Pecos River. Unaware of the accident, the mother and four daughters wrinkled their noses with disgust when they unpacked at their destination and found all of their clothing mildewed.

Ambulances and wagons carrying families, equipment, supplies, and personal belongings were driven behind the troops, which meant that the mules traveled at a walk. The entire column, which might be two miles long, either churned through mud or raised dust that smothered everything. Any images of romance and adventure remaining for the women soon vanished in dirt from what Maria Brace Kimball described as "the endless, white, dusty road (that) wound over the barren prairie from somewhere to nowhere."[26] Maria was an expert on travel. She was on her way from her honeymoon at the Acropolis in Greece to Fort Clark, Texas. Mary Maguire Carr agreed with Kimball's assessment, stating, "I had at last reached the plains and understood what the comprehensive word meant. It was like the sea. As far as the eye could reach, vast stretches of vacant land, blank and nothing in sight."[27]

When someone asked Libbie Custer what one thing she would like to have on a march, Libbie replied, "A tree."[28] An eighty-mile stretch near Fort Abraham Lincoln, North Dakota, didn't have a single one. The Burts traveled seven weeks to Fort Bridger through country totally destitute of trees. The lack of shade meant that the white wagon covers were blinding in the summer sun, and one officer's wife actually lost her sight for several days. Sunburn was another problem. Nineteenth-century women cultivated white skin much as modern women pursue a tan. When army wives first went west, they took chamois-skin masks to wear to protect their highly valued, camellia-like complexions. Heat and perspiration, however, soon caused the women to discard the masks and forget about their delicate eastern pallor. Sunburn blistered Frances Roe so badly that her face peeled until she had white strips between the tanned areas. Roe decided she resembled a zebra or an Indian with warpaint. Fannie Boyd spread glycerine on her skin as a form of suntan lotion, but the flies it drew were almost as bad as the burn. Alice Grierson wrote about "swarms of flies, bent on making a living."[29]

Face masks were not the only "Victorian" item to be abandoned. In the East a well-dressed woman put on up to thirty-seven pounds of clothing in the morning, including her large, fashionable hoop skirt.[30] In the West, hoops took up too much room in the wagons, were hard to control in the high winds on the plains, and could be dangerous around campfires. Eveline Martin Alexander, niece of the governor of New York and daughter to a railroad, shipping, and textile heiress, gave up wearing one on a two-month march to Fort Union, New Mexico, in 1866. When the column stopped to rest at Fort Bascom, New Mexico, another officer's wife offered to lend Alexander a hoop for her formal calls at the garrison. Eveline had been so long without one that she felt awkward and thought that "it looked very curious . . . to see a woman again with ample skirts."[31] For a time it had been so hot while traveling that Alexander had stopped wearing dresses entirely, staying inside with only a light robe or wrapper on, despite the presence of the enlisted man driving. Helen Fuller Davis, the wife

of a lieutenant in the Tenth Cavalry, wrote that she longed to wear knickers on the trail.[32]

The gusts of wind that swirled skirts also destroyed fancy hairdos; these were soon replaced by braids, hairnets, combs, or ribbons. And women who had to walk as their wagons were "roped" down gorges or hauled up steep inclines quickly substituted comfortable boots for soft-soled dress shoes. Army wives discovered on the trail west that the cherished clothes and adornments that had defined genteel female status in the East became burdens to be loaded and unloaded, cleaned and mended, and protected, often to no avail, from western elements.

As the women's physical environment changed, their mental outlook was also transformed. It didn't take long for boredom and the long, tedious trips to alter any misconceptions remaining about the military lifestyle. There was little that was glamorous about the two months it took the Burts to make a four-hundred-mile journey from Fort Sanders to Fort C. F. Smith, Montana, or the weeks Alice and Frank Baldwin spent on a move from Fort Harker, Kansas, to Fort Union, New Mexico.[33] Some units of the Eighth Cavalry traveled four months when relocating from New Mexico to Texas in 1875. The only exciting element of the trip may have been the nine babies that were born enroute, with their mothers resuming the march the morning after giving birth.[34]

As life on the trail became routine, families searched for ways to relieve the boredom. The Custers liked to hunt, Eveline Alexander and Alice Baldwin read books, and several wives rode horseback, a few courageous enough to try it astride. When one lady did so, she got to ride at the head of the column; she was the only woman with the cavalry detachment. When wives chose to walk from one halt to the next, they always had to be in front of the command, probably as a safety precaution. Frances Grummond understood why after she slipped out of her ambulance, perhaps to relieve herself, and the driver continued without her. Frances chased the ambulance for over a mile, wearing only cloth slippers and driven by the fear she would be captured by Indians. She got cactus needles in her feet and riding in the wagon suddenly was more attractive as she spent the next two days pulling them out. Lt. John Gibbon decided to give his wife, Fannie, driving lessons and wrote to her family in Baltimore that by the time they got to Fort C. F. Smith she was going to be very adept at handling a four-in-hand team. The family of Dr. R. H. McKay, an army surgeon, found a bear cub in the tree above their campsite. They made a bed for him in the ambulance with the family and chained him to it while moving during the day. As soon as they stopped for the evening, they released him. The cub would roam the camp, entertaining everyone and stealing whatever he could get his paws on.

Sometimes the boredom was relieved not by fun or excitement but by unpleasant or even dangerous happenings. A drunken driver almost tipped over Alice Baldwin's wagon while crossing a river, and, when Lydia Lane was traveling without her husband, the individual assigned to drive her ambulance climbed into it in the middle of the night, perhaps simply to get out of the rain. The girl from Carlisle, Pennsylvania, was so terrified that she lay holding a butcher knife, prepared to kill the man if he tried to attack her. Lane also described how an army hunter was captured by Indians, who stripped him. The naked man escaped and arrived back at camp where he tried, apparently unsuccessfully, to stay out of her sight until nightfall. The wives dreaded attack by Indians, but assaults more often came from nature. Grasshoppers invaded one campsite; the insects filled the air, ate holes in clothes and wagon covers, and even bit people as they slept. Lightning set prairie fires, and winds tore down tents and carried away belongings. Some military families lost everything. A correspondent from Camp Supply, Indian Territory, informed the *Army and Navy Journal* in 1869, "There is more wind here than in the State of Illinois about election time."[35] Josephine Buell, wife of Tenth Cavalry Assistant Surgeon James W. Buell, wrote to her mother in February 1877 that "it rained pitchforks and little Indians last night. Why, you people living in a civilized country don't know anything about a rain, a real regular old Texas rain . . . how the wind did blow, and it seemed to me that the tent would be torn to pieces."[36] Lydia Lane described how just such a storm gathered up a tent in which a small child was sleeping on a cot. Although the baby was rescued, tent and bed went sailing away.[37]

Women found that rainstorms in the Southwest often came suddenly, turning a pleasant stream into a threatening torrent. When

Eveline Alexander was on her way to join her husband at Fort Smith, Arkansas, in 1866, she traveled on a steamboat down the Mississippi River. The river was flooded so badly that she couldn't see dry land and was informed that it was from five to forty miles away.[38] Swollen by melting snow in the spring, the Rio Grande would suddenly expand to six feet deep and six hundred yards wide. One officer's wife camped beside a rising river decided that the site would soon be underwater and climbed into the ambulance to cross to higher ground. The current, however, was already too strong for the crossing. Her husband stood on shore and watched as his wife, child, driver, wagon, and mules were carried away to their deaths downstream. Had they been rescued, the victims would have been treated with the usual lifesaving method of the time—they would have been hung suspended by their feet until the water poured out of their mouths.

Frozen water caused different problems as wives were snowbound far from civilization. When an army surgeon named Brown and his wife were traveling in a snowstorm from Fort Sill, Oklahoma Territory, to Fort Arbuckle, the command had to stop for Mrs. Brown to give birth. The men worked hard to gather wood and build a fire in order to keep her as warm and dry as possible. In the otherwise successful effort, some of them got frostbite and eventually had to have fingers and toes amputated.

In its move to Dakota Territory in 1873, the Seventh Cavalry was caught near Yankton in April by a late blizzard. The troops felt the cold keenly because they had been stationed in the much warmer climate at Memphis, Tennessee, before being ordered north. Although Autie Custer was quite ill, he had the men quartered in the town's homes, barns, and sheds while the officers' wives moved into the hotel. Custer and Libbie, with just a few others, remained at the campsite about a mile from Yankton. For thirty-six hours they were isolated by the blizzard. While caring for her sick husband, Libbie struggled to provide for half a dozen soldiers who straggled in from the storm, keep everyone from freezing to death, and obtain enough food for all to survive. Because she had no liquor to warm the troops, she gave them the alcohol normally used in the little spirit lamps, a form of camp stove, and wrapped the men in carpets intended for her quarters. Only after the snow ended and rescuers arrived did Libbie break down. Custer comforted her but was embarrassed lest anyone know she had "lost [her] pluck" when the danger was past.[40] Returning west from taking her sons to school in the East, Ellen McGowan Biddle was also snowbound. However, there was no danger that she, her daughter, or the baby's nurse would starve to death during the three days they were isolated on board the west-bound train. Ellen's mother had packed delicacies such as pâté de fois gras, chicken, deviled ham, and tea to make the trip easier for her daughter who was considered very delicate. (Ellen did faint a lot—when she wasn't riding, jumping fences, fox hunting, or attending horseraces.)

Western weather could strike unexpectedly, but another element of nature—snakes—provided an even more detestable form of surprise while camping. One woman awakened to find a king snake wrapped around her neck, strangling her in its coils. She had to lie absolutely still while Col. Abner Doubleday, later of baseball legend, shot the reptile. On a move to Fort Rice, Dakota Territory, Libbie Custer said that she saw more rattlesnakes on the trail than she had seen in five years in Texas and Kansas. Elizabeth Burt depended on the frontier belief that rattlesnakes would not crawl across buffalo hair ropes, but Libbie was "loath" to lie down and sleep until the site for her tent had been cleared and the ground beaten to drive away the snakes. One night the soldiers doing so killed forty of them. Libbie said Custer "used to indulge this little prejudice of mine against making my head a reproduction of Medusa's."[41]

Every evening when the column stopped, details of four to five enlisted men went to work clearing the campsite, unloading the wagons, setting up the tents, and gathering wood and water. During the first few days of a march there was often much confusion, but as the men developed skill, it became a point of regimental pride to see which unit could make or break camp the fastest. The women thought the soldiers enjoyed the tasks and one described camp life this way: "The officers are singing and whistling and we can often hear from the distance the boisterous laughter of the men. And the wives! There is an expression of happy content on the face of each one. We know, if the world does not, that the part we are to take on this trip is most important. We will see that the tents are made comfortable and cheerful at every camp, that the little dinner after the weary march, the early breakfast, and the cold luncheon are each and all as dainty as camp cooking will permit."[42] An enlisted man unwittingly countered, "Here (on the march) we meet the greatest bothers that ever appeared in a Cavalry camp—women! Two daughters and a son of [Col. S. D. Sturgis, Commander of the Seventh Cavalry] have been riding in an ambulance all day. So they are tired and must have a wall tent put up for their special benefit. A detail is made to do this work. . . . This compels details to delay the erection of their own shelters, cooking their suppers and giving the proper attention to their horses. . . . The men do the work and the officers get the thanks."[43]

Willing or not, the men were careful to make sure the ground for the tent sites was level and free of stones. The tents they erected for the officers' wives were usually some arrangement of a fourteen-foot by sixteen-foot hospital tent or two ten-foot by twelve-foot wall tents that were connected.[44] Sometimes the wall tents were pitched facing one another with the fly of one covering the space between. If the weather was good, families could eat in the covered space. Heavy matting was available to cover the ground inside the tents, and sometimes buffalo robes were laid across the hemp to serve as rugs. One woman even had a wood floor that could be taken apart and transported in sections. When the weather was bad, the other ladies particularly envied her that substantial ground cover. Sleeping arrangements varied. Some women slept on cots, and others, probably those less afraid of snakes, spread a rubber sheet over the ground and placed mattresses on it. Libbie Custer occasionally slept on planks laid on top of sawhorses and wrote her aunt, Eliza Sabin, that she was "never happier than when sleeping in a tent. It is so comfortable."[45] She qualified the statement by adding that storms were their only trouble when camping out.

If it was cold, Eveline Alexander's husband put a large kettle full of coals in the tent opening to warm the inside. Other women used heated bricks to keep their feet warm. With so little wood, it was sometimes difficult to find material to start a fire. Women would gather any little sticks or pieces of brush that they found, and it became such a habit that they couldn't break it even when they returned east. When the Burt family camped beside sagebrush higher than their heads, Elizabeth discovered that it made excellent firewood; another family dug up mesquite roots and used them for fuel. Lydia Lane's husband chained a fatty pine log under their wagon and would chop off bits of it whenever they needed a fire. If no wood was available, buffalo "chips" were collected—there were certainly enough of those. Eveline Alexander reported that they had to have pickets around their campsite to protect them from the buffalo. Sometimes the animals charged toward the camp, occasionally running completely through it.

Campsites were always determined by the availability of water as well as fuel. When a column arrived at a site, the men had to be careful not to let the animals rush into the creek or river and stir up the mud before water for drinking and cooking was collected. Sometimes the women were delighted to find a spring bubbling strong and cold from the ground, but more often they had to clench their teeth while drinking in order to avoid swallowing the slimy sediment from some meandering stream. One officer described the Missouri River water as "too thick to drink and too thin to cultivate."[46] Military families who drank from the Rio Grande complained about its alkaline taste. Locals recommended that they purchase ice to improve the flavor, but few officers could afford the luxury, which cost almost a month's salary.

Good food was sometimes harder to find than fresh water. Sunday was the only day of the week that the column halted long enough to bake bread. On other days a woman or her cook would "pound" out biscuit dough with a bottle on top of the less-than-sterile mess kit that held their eating utensils. Fannie Boyd prepared mince pies and baked them in a Dutch oven, a broad, shallow pot shaped like a frying pan. She would lay hot coals on the lid and then place the oven in a smoldering fire. Baking this way was a fine art determined by the heat of the fire, the item being cooked, and the surrounding weather. As a new bride, Lydia Lane was just learning to cook. She and her Irish servant, Mike, didn't attempt any dish that required a great deal of skill to prepare. They burned the first batch of biscuits they tried to make in a Dutch oven, but kept on until they had a result good enough to tempt the bachelor officers to eat it with molasses. Any meat other than bacon was especially hard to prepare over a camp fire. Contractors, who were usually far away when the meal was eaten, often provided poor quality beef to the army. Even if the meat was good, wives had to get used to eating blue roasts and green ribs. The preservative the military used often turned the meat colors more appropriate for satin than steaks. When the Second Cavalry traveled to Texas in 1855, their beef contractor went with them, buying meat from local civilians and slaughtering it before the troops arrived. Then he noticed that officers' wives also purchased butter, eggs, and milk from the farmers and ranchers. The contractor bought up the supply and sold it to the women at a huge profit.

Beef was a staple of life in the army which automatically made any other form of meat a delicacy. Fannie Gibbon might have enjoyed peacefully watching ducks swimming on a pond in the East; but when she saw them floating downstream in the West she warned her husband, John, not to fire until he was sure he could kill both of them. The fastidious Eveline Alexander felt some remorse when Andrew killed a delicate fawn but still supervised skinning it and cutting it up. She also oversaw the slaughtering of a calf after deciding that she had come "into the law of the redmen, where the squaw has some onerous duties to perform."[47] Mrs. Albert Sidney Johnston was more fortunate in her tasks. She only had to collect the "grapes, raspberries, gooseberries, blackberries, walnuts and hazelberries" that were within fifty feet of her tent.[48]

Walking through the high grass to get to such delicacies extracted a toll from the women. Myriads of mosquitoes covered their clothes and buzzed around their ears, despite the ammonia the wives wore on their faces and hands to repel the insects. One woman commented that the "Father of Waters" was more accurately the "Mother of Mosquitoes."[49] Military families used smudge pots in their tents; husbands and wives sat up all night fanning each other and their children. Fannie Boyd said that wasps colonized tent canvases in such numbers that they either multiplied incredibly or "gathered recruits from all directions."[50] Gnats came "by legion." Sometimes the column was so tormented by insects that they struck camp in the dark and moved to a new location.

The weather, snakes, mosquitoes, and primitive living conditions thus presented special challenges to women who first experienced frontier life from inside an army ambulance. Those who traveled

west by stage, ship, or railroad usually had a shorter but not necessarily easier trip. Since the military protected their western routes,
stage and railroad agents provided tickets to army personnel and
their dependents at reduced rates or even free of charge. Normally
the stage fare from the Missouri River to Denver was $175, more
than a lieutenant earned in a month; thirty years later the same trip
would cost $15 by train.[51]

Stations on a stage line were usually eight to twenty miles apart
and were well constructed of logs, stone, and adobe so that they were
like miniature forts, each with a staff of two to six well-armed men.
Most served meals of hard bread and greasy, green meat, such as
Fannie Boyd had experienced, for an exorbitant 75 cents apiece.[52]
Some stations even had sleeping accommodations at "hotels," which
were accurately described by the name of one—Dirty Jules Ranch.[53]
To travel from the Missouri to the Pacific Coast by stage took seventeen days of being packed in, as Fannie had been, with up to fourteen other passengers. When Alice Kirk Grierson journeyed west, she
and her two children were lucky enough to be the only travelers inside the coach. For hours at a time Alice, the daughter of a rich Ohio
businessman, sat on the floor while a child slept on each of the two
seats. When the army wives were ordered out of Fort Wingate, New
Mexico, in January 1869 due to danger from Indians, Alice Baldwin
took her baby and traveled by ambulance and stage to the nearest
railroad junction at Sheridan, Kansas, nearly one thousand miles
away. Her husband, Frank, couldn't accompany her so the post
trader, Mr. Waters, volunteered to escort her to Fort Leavenworth.
Although Waters seemed nice, during the trip he began to drink and
became so surly that the stagecoach driver took his gun away. Since
Waters was no help, the six other passengers, all men, assisted Alice
and took turns holding the baby. Ladies and children were something
of a rarity in parts of the West. Men often responded to this fact with
such extreme gallantry and consideration that some of them wouldn't
kill a female buffalo or deer. A steamboat captain wielding a butcher
knife reportedly chased a male passenger who directed a mild swear
word at a lady.[54] The men on the stage apparently made Waters
aware of his shortcomings because, when he later sobered up, he
came to Alice and apologized for his "indiscretion."[55]

When Eveline Alexander took the steamboat *Magenta* down the Mississippi, she didn't need to depend on the captain for protection. She carried a gun, perhaps the same one she later had in the leather pocket inside her ambulance. Alexander was obviously prepared to defend herself but was somewhat amused to discover "that on retiring last night, while I took the extraordinary precaution of loading my little pistol and putting it under my pillow, I had neglected the very ordinary precaution of locking my door."[56]

As on dry land, weather often was more dangerous than men for army wives. In June 1874 Mattie Summerhayes left a cool Montana for the Southwest on a move to Camp (Fort) Apache, Arizona, which she reached on October 7. She had taken the railroad to San Francisco, sailed thirteen days down the Pacific Coast, and then up the Gulf of California to the mouth of the Colorado River, where she changed to a stern wheeler. During July, when she was sailing up the river toward Fort Mojave, two hundred miles above Yuma, Arizona, the thermometer located in a shady area of the boat registered 122 degrees.[57] Metal eating utensils in the dining room became too hot to touch, and the women wore pajamas or loose clothing in public and slept on mattresses spread out on the deck.

In the northern plains, traveling by boat became a monotonous progression of soundings, sandbars, and stops to take on wood. Even the scenery on a two-month-long trip up the Missouri River in 1867 didn't relieve the tedium for Sarah Haas Canfield. She described it as "a worse country than I ever dreamed of. Nothing but hills of dry sand, with little streaks of short, shriveled grass in the hollows and on the river bottoms."[58] Sarah might have been more content with the boredom had she known that a few days later Indians would attack the boat and kill a crew member. In 1873, Seventh Cavalry wives were probably prepared to kill one another when they were forced to share a single cabin and poor food on a steamboat for thirty-four days.[59]

Teresa Viele had more spacious accommodations when her husband, Egbert, was ordered from recruiting duty in Burlington, Vermont, to Ringgold Barracks, Texas. They left in April for New Orleans via Havana, Cuba, on the steamship *Ohio* and had "a very agreeable trip," despite the presence in the stateroom across the hall of "a family of (two or three dozen, I should think) small infants."[60]

The journey might not have been so enjoyable if they had sailed with the recruits bound for Texas—there was a mutiny on board their ship. Teresa left Havana with "its dreamy and indolent beauty deeply impressed upon my mind,"[61] but remembered a marshy New Orleans as a place where it was "necessary . . . to bury the dead above ground, in brick graves like a Dutch oven."[62] Landing in Texas didn't liberate Teresa from living on the water. She spent four more days in "sumptuously furnished staterooms" on a boat that took her upstream to Ringgold Barracks. The trip was not all pleasure—the boat was stuck repeatedly on sandbars and attacked by Indians. When Helen Blair Chapman, daughter of a prominent Massachusetts lawyer, traveled to Texas to join her husband, William, she relieved her seasickness and the tedium of the seventeen-day trip by reading Sir Walter Scott, Hume, Burke, Fielding, and Swift from the ship's small library. She reported that on arrival at the mouth of the Brazos, an "impish-looking steamboat brought us near, pitching and tumbling, till at length it seemed to throw us on the sand, I could not conceive a scene more dreary. There is nothing but sand, blown into hillocks here and there, not a blade of grass or the faintest appearance of greenness. . . . A few rough board houses set down at random in the sand, looking much like very common barns. . . . Most people could find others more unfortunate than themselves, but I did not know where those at this place could go to look."[63] Like Teresa, landing didn't liberate Helen from shipboard life. She and William stayed at the Greenwood Saloon, a beached, disabled steamboat that had been turned into a hotel at Brazos Santiago.

The Greenwood probably had house rules similar to those Teresa Viele copied from another Texas hotel at Galveston: "Gents requested not to spit on the walls," and "Keep boots off the bed cloths."[64] Whatever the method of travel, army wives gained extensive experience with a variety of western hostelries. Katie Gibson described her hotel in Yankton as a glorified barn with camp furniture and tissue-paper walls full of knotholes. Late that night, when there was a loud, drunken party in the room next door, her husband, Frank, peered through the knothole to have a look at the men playing poker in the next room. Gibson immediately gave Katie his extra gun and, taking his service revolver, went next door. He gained entrance to the room by pretending to be a gambler wanting to join the game but actually was after one of the players he had recognized as an army deserter who had stolen the camp funds. Frank marched his prisoner out at gunpoint while Katie watched through the knothole, prepared to kill any man who tried to shoot the departing Gibson in the back.

A gunfight took place in the hall outside Alice Baldwin's hotel room during her stopover at Hays City, Kansas, on the trip from Fort Wingate. The man who was killed fell against her door, which collapsed in splinters, and the dead man landed at her feet. Alice's baby slept through it all. The same child, however, cried all night because of the extreme cold when Alice stayed at the Hotel Perry in Sheridan, Kansas. The room had no carpet, no coverings over the windows, and inadequate bedding. Snow drifted down from the unplastered ceiling and mounded on the inside window sills. An unsympathetic individual in the next room shouted, "Can't you choke that brat!"[65] Alice took the child downstairs and squeezed in with the others sleeping on the floor in the heated parlor. She may have considered the accommodations good given her opinion of a typical western town as a place where "in proximity to each other, regardless of business pursuits were to be found the one 'milinary and dressmaking establishment,' next door to 'Mike's Place,' and he in turn to a butcher shop, contiguous to a pigpen."[66] Ellen Biddle described a woman who ran a hotel in Dodge City, Kansas, as dressed in bloomers with a knife and pistol stuck in her belt.[67] The floors were as thin as the walls and, when a fight broke out in the saloon below, Ellen was afraid the bullets would come through into their room.

Libbie Custer had a similar problem when traveling west with Autie and his brother, Tom, on the Kansas Pacific (KP) railroad. Since KP trains didn't run at night, the three were forced to stay in a hotel room surrounded by drinking, smoking, and brawling men. Libbie's neighbors were more considerate than the other women's had been; when told there was a lady present in the hotel, they quieted down and eventually went peacefully to bed. The Custers overslept the next morning, and the train was held awaiting their arrival. Not wanting to delay the others already on board and knowing how long it would take Libbie to dress, the men discussed "What shall we do with the old lady?" and "Can't we bundle her up and carry her?"[68] Carry her

Custer did, only partially dressed with a large traveling cloak wrapped around her; Tom brought the rest of her belongings and their bags. Once they got her on the train, the Custer men debated how to get her dressed, a pressing need since daylight was coming. Finally Tom shielded Libbie in a corner of the railroad car by spreading out her huge cloak while Custer helped her dress behind it. Libbie had not had a part in any of the discussions and decisions that affected her so intimately that morning.

She was determined to be as little trouble as possible when traveling with the troops. She willed herself to never be too hot or too cold, to forget hunger if no food could be obtained, and, finally, to control even her thirst.[69] Aboard the train, Libbie remained calm when a rifle barrel passed under her nose to get a shot out the window at a passing buffalo herd, and she tried not to flinch when a firing gun exploded too near her ear. Her comment that it was a wonder "more" people were not killed in the reckless discharge of guns inside the railroad carriage suggests that perhaps some were.[70] Sometimes all the men, including the engineer, would abandon the train for a buffalo hunt.

Since only one railroad existed with one train a day going east and one going west, there was no competition and thus no need to keep to a timetable. There was also no pressure to improve the service in certain areas. When Fannie Boyd traveled by railroad in Arizona in 1869, she had to use a ladder to climb into a caboose or a box car with wooden benches. Since the trip to meet the main line was only fifty miles long, the Boyds carried no food with them. It took them eighteen hours to cover the distance, however, and they arrived, stiff and hungry, at 3:00 A.M.[71]

Ellen Biddle's mother had provided lavishly for her on the trip west, but when traveling east to visit the sons she had taken to school, Ellen and two of her other children were forced to have breakfast at an eating shack near Kansas City. They had just been served when the arrival of a tornado interrupted the meal. Each of two men standing nearby grabbed a child and headed for nearby dugouts. Although the storm wrought much destruction, Biddle was reunited with her children and broke open a bottle of champagne to celebrate their survival.

Ellen might not have been so overjoyed had one of the rescued children been her niece, Kate. The sixteen-year-old had stayed with the Biddles at Fort Lyon, Colorado, where she learned to drive a four-in-hand team and went shooting with her uncle and the other officers. Kate was fascinated by the area and gathered a sizeable collection of western curiosities that she was determined to take back east with her. Despite her aunt's refusal, Kate had managed to sneak part of the collection into one of the packages the ladies carried on board the eastbound train. Only when they arrived at their destination did Ellen discover that the package she had carried all the way from Fort Lyon contained Kate's collection of "pickled" western reptiles.

Destination became a magic word for army wives whether they struggled with rough seas, endless prairies, or problematic railroad schedules to reach one. Getting there, however, did not necessarily mean getting there. Eveline Alexander arrived at Fort Union, New Mexico, on August 14, 1866, after a sixty-eight-day march from Fort Smith, Arkansas. The very next day the family was ordered to Colorado to establish a new post, to be called Fort Stevens. On September 7 they arrived at the spot where her husband decided to locate the new military garrison. On September 21 Alexander received orders not to build Fort Stevens but to report to Fort Garland, Colorado. Eveline arrived at Fort Garland on October 11; on October 26 the family moved into quarters and spent a hard day getting settled. That night orders were received transferring the Alexanders back to Fort Union. Eveline commented that at that point they were "somewhat disgusted."[72] They left for Fort Union on October 30, arrived November 6, and received orders relocating them to Fort Bascom, New Mexico, on Christmas day. They remained at Fort Bascom until February 16, 1867, when they were transferred back to Fort Union. In eight months, the Alexanders had made six changes of duty station. Army Assistant Surgeon and Mrs. R. H. McKay made exactly the same number of moves in a period from September to January, 1869–70. He was ordered from Fort Craig, New Mexico, to Fort Wingate in September. After two weeks there, he was moved to Fort Dodge, Kansas, where he then received orders to report to St. Louis. At St. Louis, the McKays were told to go to Fort Sill, Oklahoma, and had progressed as far as Fort Scott, Kansas, when they were ordered back to St. Louis. The family was directed to take a steamboat down the Mississippi River and up the Arkansas to Fort Smith. From there the McKays were told to take the stage to Fort Sill.[73]

To live such a life took resiliency and adaptability not required of women who remained in the East. Western life demanded that the wives have a mentality that was "practical, inventive . . . [and] quick to find expedients."[74] Women who had gone west expecting a military lifestyle of functions designed to pamper and entertain them found that they were the ones expected to provide a touch of civilization. Maria Hunter, wife of Maj. David Hunter, described the perfect army wife on the frontier: "She never annoys him with trifles, adapts herself perfectly to every situation, never frets at inconvenience, makes him perfectly comfortable, entertains company handsomely, and makes a delightful life for him."[75] In the process of meeting these demanding requirements, women at isolated posts were forced to reassess their definitions of trifles, inconvenience, comfort, and delight. As a result, army wives not only had to have courage enough to stay—they had to have courage enough to change.

A Cannon
in the Dining Room

As TODAY'S AMERICANS gather each night for dinner, the evening news on the television set serves up pictures of faraway places. An earthquake in Guatemala accompanies the goulash, and Croatia comes with the coffee and chocolate pudding for dessert. We watch the world, and, in an age of instant images, find it hard to understand how army wives of the last century did not know what to expect in their own country. In fact, when these women went west to new homes on the frontier, many spoke and wrote of leaving the United States since they were traveling to areas that were only territories belonging to the nation. To go west in 1869 was not simply a journey, it was an adventure similar to a lunar landing a century later.

In the Union Pacific Railroad Station in Omaha, Nebraska, around 1870, a crowd of men and women waited nervously for the westbound train to Promontory, Utah, the connecting point for the Central Pacific Railroad and California. Those who claimed to know the frontier endeavoured "to excite the fears of the timid and the apprehensions of the excitable" by enlarging on "the dangers incident to a line constructed too hurriedly" and drawing "ghastly pictures of perils to be faced in the event of the wild Indians putting obstructions in the way of the train, and attacking the passengers."[1] The stories inspired brisk sales when a railroad agent passed through the crowd selling insurance before the train departed. That was the real reason the tales were told, but people believed them, just as they believed the dime novels and Fenimore Cooper, because it was the only information available.

When the Seventh Cavalry received orders to Dakota Territory in 1873, Libbie Custer had to look up the destination in an atlas. She not only was unaware of the living conditions she would find there, she didn't know where "there" was. Women who lived near eastern military establishments such as Carlisle Barracks, Pennsylvania, or Fort Monroe, Virginia, may have thought with a sense of superiority that they knew what life was going to be like at a western outpost. Fannie Boyd had automatically assumed that whatever was there would be like the "rose-colored" West Point, which had a large complement of troops to care for it and a surrounding community of doctors, schools, churches, transportation facilities, and other amenities of civilization. More than miles, however, separated assignment at such a post from a home at Fort Davis, Texas, or Fort Laramie, Wyoming. At West Point, stables were for horses, chicken coops housed chickens, and cellars were for keeping roots in. On the Platte River or the Rio Grande, they were prime real estate.

The government, believing that the Indian "problem" was a temporary one, originally constructed only makeshift forts with rudimentary facilities in the West. In 1860 there were seventy-three such posts in the region, each with an average garrison of 180 soldiers.[2] The jury-rigged establishments came and went: Fort Webster, New Mexico, was relocated on the Rio Grande and became Fort Thorne; Fort Conrad was moved eight miles down river and became Fort Craig; and Fort Massachusetts, Colorado, became the longer-lasting Fort Garland. There were twenty-four military posts in New Mexico during the 1850s, but no more than ten of them were garrisoned at any one time.[3] Troops were constantly shifted to meet demands for military aid and protection as the Gadsden Purchase added thirty-thousand square miles of land to the American Southwest about the same time that gold was discovered in California. Posts such as Fort Davis, Texas, were established to protect the southern route to the gold fields laid out by Col. (later Confederate Gen.) Joseph E. Johnston. The road and the people who traveled it needed protection, as it crossed the raiding trails of the Mescalero Apache, the Comanches, and several other hostile tribes.

As the Civil War began, regular army troops were moved east to fight Confederates instead of Comanches, and western forts were manned largely by volunteers who had little interest in maintaining them. When the regular army was ordered west again in 1866 to deal with the continuing "temporary" threat from the Indians, they found buildings collapsed, wells silted up, and government property decorating the houses of local families.

Concern about the Native Americans was especially pressing because of the mounting migration westward. From February 1 to September 28, 1867, more than 5,000 people passed through one Texas post: The fort gave the complete breakdown as 3,024 wagons; 4,587 men; 556 women; 587 children; 5,738 mules; 11,096 oxen; and 1,061 horses.[4] With so many people and so much property to protect, the government realized that abandoned western posts had to be reoccupied. One settler expressed a common view when he said, "If once you get a foothold in the country, the military are bound to come to the rescue and support you."[5] A new line of forts also had to be established along the Bozeman Trail, the route to the newly discovered gold fields in Montana, and on the older Oregon Trail. Despite the fact that the army was reduced from fifty-seven thousand men in 1866 to twenty-seven thousand by 1874, almost twenty-three thousand of the soldiers were assigned to duty at 111 frontier posts.[6] Where the army went, "camp followers" would undoubtedly accompany it. To the chagrin of the officers' wives, this official military term included them.

Forts literally came into being in a day. One morning in Wyoming in the summer of 1866 troops staked out the dimensions of a new post located deep in Sioux country. Wagons were driven repeatedly around the four-hundred-foot by four-hundred-foot perimeter to form streets that delineated the parade ground, a sort of "town square." A mowing machine cut the grass in the middle, and people were forbidden to cross. Tents were pitched surrounding the parade area, marking building sites for officers' and enlisted quarters, the sutler's store, bake houses, headquarters, and other structures. By noon, Fort Phil Kearny, Wyoming, looked like it had been in existence for weeks.[7] A stockade of pointed pine logs eleven feet long buried three feet in the ground would soon be added. Sentries would patrol the blockhouses (square, raised, defensive fortifications with firing platforms) that were quickly erected on two diagonal corners of the stockade.[8] While construction was going on, a Cheyenne warrior dressed in breech cloth, moccasins, and carrying a brightly colored umbrella warned the garrison that the Sioux were going to attack the post.

Living conditions for military wives in the West were governed by several factors: climate, location and age of the facility, how far the assignment was from civilization and the army supply line, and especially, the friendliness of the "neighbors." Relocating to the new Fort Kearny, five officers, one wife, her child, and ten enlisted men serving as an escort were attacked near the post. One of the officers was killed, scalped, and mutilated, while a chaplain traveling with the group reminded the others of Oliver Cromwell as he alternately prayed and fired.[9] Frances Grummond arrived at the outpost as another wagon entered the area containing the naked and scalped body of a soldier. A newspaper correspondent was killed on a Sunday morning while walking near the post. From July 26 to December 21, 1866, in the area of Fort Phil Kearny ninety-one enlisted men, five officers, and fifty-eight citizens were killed, and twenty individuals were wounded. Natives made fifty-one different attacks near the post, half of them within eyesight of the women and children of the garrison.[10] Margaret Carrington, the commanding officer's wife, wrote sarcastically that when a woman observed "men shot within thirty yards of the gates . . . and saw five wagon-loads of bodies . . . she acquires *somehow,* whether by instinct or by observation . . . an idea that Indians *will fight,* and sometimes do become quite . . . dangerous."[11]

Frances Grummond was so discouraged by these surroundings that she seriously considered suicide. If Frances could have foreseen the future, she undoubtedly would have demanded that her husband take her back east immediately. He was killed with approximately seventy others on December 21, 1866, when a rescue party under Capt. William Fetterman was sent to assist a wood detail that had been attacked by a large force of Sioux and Cheyenne warriors. Frances sat and listened to the hammering as enlisted men built his coffin next door. When Col. Henry Carrington set out with a large body of troops to retrieve the remains of soldiers who had been killed, he was afraid the fort would be attacked while he was away. He left instructions with the officer of the day; "If, in my absence, Indians in overwhelming numbers attack, put the women and children in the magazine with supplies of water, bread, crackers, and other supplies that seem best, and, in the event of a last desperate struggle, destroy all together, rather than have any captured alive."[12] Carrington himself set the fuses so that a single match would destroy everyone. The situation became so severe that on January 23, 1867, women and children were ordered to retreat sixty-seven miles through a blinding snowstorm to Fort Reno, Wyoming.

Even when "camp followers" could live safely at a new post or temporary cantonment, the lack of facilities often made for a very spartan existence. Sometimes the wives just continued to live in the tents they had used on the trail. At Camp Halleck, Fannie Boyd occupied two eight-foot-square tents with only one narrow opening, so that she felt like a prisoner inside them. As she lay in bed, desperately homesick her first night at the post, she suddenly heard the sound of a piano from a nearby officer's tent. Remembering the journey she had just completed, Fannie was amazed to discover the large musical instrument so far from civilization.

Wives moving to a fort that had been in existence for a period of time usually were offered better accommodations. Army families already in residence opened their homes to new arrivals and visitors so often that one wife said she felt capable of running a hotel after a year on the frontier. Col. and Mrs. John Dent housed several members of the LaTourrette family who arrived at Fort Union, New Mexico, in 1877. Dent, the brother of Julia Dent (Mrs. Ulysses S.) Grant, had been a post trader at Fort Union for many years. The Dents were "selling out" before moving back east, and the LaTourrettes bought much of their furniture, including a bedroom suite that had been used by General Grant.

The bedroom furniture Maj. and Mrs. Henry Noyes offered Andrew and Elizabeth Burt when they arrived at Camp McDowell was not quite so prestigious. The Noyes moved seven beds into the yard and eventually persuaded the Burts that it was simply too hot to sleep inside the quarters. Years before, the Summerhayes had made the same discovery. Jack and Mattie, along with most of the garrison, had set up cots on the parade ground at Camp McDowell, placing the legs in cans of water or turpentine to keep the ants away. The temperature during the Summerhayes's stay in Arizona reached 120 degrees.[13] The facility often competed with Yuma to see which was hotter. A popular army joke told of a particularly reprehensible soldier who died at Fort Yuma and went to hell. He soon reappeared to his former comrades, begging for blankets, suggesting that the climate at his new location was a lot colder than Arizona in the summer.

Conversely, it was so cold on the northern plains that at some posts men walking guard duty had to be relieved every half hour. When the temperature reached minus fifty degrees at Fort Ellis, Montana Territory, the wood in the log cabin quarters froze and popped like it was shot from a pistol.[14] Roofs extended giant tentacles of ice to the ground; inside walls that were not close to a fireplace were covered with frost. Food froze and wives had to "cut" bread with an axe. The Burts awakened one morning at Fort Bridger to find themselves in complete darkness because snow had covered their entire hut. As the temperature dropped so low that the mercury froze in the thermometer, soldiers at the post dug tunnels from house to house. Details transporting wood couldn't function, and the family huddled together as supplies of fuel ran dangerously low. In the winter of 1868–1869, snow was piled twenty feet deep across parts of Wyoming.[15]

When a blizzard banked snow high against the front of the Biddle's quarters at Fort Lyon, Colorado, James went through the rear door to see what was exciting the horse, whom he could hear kicking and neighing in the stable. Biddle tried to get out the back gate, but it wouldn't open. He climbed to the top to look over and was amazed to discover that a herd of buffalo had taken shelter behind the fence during the recent storm.

Margaret Carrington had no such place of shelter when the women and children were ordered to retreat from Fort Phil Kearny. The wagon train started at one in the afternoon and traveled through waist-deep snow until 10:00 P.M., covering only six miles in the nine hours. In an effort to keep ahead of the Indians, the bugler sounded "boots and saddles" at 1:00 A.M. As the aurora borealis provided light, the group struggled forward through what one officer called "stunning cold." The temperature hovered at minus thirteen degrees. When they camped at Crazy Woman Fork that night after struggling for twenty-five more miles, even a hatchet wouldn't cut the bread, merely shattering a loaf into chunks. Women and children snuggled around stoves set up inside the wagons in an effort to keep warm and defrost food. Margaret described "[a] lady sitting on a pile of wood, with feet to the stove, though these were covered with high buffalo boots, her head enveloped in a beaver hood, her form wrapped in linsey woolsey and buffalo skins, and her hands stirring something like turkey knobs and bread chunks over the stove. In the background, in a perfect nest of wolf skins and beaver, two boys with caps, boots, and coats trimmed with the same material, and pushing themselves as close to that little sheet-iron [stove] arrangement as safety and culinary duties would permit; on the right and left a saber, shotgun, rifle, and revolver . . . at the extreme end, a thermometer, worn out and desolate."[16]

The temperature, forty below that night, drove the mules crazy. They bucked and snorted, breaking their halters. The mules brayed, the men chasing them cursed, others stomped the ground trying to keep warm, and children cried continuously. Anyone who lay down froze to death, and others, including the Fort Phil Kearny surgeon, lost fingers and toes. On the third day it took the wagon train three hours to go one-sixteenth of a mile as frozen hands tried to rope the wagons up a rock-strewn gorge. The exhausted cavalcade didn't reach safety at Fort Reno until after dusk that night. Despite the threat of Indians and the debilitating cold, the most persistent concern, according to Margaret Carrington, was the urgent need for food.

As the women had discovered, nature provided a persistent, sometimes overwhelming, and even bizarre challenge on the frontier. At Fort Ellis, a deluge forced hundreds of gophers out of their holes, where they were then beaten to death by hail the size of hens' eggs. The hail also pounded roofs and broke every one of the nine hundred panes of glass at the post. The ground was littered with animal bodies, shards of glass, and eight inches of hail.[17]

The Boyd's quarters at Fort Bayard, New Mexico, sat on the brow of a hill. During rainstorms, water entered through the back door of the log hut and left by the front; Fannie sat on top of a table to avoid a mud bath in the dirt floor. Others commented that it was a hard way to "mop" the kitchen. When an officer at Fort Bayard went east and returned with a wealthy young bride from New York, she decorated their quarters with expensive carpets and lavish curtains. The furnishings were destroyed by the next rainstorm in a deluge of mud. As money was no object she immediately sent east for more, which never arrived. The disappointed wife learned a lesson many wealthy women discovered on the frontier—money could not guarantee happiness or necessarily buy contentment.

Frances Roe was out riding with two officers near Fort Lyon when the sky began to darken with a sandstorm. A loud, continuous roar like a waterfall rolled over the terrain. As the riders headed for the post, hurricane-speed wind tore at Fran's hair, and grains of sand pitted her face like smallpox. Although the officers warned her to stay with her horse, the frightened woman slid from the saddle and ran to a picket fence she had glimpsed during a momentary lull in the storm. She lay there clinging to the pickets as the wind swirled over her, carrying away the roofs of buildings and most of the post's laundry.[18]

The low, whitewashed facilities at Ringgold Barracks, Texas, sat on a high bluff made of sand. It reminded Teresa Viele of the story of the foolish man in the Bible who built his house on the sand. There was not a single blade of grass in sight. When Teresa first arrived in Texas, she had noticed a house that spoke of misery and squalor. When departing the area, she passed the same building. This time it appeared quite comfortable because, during her stay, she had seen many that were infinitely worse.

There were also whitewashed buildings at Fort Clark, Texas. Fannie Boyd reported that they were blinding in the sun but very romantic at night when the regimental band played by moonlight on the parade ground. The ladies in fluffy white dresses and "gallant officers in uniform" sat on the porches listening to the music.[19] Fannie had learned to appreciate these simple pleasures. When she arrived at the low, malarious Camp Date Creek, Arizona, in 1869, she was the only woman within fifty miles. The Boyd's quarters there had just one room with a door at either end and two windows on each side. Typical windows were small and near the ceiling so Indians could not fire arrows through them. Wives sometimes had to stand on chairs in order to look out. A curtain divided the single room into a sitting area and bedroom. The building was constructed of unplastered adobe that soon began to crumble, leaving additional "doors" for scorpions, rattlesnakes, and centipedes. The floors of rough, uncured planks had shrunk, resulting in two-inch wide gaps. Dropped articles invariably disappeared through the openings.[20] Some "dobey" quarters had roofs made of logs with mud packed between them. After a gentle rain, flowers would grow in the mud, giving the quarters a sort of roof garden. Sometimes cottonwood logs even sprouted leaves.

At several posts officers lived in duplexes with a common porch or breezeway between called a "dog run." The family dog(s) usually occupied it—hence the name—but it also provided extra sleeping space for overflow guests and a place to hang riding equipment or wet laundry on a rainy day. When Col. Albert Sidney Johnston and his wife, Eliza, occupied one side of such a duplex, they decided to enclose the dog run to gain an extra room. The construction ordered by Johnston, the post commander, left the family in the other half to come and go through one of their windows since the only entrances to both sides of the duplex were off the breezeway. Sometimes a long series of quarters would be connected by dog runs. All the entrances and exits were aligned to provide a covered retreat from one set of quarters to the next in case of attack.

Given the single-wall construction in the duplexes, sounds carried easily and privacy suffered. Many army couples took a walk on the parade ground late at night when they wanted to have a "discussion" that might otherwise be overheard by their neighbors. Sharing a single house was an acceptable arrangement *if* the couples doing so were congenial; there was constant friction if they were not because the occupants had to share a yard, garden plot, hen house, and, after it was built, a privy.

Some posts had duplexes that consisted of three rooms on each side and a full-length porch that covered the front and back but no opening between the two sides. Mattie Summerhayes occupied such a house when she first arrived in the West and was depressed because she didn't think she could live in only three rooms, even if each was eighteen square feet in size. This was actually generous, given that army regulations allowed only one eighteen-foot-square room and a kitchen for a second lieutenant and his family. But it was cramped compared to what a woman of Summerhayes's social status could expect in the East. One lieutenant's wife expressed her dissatisfaction with army quarters in a poem:

I know 'Uncle Sam' must be an old bachelor,
For he made no provision for an officer's wife:
And the very worst fate that I ever can wish him
Is one room and a kitchen the rest of his life.[21]

Lieutenants certainly did better at Fort Leavenworth, Kansas. The fact that the post was a major supply depot undoubtedly contributed to its excellent living conditions. When Lt. Albert Barnitz wrote in 1866 to tell his wife, Jennie, that the Seventh Cavalry would be spending the winter at Fort Leavenworth, he assured her that they would "have a kitchen and dining room and two servants rooms, etc. in basement etc, also a cellar. A large balcony, hall, sitting room, sleeping room and dressing room on first floor and two rooms on 3d floor and many clothes presses and closets. . . . The rooms are not large—only about 15 or 16 feet square, but they are very cozy—a fireplace in each room and stoves—ornamented—will be furnished by the quartermaster."[22] The fact that Barnitz acknowledged to Jennie that the fifteen- or sixteen-foot-square rooms were not large suggests something of the standards she was used to. Andrew and Elizabeth Burt's quarters at Fort Leavenworth were similar to the Barnitzs' and even had a cistern in the back, but neither family had a watercloset or bathroom.

At a time when indoor bathrooms were an essential part of middle- and upper-class homes in eastern cities, it would be twenty-five years— and Burt would be a major—before any of the western quarters he and his family occupied had one. That made it virtually impossible to follow the War Department order that army personnel bathe once a week. "The regulations say the men must be made to bathe frequently; the doctors say it should be done; the men want to do it; the company officers wish them to do so; the Quartermasters' Department says it is important. Yet we have no bathrooms."[23] Flora Cooper did have a bathtub at Camp Supply, Indian Territory, in 1871; it was made from half a whiskey barrel that had been seared inside to burn out the odor. With no bathrooms and the heat and dirt prevalent at some posts, the smell became ferocious. Even noses had to adapt to the western environment.

Alice Baldwin was surrounded by dirt when she arrived as a bride at Fort Harker, Kansas, in 1867. She lived in a dugout, furnished with a camp chair, two empty candle boxes, and a packing box that served as a kitchen table. Eating utensils were scattered over the earthen kitchen floor, and a huge box stove was covered with rust and grime. The unplaned parlor floor contributed splinters to her feet; the canvas covering the walls and ceiling sagged in the middle. She could hear rats and mice scampering above her head. A blanket strung across one end of the parlor partitioned off a bedroom. The Baldwin's first meal in these quarters was cooked by a Dutchman named John Lick, who cooked fried bacon and apples, stewed peaches, and coffee made from the grounds of several earlier pots. The food was served on a packing-box table with newspaper for a tablecloth and napkins cut out of flour sacks.[24] If the Baldwins were typical, the dishes and serving utensils holding the sparse meal would have been made from the finest china, crystal, and silver.

Small items were all that a military family could afford to carry with them. The army provided an officer with accommodations for himself and two horses, fuel and light for his quarters, and food for the animals. Everything else, including moving expenses for his family, came out of his pay. A change of station could cost a staggering amount, especially during a period when a lieutenant's annual salary was only $1,400 and a colonel's $3,500.[25] The weight allowance for a lieutenant's personal baggage (furniture, housewares, clothes, books, etc., for his entire family) was one thousand pounds.[26] Anything beyond that had to be shipped by civilian freight haulers at a rate of two dollars per hundred pounds in 1878.[27] Moving expenses could quickly dissolve savings, and the wealthy relatives of army wives were frequently applied to for financial assistance. Frances Roe found it particularly hard to meet their moving expenses when her husband's unit was ordered to Montana in 1877. Congress had adjourned that year without passing a military appropriation bill, and the men received no pay from June 30 to November 17.[28] Even when it finally received money, the army was paid in greenbacks, which were often discounted by up to 30 percent.[29] Unless one was a very senior officer, freight costs and the frequency of moves made it hard for military families to assemble household goods. Mattie Summerhayes discovered that consolidated packing was a required skill. She took lessons, while kneeling on a pillow, from a major's wife, who taught her how to cram everything into the three army chests the Summerhayes were allowed to put in the company wagon. Large items such as carpets and bedding could be rolled. Maria Kimball bragged that she could do up all of their belongings in sixty packages.[30] Perhaps to save transporting it, Autie Custer would always announce a move by smashing a homemade chair to pieces and throwing it into the kitchen at Libbie's feet.

The Custers were unusual in that they had a chair to demolish. The Cooper family also had a chair—it was the only piece of real furniture in their whole house. The object was so revered as a place of honor that no one could be persuaded to sit on it. When Flora Cooper finally prevailed on her husband, Charles, to try it out, the chair collapsed under him, and the family went back to the soap boxes they normally used for sitting.

The Coopers also discovered that beds were another large item that couldn't be transported from post to post. The family made do with flat boards nailed to short posts that had been driven into the dirt floors; mattresses were feed sacks filled with straw and covered with buffalo robes. Marian Russell believed that her bed, made out of a six-foot-long log split in half and covered with cedar boughs, was the best she had ever slept in. Officers' wives who were able to borrow army cots from post hospitals considered themselves fortunate. Ellen Biddle borrowed cots when the inspector general and two staff officers came to scrutinize Fort Halleck and were assigned to stay with her family. During the hospital inspection, the IG discovered that three beds were missing and ordered them returned at once. He was instantly obeyed. That night the inspector general and his staff slept on the floor.

The cots were actually a luxury. Usually makeshift furniture constructed out of trunks, planks, and boxes filled army quarters on the frontier. Sofas were made out of low trestles with boards spread between them that were then covered by buffalo robes or Indian blankets. Ellen Biddle had a "lounge" and two chairs built by a soldier from packing boxes and some springs she had carried west with her. The Custers designed "composite" furniture. Moving chests formed the foundation for a lounge; packing boxes with shelves doubled as bureaus when they were covered with calico.

Quarters' windows were hung with unbleached muslin curtains trimmed with red material dyed from beet juice. Spikes driven into the walls held clothes. Dirt floors were covered with layers of hay, newspapers, army blankets that were sewn together, and carpets if the family had any. Libbie Custer and other Seventh Cavalry wives presented the Gibsons with a rag rug they had made: The blue center came from an old pair of Autie Custer's pants, the yellow section from the trim on cavalry uniform trousers, and the black border from the mourning veil Katie had given up wearing on her train trip west. If the earthen floors weren't covered, toadstools sprang up overnight during rainy periods and had to be "harvested" with a broom each morning. Gaping holes in wooden walls were covered with tarps or papered over with old newspapers. One summer at Fort Sanders, Wyoming, a whole newspaper morgue couldn't have hidden the "holes" in the quarters assigned to Andrew and Elizabeth Burt. The post was so crowded that the Burts had to occupy a corner blockhouse where sentries normally marched and kept watch. The blockhouse walls extended only halfway to the ceiling; corner supports held the roof in place. If there had been a prize for make-do furniture on the frontier, it probably would have gone to the Burts. They had a cannon in the dining room of their blockhouse, which guests could lean against, eat on, or sit astride as the need arose.

Lighting in army housing was provided by mineral lamps when residents were able to get oil. The cans transporting oil to one frontier post leaked so badly that, when the shipment arrived in the West, they were empty. Among Lt. Cooper's personal belongings shipped to Fort Sill in 1871 was a five-gallon can of coal oil. It had shared a wagon with Capt. Nolan's prize carpet and leaked all over it. The wives did not speak for days. Sutlers, who contracted to run stores at western posts, usually carried oil, but sometimes it was too costly for officers to afford. Tens, often hundreds, of miles from civilization, the sutler had a monopoly, with limited restrictions on what he could charge for his goods or services. The rough-hewn counters and shelves at Fort Wingate held a wide variety of goods, and there was a back room where officers "in need of benign retirement" could enjoy a wide variety of special "services."[31]

The post quartermaster controlled the supplies as well as the workmen who could improve the quality of life at a post. A sympathetic officer would allow the wives to use leftover scraps of government paint on the quarters, which often resulted in a rainbow of rooms. At Camp Halleck, one of Ellen Biddle's rooms was red, a mystery since the army didn't normally use red paint. Many of the enlisted men had professional skills. The enlisted ranks often included carpenters, stonemasons, bricklayers, and other specialists who were ordered to construct and repair buildings at a western fort. The quartermaster could draw on their talents and frequently did, usually to improve his own quarters first. Invariably his house was freshly painted and had closets and extra shelving for books, cooking utensils, and storage requirements. Libbie Custer reported that the wives at a particular post were delighted when the quartermaster's doorbell rang (they had none) before dawn one Christmas morning. A drunken camp woman standing on his porch muttered, "It's cold and my nose bleeds."[32] Then she wandered away. After that, when wives at the post needed anything, they announced, "It's cold and my nose bleeds." Orsemus Boyd was lucky when he was acting assistant quartermaster at Camp Date Creek. Since Fannie was the only woman at the post, there were no other wives to envy them their crumbling home.

Using company workmen could prove a mixed blessing. When the Custers arrived at Fort Abraham Lincoln, enlisted personnel were assigned to construct their house. After the exterior was completed, Libbie took pains with the inside "to give it a permanent character. . . . For three months I kept painters and carpenters at work steadily. We curtained about twenty windows, carpeted almost all the floors."[33] Only a few weeks later the house was destroyed by fire, and Libbie lost most of her belongings. A woman guest staying with the family had only one party dress left out of all the clothes she was carrying on her trip. An investigation showed that the workmen had designed and erected a faulty chimney that started the fire. All the chimneys at the post were then discovered to have potentially hazardous defects.

If fire was a special threat to officers who lived in wooden quarters with thatched roofs, so was rain. Horse manure was used as a bonding agent to hold the thatch together, but the roofs leaked badly. Umbrellas became an important part of the furnishings. Flora Cooper arrived at her Camp Supply quarters to be greeted by a chunk of "bonding agent" that fell on her head. When the ambulance had initially stopped at the cabin, Flora had refused to get down. "Not at these stables," she told her husband, assuming he was teasing her.[34] When she found out that he wasn't, she sat down on her trunk and cried, vowing to return to her comfortable and dry home in Philadelphia. However, she forgot "her determination to desert the army" and eventually "grew accustomed" to life on the frontier.[35]

Rain was not the only thing that seeped through the roof. Snakes managed to enter the houses by climbing the latchpole frames for kitchen lean-tos and then falling through the thatch into the interior of the buildings. Wives then discovered the reptiles curled up on mantels, stretched out on beds, and hidden inside the boxes and trunks that served as furniture. At Camp McDowell, the Burts filled their shoes with crushed papers to keep out the snakes. Fanny Boyd found so many rattlesnakes that she kept a collection of their rattles. Katie Gibson was greeted by surprise visitors that came down the chimney. As the mother rattlesnake and her offspring crawled across the floor, Katie climbed out the window. She ran to the kitchen, where her servant, Lizzie, had a pot of water boiling. On learning of the problem, Lizzie entered the living room in her stocking feet, carrying a set of kitchen tongs. Catching the snakes with the tongs, Lizzie plopped them in the boiling water and announced that lunch would soon be ready. Katie refused the menu at first but was goaded into trying some when a visiting officer said she had no nerve. She was surprised to find that the meal was not only good, but very good.[36]

Grasshoppers were a less deadly but often more destructive visitor to frontier posts. Ellen Biddle described how the sky began to grow dark at three on a Sunday afternoon at Fort Lyon, Colorado. She thought a storm was coming but soon realized that the sky was obscured by hordes of grasshoppers. They overwhelmed the area, eating everything in front of them. They decimated anything green on the post and devoured hundreds of watermelons in the troop garden. It took the rest of Sunday and all of Monday for the insect army to pass.[37] Col. Benjamin O. Grierson wrote his wife, Alice, about a similar invasion of Fort Leavenworth. "They (grasshoppers) were impolite and unceremonious enough to hop up, get up or in some way make their merry way up under the hoops and skirts of the ladies who were bold enough to promenade among them."[38] Destruction by the insects was so severe in 1875 that army officers worked from February 2 to March 25 enrolling people for relief assistance after the recent plague.[39]

Teresa Viele believed that, "Vermin are the scourge of this country. . . . This portion of the world may be set down as the birthplace of the flea; those found in other parts are merely occasional wanderers from this, their native land."[40] Emily McCorkle FitzGerald wrote to her sister from Fort Lapwai, Idaho, "We are being devoured here by moths. They eat everything—our best clothes hanging in closets, our blankets on the beds, and coats and hats on the rack!"[41] According to Fannie Boyd, Texas had giant cockroaches so large they made the kitchen floor appear black, wood ticks that burrowed into the skin, and a small red bug that could infiltrate anywhere. Despite larger and more potent threats from nature in the West, Fannie decided that the real annoyances were these small insects along with wasps, gnats, fleas, flies, and mosquitoes.

The wives occasionally faced danger from larger animals. At Fort Russell, the Summerhayes' bedroom window opened onto the prairie outside the post. They were awakened one night to find that a mountain lion had decided to join them in the bedroom. Jack grabbed his saber and, brandishing it, chased the cat around the house, no doubt with much noise and confusion. As Mattie cowered under the covers, the uninjured animal eventually returned to the bedroom and departed the house the way it had come.

When the Seventh Cavalry was assembling near Fort Lincoln in preparation for a campaign, several wives decided to join the men in camp for a few days. Katie Garrett went along to visit her soon-to-be fiancé, Lt. Francis Gibson, and stayed in a tent by herself. Something that appeared to be a dog crept under the canvas. Katie knew that Custer had ordered all the dogs in camp tied up so they wouldn't fight with the wolves and coyotes. If she got someone to take the dog away, she was afraid the soldier who had been responsible for tying it up would get in trouble. Katie decided to keep the animal in the tent until morning and then let it out when the other dogs were released. She tried to coax it closer with every canine name she could remember. She got no response until she recalled she had a piece of hardtack (a hard biscuit) under her pillow. She held it out to the animal, thinking he might eat it and go to sleep. The "dog" grabbed it and wiggled under the edge of the tent. Immediately a rifle shot rang out. The girl grabbed her robe and ran out just in time to hear a sentry report to Custer that he had shot a wolf coming out of Miss Garrett's tent.[42]

Katie had left behind in the East only weeks before a safe and comfortable world of elegant Victorian houses, servants, gas lights, and wild animals only in zoos. When she experienced the frontier military environment of canvas walls, fur rugs, unpainted chairs, and dining tables made of wooden planks, she had glanced at her sister, Mollie, "who had been brought up on family antique mahogany and rosewood . . . and was unable to understand her complete contentment, and resolved that nothing would ever induce me to abandon the comforts of the East."[43] Yet only a few weeks later love and Lt. Gibson persuaded her "to forsake the culture and green vegetables of the East for the crudities, hardtack, and perpetual canned beans of the army and the West . . . surrendering herself . . . into the very jaws of a rough, tough existence."[44]

Not only did Katie and other wives have to adjust to the privations of frontier life, they learned that it didn't always pay to try to improve living conditions, especially if married to a junior officer. If a wife made their quarters too comfortable and attractive, it was an invitation to get "ranked out." This army tradition allowed a senior officer to evict a junior one so that he could occupy the desirable quarters himself. In what has been called "army musical chairs," the tradition meant that a post with a high turnover of officers was constantly in flux.[45] Lt. and Mrs. James K. Thompson were ranked out by a senior bachelor officer in 1891 because they had equipped their house at Fort Davis with a bathtub.[46] An officer only twenty-four hours senior wanted to rank the Coopers out of their house although an identical set of quarters was already vacant. Flora discovered that the senior officer's wife wanted their quarters because of the large madeira vines that sheltered the porch. Overhearing this, Forrestine, the Cooper's five-year-old daughter, went outside and pulled every vine out of the ground. The other officer accepted the vacant quarters. At Fort Clark, the Boyds occupied a lovely limestone house with several rooms. Six senior officers who arrived the following year claimed it, with a bachelor captain winning the date-of-rank "lottery." When the post doctor declared Fannie, who was about to give birth, too ill to relocate, the captain moved into the one-room quarters the Boyds were going to occupy. The next day Fannie almost died while giving birth to a son, and all three children came down with whooping cough. Despite this, a week later the captain took possession of the large house, and the Boyd family was crammed into the single room.

This privilege shocked women who were accustomed in the East to living in the same large, comfortable house for many years. The first time the Summerhayes turned someone out, Mattie felt sorry for them. "To me, who had lived my life in the house in which I was born, moving was a thing to be dreaded.[47] This "bumping" of lower-ranking officers applied the domino effect as each man took the quarters of the individual below him until the most junior lieutenant usually ended up in a chicken coop or a tent. Ranking out added tremendously to the friction at frontier posts. When Alice Baldwin's husband went to the quarters of Lt. William Foulk, an officer he had bumped, Mrs. Foulk attacked him with a bullwhip while her children threw books at him. Foulk was soon transferred to a more remote post. Increased isolation or "quarantine" of the family was apparently considered a greater punishment than court-martial of the officer.

Mrs. Foulk's outrage was definitely the exception; most army wives eventually became accustomed to the instability of not knowing how long they would remain in a given place. Frequent relocations were an experience they shared with their civilian sisters on the frontier, who moved an average of four to five times in their lives. Over the years constantly starting over in a new location contributed to a military mindset that accepted perpetual motion. When army wives returned to the East, in fact, many soon became bored with the more settled existence.

Military wives like Katie Gibson responded variously to the challenges of living in the West. Eveline Alexander began to handle the family's finances, deciding that her husband had "to attend to Uncle Sam's interests, and it is as well for one of us to look after . . . family affairs."[48] Before the next move, she sold the large household items and shopped for a new ambulance. Mattie Summerhayes recommended to her husband, "If we must live in this wretched place [Ehrenberg, Arizona], let's give up civilization and live as the Mexicans do!"[49] She longed to wear loose clothing and have the freer lifestyle of her Hispanic acquaintances. Teresa Viele complained, "Little does the casual observer at West Point know of the after existence of its graduates, and their lives of exile and privation on the frontier, passed in lonely seclusion from the world, a stranger to its luxuries, almost a stranger to the ordinary comforts of civilization."[50] In a letter to her aunt, Alice Grierson, who was also an army wife, Helen Davis countered Viele: "Roughing it seems to be good for us. I am surprised to find that we can be comfortable with so little."[51]

The instability of frequent moves, the primitive houses that certainly weren't fit even for Capt. Marcy's horse, the lack of creature comforts, and the danger from nature, animals, and Indians all demanded great adjustments on the part of army wives. The women soon began to take pride in creating a civilized existence for their families without realizing that their definition of civilization was changing.

Servants, Shortages, and the Sutler

❧ OFFICERS' WIVES WHO traveled west discovered that it was a land of opportunity as well as a great equalizer. Their worth in the East had depended on a display of wealth governed by rigid social practices and strict class distinctions. In the West, the women's true value was revealed by how they dealt with insufficiencies, losses, and hardships that were alien to their former lives. In an area of shared danger and deprivation, money and social status no longer guaranteed what Victorian society had assured them were the necessities of life.

One of the most important "necessities" to army wives was servants. Twenty-five percent of American households had them at the time.[1] The majority of officers' wives came from a class level where household labor was performed by hand—a servant's hands. Even for wives who had attended an eastern ladies' college, their education there had stressed feminine or homemaking arts such as embroidery, painting, and decorative talents. Classes teaching practical skills tended to be limited to household management and a little plain sewing, such as making a tablecloth or napkins. When Ellen Biddle's mother, who had been a navy wife, discovered that her daughter was going to marry an army officer, she insisted that Ellen learn to cook. James Biddle offered to pay his wife to learn how to sew and presented Ellen with a twenty-dollar gold piece when she completed her first dress.[2] Many prospective officers' wives, however, had no experience with or knowledge of the physical drudgery presented by cooking, cleaning, sewing, or taking care of children.

Caring for a large household took hours of heavy labor, even in the East where "modern" conveniences such as the carpet sweeper and a

fantastic invention called the "washing machine" were slowly becoming available. Officers' wives were determined to maintain an orderly home wherever they were located. If they didn't, the literary advice of the period informed them that they would be responsible for
their husband arriving "at evening from his hard toil . . . repelled by
the sight of a disorderly house and comfortless supper . . . and [mak-
ing] his escape to the grog-shop or . . . gambling room."[3] The wives
knew how difficult it was, even with servants, to meet Victorian standards of order and cleanliness even in an eastern area, where streets
were paved and plumbing was not considered a luxury. Without servants, the women were convinced it would be impossible to maintain
a proper home on the frontier. Officers might live in a chicken coop,
but their wives were determined to have someone to help them sweep
up the feathers every morning.

In the East, the minimum servant requirement for a genteel household was a cook, a maid, and a nursery attendant or nurse. In the
West, officers' wives were ecstatic just to have one of the three. When
Mary Swanson wrote her family that she had no servants at Fort
Davis, Texas, her grandmother didn't believe her. The woman had
chided her granddaughter for not writing, and the girl responded that
her grandmother had no idea what it took to care for a house and
baby.[4] One rich young wife was so desperate for help that she offered
fifty dollars a week, a small fortune at that time, for someone to care
for her and her baby daughter, but no one applied for the job.[5]
Frances Grummond was astonished at the mere idea of a servant
shortage—her father had owned slaves.

Frances Roe decided that the only advantage offered by her husband's duty as an officer with a newly established black regiment was
that they could always have servants who were excellently trained.
Many of the enlisted personnel in the Ninth and Tenth Cavalries and
the Twenty-Fourth and Twenty-Fifth Infantries were former slaves
who had been house servants in the South. An officer at Fort Fred
Steele, Wyoming, desperate for household help, wrote his wife that if
slavery had not been abolished he would be "inclined to buy some
old black Aunty and make her a regular member of the household."[6]
The Custers' cook and family friend, Eliza Brown, was a freed slave
who had "jined up with the Ginnil."[7] Libbie said that Eliza, who had

to cook in a tent, "had a right to be in a fury, and why she did not set the tent on fire, or take a skillet and brain those who brought her out there, was, and is, an unsolved problem."[8] Disliking the cold weather when the Custers moved north, Eliza eventually married a black lawyer from Ohio and was replaced with another Negro cook, Mary. Mollie and Donald McIntosh employed a black cook named Iwilla. (She had been christened "I Will Arise.") Teresa Viele hired a black servant, Joseph Williams, who had been trained by navy officers. Williams had accompanied the officers on overseas cruises and was very cosmopolitan. He served the Vieles "with grace and elegance" and "prided himself on keeping up the style of the family."[9] The food might have been plebeian but the silver, glass, and china always gleamed. Teresa commented that she "never dreamed of interfering with the [way Joseph ran the] household."[10]

Wives who weren't lucky enough to have an Eliza or Joseph tried to overcome the servant problem by bringing female employees with them. One lieutenant's wife, while visiting in the East, hired a young Swedish woman who had just immigrated to Pennsylvania. The girl married immediately after her arrival at Fort Davis so the family sent for an immigrant Polish servant. She, too, quickly found a husband. Given the scarcity of women on the frontier, the wives soon discovered that they were essentially running a marriage bureau. Libbie Custer chose plain, middle-aged women to take west and then described how they began to "metamorphose" in a world of admiring men at an isolated post. Officers' wives always considered it a bad sign when servants began to "primp and powder."[11] It was said that pretty maids or cooks could be married within two weeks, the homely ones within a month.[12] It took Dr. Buell's servant, Sarah Knapp, exactly three weeks to get a proposal from Ordnance Sgt. Joyce at Fort Concho, Texas, in 1877. Feeling responsible for Sarah, Josie Buell inquired of Alice Grierson, the commanding officer's wife, about the man's reputation. Col. Grierson later assured Mrs. Buell that the only thing he had against Joyce was that he was a Democrat.

Ellen Biddle should have checked on the quartermaster sergeant who was engaged to her plain, thirty-year-old nurse, Bridget. He deserted, taking the Irish woman's life savings of three hundred dollars and the money from the quartermaster's safe. He was eventually tracked down and killed in a gun battle with his pursuers. Ellen couldn't understand why Bridget grieved more for the loss of the man than the money.[13] The Biddles apparently learned from the experience because later, when an army clerk proposed to their maid, Mary Broderick, Ellen made him prove that he could stop drinking before the wedding took place.

Some of the women themselves overindulged in what they called "strong water." Female servants at Fort Robinson went on a binge with "hunter rye whiskey" and locally purchased cocaine and laudanum. For six months, Frances Roe employed Scotch Ellen, a "real treasure," who may have been named more for the whiskey she consumed than for her homeland. Caroline Frey Winne wrote of a previous cook, "I have heard of my good Fanny (and really if she wouldn't drink so, I never would ask for a better servant) in jail two or three times lately."[14] The FitzGeralds' Eskimo servant, Jennie, went on a "bust" just as Emily was preparing to entertain the officers of the garrison and their wives at a card party. FitzGerald wrote to her mother, "Now I know you will say I ought to talk to her and reform her, etc., but I would just like to know how you would go about it."[15] Fannie Boyd's male cook demonstrated that he had a similar addiction. When Fannie gave a luncheon with several friends at the dining table awaiting the meal, the cook reeled in, declared he was no slave, said he hadn't signed on as a hotel cook, and refused to serve lunch. The problem was so common on the frontier that the guests laughed and were satisfied with bowls of bread and milk.[16]

Used to a broad selection of applicants in the East, wives quickly learned that the limited employment pool in the West meant that they must be willing to overlook certain "deficiencies." Fanny Corbusier's servant, Louise, from Elmira, New York, was an excellent cook. She could throw things together and come up with a magnificent meal. Unfortunately at least once a month she also threw a tantrum and everything else—pots, pans, and flatirons. It became so severe that she had to be committed to a mental institution. One lieutenant's wife at Fort Fetterman was reported to have hired a woman who had been a teamster at the post, but the servant turned out to be an excellent cook who was very good with children. The cook's name was Martha, but most people addressed her as Calamity Jane. Alice

Grierson's servant, Maria, was accused of arson at Fort Gibson. When an officer was sent to arrest her, she fled to Alice for protection—and received it. Mrs. Col. Grierson sent the major on his way without the prisoner he had come to claim.

The Roes experienced a long string of servant problems. They hired a "lady tourist" who condescended to let them pay her way west before deciding that home was better after all. Next was a young woman who was insulted because she had to take her meals in the kitchen rather than eat with the family. Then came a Russian who was wonderful at cooking but terrible at keeping to a schedule. She believed that guard mount and other functions of the post should be planned around her cooking rather than vice versa. Then came a gambler's wife "with dull red hair . . . twisted in a knot as hard as her head."[17]

Frustrated at keeping female help, Fanny Corbusier considered hiring a local Indian for the job. One candidate assured his prospective employer that he was a "good Injun, me only kill one white squaw, me no hurt you."[18] Mattie Summerhayes faced a different kind of "danger" when she hired a young Indian servant named Charley who wore only an extremely scanty loincloth. Summerhayes wrote that he "appealed to my aesthetic sense in every way. Tall and well made, with clean cut limbs and features, fine, smooth, copper-colored skin, handsome face, heavy black hair done up in pompadour fashion and plastered with Colorado mud, which was baked white by the sun, a small feather at the crown of his head, wide turquoise bead bracelets upon his upper arm, and a knife at his waist—this was my Charley, my half-tame Cocopah, my man about the place, my butler in fact, for Charley understood how to open a bottle of co-comonga [wine] gracefully and to keep the glasses filled."[19] When another wife suggested that Mattie clothe him, Summerhayes responded that her friend needed to cultivate an appreciation of "nature" but decided later "that a life spent mostly in a large city had cast fetters around her imagination."[20] Charley and his clothing, or lack thereof, became a familiar attraction as he wheeled the Summerhayes's baby down the street at Ehrenberg. When the young man left the baby carriage in the middle of the road while he peered in a nearby store window, the child was almost killed by stampeding cattle. It may have been his aesthetic appeal that saved Charley from being fired.

The Roes decided to employ a Chinese servant, also named Charlie. The man read extensively and proved to be resourceful and talented in the kitchen. He even designed and built a sort of cooler in a local stream to keep milk and butter cold. The Roes were extremely upset when the other Chinese at the post forced him to leave. The family discovered later that Charlie was a "highbinder," a member of a secret Chinese society of assassins and blackmailers.

Despite this experience, Frances Roe wondered why more officers didn't use Chinese help. She believed that Asian men did the work of two women and said that, once an individual had won their confidence, the "Chinamen" would do anything for them. So many families employed Chinese servants at Fort Union, New Mexico, in the 1880s that the soldiers became angry because there were no women employees to invite to post dances. The troopers threatened the Asians and harassed them at night until no Chinese servants were willing to stay at the fort. The twelve-year-old Chinese boy hired in San Francisco by Fannie and Orsemus Boyd was certainly not eager to stay with them. No woman servant had been willing to accompany the Boyds on their coming move to Arizona because of the increasing Indian threat. At Los Angeles, the Chinese youngster heard graphic stories of Indian atrocities from hotel employees and changed his mind. He was afraid that his long queue (pigtail) would be an added enticement for the Indians to scalp him. He didn't want to lose his hair, and the Boyds didn't want to lose his service, so they kept him locked up until they left for Arizona. As they traveled across the desert, with only two soldiers for protection, the boy was so terrified that he literally turned green.[21] After the Boyds arrived at the new assignment, the Indians were in fact fascinated by the boy's hair, but mainly because they couldn't decide whether the young Chinese was a male or female. Finally the boy got so disgusted with the notoriety that he sawed off his queue. In response to Fran's comment that now he couldn't go back to China, the youngster, who was also changing in this new western world, responded, "Me no care. Me want to be 'Melican man.'"[22]

The Mills' Chinese servant, Sam, was already enough of an American man to have become extremely proficient at poker. When he won a great deal of money from several of the soldiers, one of them threatened to kill him because the trooper believed he had been cheated in the game. That night Sam cooked and served an excellent meal to several dinner guests, cleaned up the kitchen, then went to his room and shot himself to death with a small derringer. The next day all the Chinese servants at Fort Shaw, Montana Territory, buried him near the post cemetery, laying clothes and food across the top of the grave to sustain his spirit until it could reach "Happy Land." During the night the coyotes ate the food, but the Chinese firmly believed that Sam had enjoyed an excellent last meal.

One of the greatest difficulties faced by officers' wives with male servants of any nationality was the issue of authority. Mattie Gilbert was so successful that her Chinese cook left a note for his replacement that read, "Mrs. Gilbert heep good woman, good job, but you watchee out. Mrs. Gilbert heep spunky, she punchee head with stick of wood."[23] Grace Paulding employed Wo, a Chinese servant she described as wonderful, but who did not like to obey "Missy" until he realized that she was the one who was going to pay him each month. When Grace read him an extensive list of duties and instructions she had prepared, Wo responded, "Can do," and did.[24] Some months later he refused adamantly when Paulding told him to wash the windows. The task wasn't on her original list. The army wife had to hire someone else to do the job.

Frances Roe believed that household discipline was a special problem when officers were away for a long period of time. In addition to their Chinese cook, Hang, the Roes employed a German striker (an enlisted man hired to act as a servant for an officer) named Volmer. While Lt. Roe was in Washington caring for his sick father, Volmer asked Fran if he could take out the family buggy and horses. Keenly aware of her responsibility for the thoroughbreds, Fran adamantly refused. Volmer, a giant of a man with a furious temper, raged at her until Hang, hiding in his room, was afraid the enlisted man was going to kill her. Hang had reason to be concerned. When he first arrived in the house, Volmer, apparently to exert his authority over the newcomer, had spread-eagled the Asian on his bed with a picket rope. Now Hang listened and was impressed as Fran successfully ordered the menacing Volmer out of the house. When the striker returned later to apologize, Roe lectured him firmly him on his language and behavior, knowing it would be deadly to reveal the terror she actually felt.

Despite a law passed by Congress in 1870 forbidding the practice, most officers employed enlisted personnel in some capacity. A man would be hired to take care of the horses, cut the grass around the quarters, and perform heavy tasks such as chopping firewood and hauling water. Mattie Summerhayes considered their striker, Bowen, invaluable. Though he was an excellent cook, the talent she most appreciated was his ability to scavenge. He even managed to acquire, in the land of wooden crates and crystal, a real table for the family. The derisive title, "dog robber," which other enlisted men often applied to strikers, perhaps was really accurate in Bowen's case. The term implied that an officer's dog was robbed of scraps from the family table by the presence of a striker. The job offered enough benefits, however, to overcome the stigma. Strikers earned an extra five to ten dollars per month at a time when their army pay was thirteen dollars for the same period.[25] They had a chance to live in a family environment at the officer's quarters rather than in the noisy and crowded barracks. Sometimes the job even allowed them to escape more onerous military duties.

How easy the work was often depended on the personality of the officer's wife giving the orders. Jennie Barnitz, described by her family as imperious, wrote her mother from Fort Riley, Kansas, that the "poor privates are perfect slaves. I do pity them. . . . The Army life is delightful and is eminently suited for me, as I do love so much to be waited upon."[26] Barnitz's granddaughter later wrote that Jennie possessed "the soul of a Major General, who ran everyone, and ran them ragged."[27] The striker who worked for the Barnitzes undoubtedly got more toil than tidbits.

Libbie Custer was adored by everyone, and the family striker was no exception. Custer left a soldier named Keevan to care for his wife and the house while he was away on the Black Hills Expedition. The instant the returning officer was sighted in the distance, Keevan informed the cook, Mary, that he had been honor bound to behave properly while Mrs. Custer was in his charge. Now that the general was back, Keevan intended "to celebrate their return by going on a tremendous 'bum.'"[28] It must have been the quickest binge in history.

Custer marched up the steps to his quarters barely ahead of the stumbling striker.

Tygret, the Kimball's enlisted servant at Fort Wingate, braved a fire to save family belongings. The Boyds' striker at Fort Halleck did the laundry rather than have Fannie suffer the humiliation of doing so when the post laundresses refused to wash the family clothes. He was prepared to face ridicule—and did—rather than have her exposed to it. Joe Bowers provided Alice and Frank Baldwin with plum brandy he had made out of wild fruit from the prairie. Joe undoubtedly gave Frank a glass before he handed one to Alice; the Baldwins could never teach him to serve ladies first. As an enlisted man, he had been well trained that officers took precedence over everyone else. Fannie Boyd was always upset to see enlisted men punished because "most of the kindly help which made life on the frontier endurable . . . came from these men . . . [and it] would have been necessary for me either to have cooked or starved but for their ever-ready service."[29]

After a hard day's march on a move to Fort Whipple, Arizona, Lieutenant Summerhayes was starving—for donuts. In response to Mattie's comment that she had no eggs or proper cooking utensils, her husband replied, as he increasingly did, "you're on the frontier now; you must learn to do without."[30] Mattie could have told him to do without the donuts, but she had been brought up to defer to a man's wishes. Despite a hot day on the trail and lacking ingredients and cooking experience over a campfire, the dutiful wife began to prepare donuts for her husband. When a sandstorm interrupted the process, Colonel Wilkins's wife advised Mattie to let Bowen cook over the campfire in the future since he knew how to do it. Frances Grummond could have used similar advice. When she experimented with starting a cooking fire at Fort Phil Kearny, sparks from the wood shavings she was using blew under the commanding officer's quarters and set it on fire. Emily FitzGerald was so overwhelmed at the thought of such tasks that she was "always in constant terror for fear sometime my domestics will suddenly depart and leave me alone."[31]

Such women were amazed that the strikers were excellent cooks despite the harsh conditions. Before the Civil War the army had employed no professional cooks so KP (kitchen police) was rotated among the troops. The military provided detailed instructions for baking bread and for preparing meats by every method known except frying. The manual even informed cooks that the best way to determine oven temperature was to insert a hand into the oven and count the number of seconds before a burning sensation developed. Experience during the war probably explains how many soldiers came to be so proficient at cooking over a campfire, a hot and difficult task. One woman found an enlisted man who was a marvelous cook and unwisely invited the commanding officer to dinner to show off the striker's ability. The next day the colonel ordered the man reassigned—to work at his house.[32]

Good cooks were especially valuable because of the scarcity of food on the frontier. Maria Kimball commented that army men studied tactics and added that their wives also had to do so in a land where there were no stores. In Charleston or Philadelphia, one simply sent a servant to the butcher, the fishmonger, or the farmers' market to gather the ingredients for that night's dinner. In the West, eggs, butter, and milk were so rare that they were exchanged as presents. When a drought lowered the water level on the Rio Grande, supply boats couldn't get through to Ringgold Barracks, Texas. The same drought had parched the surrounding countryside until no food was available locally either. Teresa Viele reported that "the subject of food was one that was dropped by mutual consent."[33] There was no sutler's store at Fort Halleck, Nevada, when Fannie Boyd arrived. For two years she and Orsemus lived on the soldiers' ration of bacon, flour, beans, coffee, tea, rice, sugar, and condiments. The only "luxury" was dried apples, which Fannie served baked, fried, stewed, in pies, and out of pies. Libbie Custer said that eating such food was passable if it was flavored "by that inexhaustible 'sauce,' good appetite."[34]

Andrew and Elizabeth Burt and the garrison at Fort C. F. Smith, Montana, had been on short rations in the spring of 1868 when a wagon approached from the north. The officers were amazed because in that direction were some very hostile Indians who had been threatening their supply line. In the wagon were two men with a load of potatoes, onions, and a little butter. The cost was fifteen dollars a bushel for the potatoes and two dollars a pound for the butter. The Burts paid but considered it daring prices for a daring journey.[35]

As Ellen Biddle learned, housewives in the West had to "make the best of everything that [came] within reach."[36] Wives began to take pride in knowing how to use substitutes or make concoctions out of almost nothing. Frances Roe served a dinner in 1872 with twenty-two dishes that were all "frauds."[37] Chicken salad was made of veal, and a turkey dish was prepared using a goose. Biddle herself had a popular recipe for apple pie without apples. She soaked soda crackers in warm water until they were soft, then added essence of lemon, sugar, and a great deal of nutmeg. The mixture was cooked inside a pastry shell. People who didn't know what it was assured others that Ellen Biddle really knew how to make a great apple pie.[38]

Ellen also cooked custard without eggs. She took six tablespoons of cornstarch, added enough water to make it thick and creamy when cooked, then flavored it with lemon and sugar.[39] Other women copied this recipe because, as Mattie Summerhayes had discovered, eggs were always hard to obtain on the frontier. It was a very serious issue when army wives debated the best method to carry or preserve them. Frances Roe moved fourteen dozen eggs to Fort Maginnis, Montana Territory, in boxes packed with salt and required her cook to keep an exact account of his use of them.[40] On Christmas 1876 the trooper transporting the mail from Bismarck, North Dakota, to Fort Rice carried eggs wrapped in cotton inside his shirt to keep them from freezing. Conversely, those left in the summer sun in Arizona cooked inside their shells. Randolph Marcy's wife carried fertilized turkey eggs west from New Orleans inside her bodice so that Marcy wrote "the corsage of my dear wife bulged."[41]

The shortage of poultry and the cost of up to $2.50 a dozen for eggs inspired women, whose eastern experience with animals had largely been limited to riding horses or petting dogs and cats, to become "chicken farmers."[42] Mrs. Marcy was so concerned about her fowl that when she saw a "dog" running off with one of her turkeys, she brained the animal with a skillet and returned the bird to its pen. When her husband arrived home later, he inquired about the dead wolf lying in the yard. The turkey had been saved, and Mrs. Marcy got a new wolfskin hat and muff out of the rescue effort. Ellen Biddle went into business at Fort Whipple and eventually sold more than 200 chickens and 14 turkeys.[43] Mrs. D. B. Dyer raised over 250 chickens her first year at Fort Reno, Oklahoma Territory.[44] She discovered that feeding them sunflower seeds produced extremely shiny feathers, making the birds look healthier. Fannie Boyd kept chickens and cows, selling enough butter and eggs to save fifty dollars a month, almost half of her husband's income for the same period.[45] Of course there was an added risk to business "stock" in the West. The Carringtons drove two milk cows six hundred miles to a new post only to have the animals stolen by Indians soon after their arrival. Then wolves ate their turkey hen just when she was preparing to hatch a brood of future merchandise.

Cows were particularly valuable because they produced milk and butter, which were scarce. Unfortunately, the quality of the product varied with the time of year. In the spring the wild onions and garlic eaten by cows on the Texas plains made their milk and butter inedible. In the summer the heat in Arizona caused butter to separate into layers—dead white, deep orange, and a lilac shade of purple. Fannie Boyd asked one army bride if she was not bored by the forced inactivity of a broiling western summer. The woman replied that she was busy trying to keep the family's supply of butter and milk cool by putting wet rags around the jars that held them. Marian Russell cooled their milk at Fort Bascom, New Mexico, by placing it in the fireplace, where a current of air constantly passed over it. Hearing the pans rattle one day, she went into the living room to find that two rattlesnakes had come for breakfast.

As indicated earlier, beef was a staple in the military diet. The army ate so much beef, in fact, that Autie Custer suggested "Give us this day our daily bread" be changed to "Give us this day our daily beef."[46] Out of the twenty-one meals a week prepared at the army post near the Cheyenne River Indian Agency, beef was usually served at ten of them.[47] Soldiers came to the Summerhayes's quarters at Camp Apache to take monthly orders for meat. Mattie had to tell them how much beef she needed and what cuts she wanted for the coming weeks. A family would eat beef almost every day of the year unless they could procure some sort of substitute. Capt. R. T. Jacob at Fort Cobb, Oklahoma Territory, traded a half-pound of tobacco for a turkey and got a whole venison for two to three pounds of sugar.[48] Other officers and some of their wives hunted, bringing down buffalo, antelope, deer, rabbit, and game birds to relieve the boredom at the table. Those on the northern plains discovered that the mountain goat was particularly tender and juicy. A more limited number developed a taste for bear meat. Letting the "wild" meat hang outside for a few days usually removed most of the gamey flavor.

At Fort Rice, soldiers caught one thousand pounds of fish by spreading a seine in the Missouri River.[49] During the winter officers went ice fishing for rainbow trout, and in the spring and summer wives often joined them in the sport. Ellen Biddle was determined to serve something other than beef when Gen. Orlando Wilcox, an old family friend and the departmental commander, came to visit. She requested that officers assigned near the Verde River get her fish, and they procured some by "blowing up" the river. Ellen made very sure that James Biddle, who was now inspector general, didn't find out that she was the one responsible for the dynamiting.

While most personnel liked meat, the dried fruit and vegetables the army experimented with were not popular. When Margaret Carrington first tried to cook them, she broke off a desiccated chunk and added water. As the vegetables cooked and swelled like rice over the top of the pot, Margaret searched frantically for other containers to handle the overflow. Quantity did not in this case reflect quality, because most agreed that the taste of the dried food was terrible. Caroline Winne, the wife of an army doctor, wrote her brother that having real vegetables was "a treat."[50] The Winnes were delighted when an officer and his wife shared with them part of a package they had received as a gift from their son in California. It contained peas, potatoes, asparagus, pie plant, and radishes. Although Helen Davis looked forward to an upcoming visit by some of her family from the East, she was much more excited about the anticipated arrival at Fort Davis of a shipment of potatoes and onions.

Real fruit was even harder to obtain than vegetables. Helen Davis wrote to Alice Grierson that she longed for fruit more than for society, money, or furniture.[51] Mary Swanson declared that she craved oranges and lemons.[52] One wife, in an "orgy of extravagance" paid $1.50 for a dozen bananas and twenty-five dollars for a barrel of apples.[53] Swanson was luckier; her grandfather sent the family a barrel of Northern Spies (apples) from Pennsylvania as a present. He chose that variety because of its hardiness during the two-month trip to Texas. When someone wanted to give Libbie Custer a gift, they brought strawberries to her from St. Paul, Minnesota. The strawberries were the only ones she would have in eleven years on the frontier. Wives at Texas forts could occasionally obtain grapes and peaches from Mexico, but the supply depended on the state of political relations between the two countries. A can of peaches at the sutler's store could cost up to two dollars.[54]

When Elizabeth Burt visited Salt Lake City in October 1866, she was delighted to be able to purchase a bushel of peaches to take back to Fort Bridger. On the second day of the three-day trip home, however, it began to snow. The party tried to follow the telegraph poles, but it became clear after dark that they were lost in the storm. At dawn, they still couldn't see more than two feet ahead of the horses. When a wood party from Fort Bridger finally stumbled across the wagons, the train was less than one quarter mile from the post. The peaches had frozen by that time, as well as all the fort's supplies for the winter, which were being carried in the other wagons. The dried apples and pickles that survived the storm at least prevented a severe outbreak of scurvy at the post. It was a disease common at many frontier locations. In 1853, of 4,450 men stationed in Texas, 510 had scurvy. Three died from the disease.[55]

Soldiers at several forts planted gardens in an effort to avoid scurvy and earn some extra money by meeting the demand for fresh food. In 1869 the garden at Fort Laramie contained 6,000 strawberry plants, 250 raspberry, 250 blackberry, 600 asparagus, and 50 rhubarb.[56] When a unit at Fort Limestone, Kansas, cultivated four or five acres in 1872, "the company did the work of planting . . . but the rabbits did a large part of the eating."[57] The men decided to get their vitamins by shooting and eating the rabbits. No shooting was allowed at Camp Supply that same year when forty or fifty young Indians "out for a frolic" deliberately trampled the vegetables and watermelons growing in the post garden.[58] As the Indians knew, the troops were not permitted to fire on them for fear of bringing on an uprising. Army wives also tried gardening and battled drought, animals, poor soil, and even the army itself to obtain additional food for their families. Libbie Custer reported that one cavalry wife planted gardens for twelve successive springs but was never at one post long enough to harvest a single crop.[59]

Tinned (canned) food was available at the sutler's store but, in the law of supply and demand, the prices for all the products offered were frequently exorbitant. Kerosene was normally about five dollars per gallon, but during a shortage could run as high as fourteen dollars.[60] Purchasing a five-gallon can—the usual amount—required almost 70 percent of a lieutenant's monthly income. Supply levels within the stores themselves often varied. When the Burts arrived at Fort C. F. Smith in November 1867, there were only enough canned goods to provide each officer with one can of currant jelly, corn, and tomatoes per month.[61] Conversely, the sutler's store at Fort Atkinson, Kansas, had a stock inventory worth twenty thousand dollars.[62]

Fort Gibson's sutler offered a variety of 813 items, including 142 different kinds of textiles and sewing supplies; 214 items of clothing and accessories, 72 of which were specifically for women and children; 77 varieties of grooming and hygiene supplies; 31 types of hardware; and 184 houseware items.[63] An officer's wife could buy the finest black silk for a price so shocking that it wasn't even listed on the store manifest. If she longed for a new hat, it cost $2.00; she could drop a silk handkerchief for 56 cents. Her husband could purchase a set of French "dancing pumps" for $1.25 to wear with his $5.00 silk shirt. While he was dressed appropriately, he could puff his way through three Havana cigars for 12¢. The stock level of cigars for men was one thousand, but the sutler only had one bag of marbles for little boys at the post.

Eleven of the thirty-one types of hardware were padlocks, perhaps surprising in a land where people claimed to never lock their doors. Mosquito nets, always in great demand, were a dollar apiece. A family could purchase a gilt lamp as a wedding present for $8.50 or give a more practical set of dishware for 87¢. A damask tablecloth, to cover the wooden box serving as a dining table, was $3.50; the napkins to go with it were 43¢ apiece. A chamber pot, a real necessity of life, especially on cold winter nights at northern posts, cost from 62¢ to $1.25 each, depending on the discriminating taste of the user.

Only 82 of the 813 items offered at Fort Gibson were food products. There were 8 kind of cookies, 7 varieties of pickles, 10 types of candy, and 8 sorts of fish. An officer's wife could buy oysters but not

eggs. Mushroom and walnut ketchup was available but not tomatoes. Biscuits could be purchased but not the butter to spread on
them. There was sugar plum candy but no plums. Not a single vegetable was offered, and figs and raisins were the only type of fruit the
sutler carried.

Items that couldn't be obtained locally at western posts had to be
ordered from the East or the West Coast. Before returning to "civilization" for a visit, Seventh Cavalry officers received shopping lists
for intimate ladies' apparel from army wives on the frontier. It was
much more embarrassing when the young bachelors tried to communicate their needs to eastern shop girls. Women ordered items
such as shoes from catalogs published by Altman's or Sears. Good
shoes and boots, which were especially hard to get in the West, could
be ordered for five dollars a pair.[64] The problem was that the eastern
firm often shipped the shoes separately; the left might come in this
month's mail and the right sometime the following month.

Women sewed as a way to overcome the clothing shortage and ordered Butterick patterns in order to keep up with eastern fashions.
Mary Swanson wrote to her mother in Philadelphia asking her to
send to Fort Davis fashion plates and swatches of silk. Autie Custer
bought Libbie a sewing machine that Godey's Ladies Book called
"The Queen of Inventions."[65] This significant labor-saving device for
women cost between fifty and seventy-five dollars and produced a
man's shirt in only one and one-third hours. It took more than fourteen hours to make one by hand. Libbie enjoyed sewing her own
clothes and even made underwear and nightshirts for her husband
and brother-in-law, Tom. Ellen Biddle discovered that the hardest
part of sewing for anyone was putting pockets in her son's pants; she
tried unsuccessfully to bribe him into doing without them.

Women who were adept at making their own clothes found it more
of a challenge to prepare their own toiletry items. Wives learned to
make toothpaste with borax, hair dye from sulphur and lead, and
skin softener from a lard concoction. They combined Epsom salts,
borax, sulphur, and quinine to make a "face bleach" that would get
rid of freckles brought out by a blazing prairie sun. They spread a
mixture of lard and plug tobacco on their hair to cure the inevitable
head lice. A mouthwash of cloves or nutmeg was used to sweeten the

breath; however, if a woman's breath was bad enough to make her a "walking sepulchre," she could also hold a piece of charcoal the size of a cherry in her mouth, then slowly chew it up.[66] Perfume was concocted by alternating layers of flower petals and soft cloths soaked in olive oil. A mixture of water, aqua ammonia, salt peter, and shaving soap allowed to stand for a day could be used to shampoo a lady's hair—or clean grease spots, kill bed bugs, and remove the paint from a wooden board.

Not that there was much wood to paint. As Libbie Custer's lament about the lack of trees suggested, wood for building or burning was hard to obtain at western forts. A cord of wood that cost $6.50 in a forested area was priced at $105.00 on the frontier.[67] Lumber to build the sutler's store at Fort Reno, Wyoming, had to be freighted over two hundred miles.[68] Wood was so scarce at one Texas post they didn't have enough to make a coffin for an officer who died; he went to his rest in a box marked, "200 lbs. bacon."[69] Another was carried to the cemetery in a barrel, in what must have been a mind-boggling military funeral. An enlisted man was interred in a wooden crate that had stenciled on it, "40 pair cavalry trousers."[70] He was government property to the end.

The lack of trees was not surprising given the scarcity of water on the plains. Although one of the prerequisites for the location of a frontier fort was a dependable source of water, its conservation, sanitation, and distribution was a constant struggle for the military. Some forts placed two water barrels outside each set of quarters, and they were filled once a week by enlisted men. The uncovered barrel held water for washing clothes and bathing while the other stored water for cooking and drinking and had a lid fastened with a stone on top. Inevitably both collected leaves, grass, and dust, and eventually mosquitoes began to breed.

Several posts had an acequia (ditch) surrounding the parade ground, which was used to distribute the water supply. At Fort Stanton, the ditch was fed from a nearby mountain stream. Occasionally people dipping water would catch a trout in their bucket. Fort Davis was unusual; it had a nearby spring that provided water at nine hundred gallons a minute.[71] Wives filled ollas (large clay pots) with the water and hung them in the shade to cool. When the weather was very hot, they wrapped wet flannel around the jars just as they did for butter and milk. Mattie Summerhayes reported that it worked because, when the outside temperature in Arizona was 120 degrees, the water in her olla was 86.[72] When suspended in the house, the ollas even served as an early form of water cooler as the liquid evaporated.

Fort Sill built a huge storage tank and supplied water to the quarters in pipes made from old telegraph poles. After a few years, when the water began to taste bad, officials decided it was time to clean the tank. At the bottom they found a two-foot deep layer of dead pigeons.[73] The water the garrison drank at Fort Terrett, Texas, was almost that dirty to begin with. The nearby Llano River formed pools with little or no current, resulting in a thick scum of brownish green moss that gave off an offensive odor. Mattie Summerhayes described the Colorado as looking like "melted chocolate."[74] Those women at posts that drained water from the Rio Grande either used charcoal filters or had to let the suspended matter settle out. Water from such sources was hard, but wives were not inclined to take the military's advice that they mix in extremely valuable egg whites to soften it.

Women who lived beside the bubbling creek that ran through Fort Bridger or enjoyed the spring near Fort Davis were fortunate and knew it.[75] When Autie Custer returned from the Black Hills Expedition, he brought Libbie a present she had not seen for years. It was a keg of clear mountain stream water. The wife who had learned "to take a bath in a thimble" was thrilled with the gift.[76]

When the Custers returned east to be "stationed in the States for a short time," they rented a house that they shared with another officer and his family.[77] They "reveled" in the space and were amazed at the "delicacies" procurable for the table. Libbie commented that the wives had forgotten how to prepare meals with an abundance of food. They cooked as they had done in the West, leaving some things out and substituting for originals that were now readily available.

When Mrs. Frank Walborn's servant, Annie Noble, decided to marry a musician named Hantz at Fort Stevenson, Dakota Territory, in 1868, the Walborns held the wedding and reception in their quarters. Following the simple festivities, Mrs. Walborn reflected that the couple were "as legitimately and firmly united as if priests, ministers, magistrates had taken part in it . . . with all the pomp of ceremonies.

. . . It is the same with most things in civilization. A great many com-plications and useless things. One must come to live in Dakota to get things back to their real value."[78]

Margaret Carrington said that those army wives who went west discovered the truth of the scripture that "a man's (woman's) life con-sisteth not in the abundance of what a man (woman) possesseth."[79] The women learned to value the clothes they wore, the water they drank, the food they ate, and the hands that prepared it. The wives were more grateful for the sweetness of life when they had to pay a trader 10 cents each for the privilege of licking a knife dipped in a can of honey. When back in the East, these women could not peel a banana, see a small boy put his hands in his pants pockets, or watch a well-trained butler pouring wine at dinner without remembering when they went without such "luxuries." Their lives in the West had given them a new appreciation for the true "necessities of life."

Holidays, Horse Races, and Hops

OF ALL THE SHORTAGES suffered on the frontier, none was as damaging to morale as the lack of diversion at isolated posts. The short interludes of danger or excitement from Indian threats or a change of duty station were overwhelmed by months of monotony. Boredom often inspired troublemaking in the ranks, which is why the Army "made" work for enlisted men during the tedious days of garrison duty. Posts without some form of positive recreation saw a jump in alcoholism, venereal disease, and gambling. Violent confrontations often followed as at Fort Davis, where three murders occurred in two years.[1] Although the January 1869 report listed no desertions, drunkenness, or insubordination at Fort Davis, seven percent of the command was in the guardhouse.[2] Duels occasionally took place between officers as incidents became magnified in the isolated environment. At one fort tension ran so high that every officer brought court martial charges against every other officer. The men of the Fifth Cavalry had constant disagreements when they were stationed in Arizona but when they were transferred to Fort D. A. Russell—and their wives were allowed to join them—everyone suddenly got along much better.

In part that was because army wives in the West took seriously the colonel's command to his bride, "You will entertain me." In the East husbands were away from home most of the day immersed in business. At a western post, where duties were light, Fannie Boyd said the men "were ever ready to be amazed or amused . . . with the results of our industry, and absolute delight was manifested over the most trifling plan for social enjoyment."[3] As women worked to develop new skills and organize opportunities for entertainment, whether for themselves, their husbands, the other officers and their wives, or the entire garrison, they relieved their own boredom and sometimes brought a greater sense of cohesiveness to the unit. Some of the leisure activities they planned crossed class barriers between officers and enlisted men, ladies and laundresses. Recreation and entertainment under such isolated conditions often required a special level of involvement and ingenuity by everyone.

At Fort Clark wives organized a theatrical company and stripped their quarters of the scant furnishings to provide props. They gave charity performances before packed houses. The money went to renovate the building that served as the post chapel, school, theater, and ballroom; to purchase a Christmas tree and presents for the one hundred children of the garrison; and to feed the "famishing Irish." The last was "especially successful."

One of the most popular entertainments at Fort Davis was when officers and their wives performed a minstrel show for the black troops of the Tenth Cavalry. On another occasion, a quiet, reserved officer's wife from Charleston, wearing a brilliantly colored dress with a kerchief on her head, was a great hit when she performed a wild African dance she had learned from her slave nursemaid.

The soldiers at Fort Rice converted an old sawmill into a theater and gave benefit performances to raise money for a billiard table and bowling alley equipment. When one enlisted man who was a particularly talented actor had to march guard duty, he would announce the passing hours to listeners, "adding with a flourish [at the end] 'And all is well, my lord.'"[4] Indians were so involved in their "performance" when a mock battle was arranged between a troop of cavalry and some nearby Pawnees, that the natives fired their blanks directly into the faces of the "attacking" troopers. One enlisted man was in danger of losing his sight as a result of the powder burns. People were so desperate for entertainment that "every seat was occupied, every corner packed," at the benefit performance the Roes staged at Fort Shaw, Montana Territory. The crowd came from miles away despite the fact that the path to the theater was cut through snowdrifts higher than their heads.[5]

When cold weather froze the river at Fort Laramie, wives helped to organize a skating party that was attended by the entire garrison. Ladies who couldn't skate were pushed around in chairs on wooden slats. Ada Vodges said that the activity reminded her nostalgically of Central Park.[6] The cold inspired the Seventh Cavalry to have sleigh rides in minus forty-five degree weather, and some individuals were hungry enough for trout to go fishing through five-foot-thick ice. Frances Roe continued to ride horseback in the winter, wearing a sealskin cap with earflaps and gauntlets of the same material; her leggings and mocassins were of beaver with the fur turned inside out. And the mare she rode was decorated with "icicles two or three inches long hanging from each side of her chin."[7]

One of the first questions officers' wives were asked when they arrived in the West was, "Do you ride?" Katie Garrett, who could not, said she was asked the question so many times that she quickly became sensitive about her "military shortcomings." For most, however, the answer was yes. In the East riding was another indication of affluence. It cost a great deal of money to stable a horse and buy the proper equipment and clothes for the sport. A ride through Central Park or a fox hunt in Virginia was the epitome of social acceptability. In the West, with its vast distances and potential danger from a buffalo stampede or Indian attack, riding was not just a social grace, it was often a saving one. It was important that women have a "tight" seat in the saddle. Frances Roe bragged in a letter home that she had been on twenty-two different horses never before ridden by a woman and had not been unseated once.[8] When a cavalry horse tried to run away with her, Roe's escort suggested she change animals. "Dismount before Lieutenant Golden, a cavalry officer and Faye's [her husband's] classmate, and all those staring troopers. . . . Never!"[9] Frances had a sergeant tighten the cinch and put a harder bit in the horse's mouth, and then she proudly rode the animal to a standstill. The infantry wife was so pleased with her equestrian skills that she acquired a riding habit modeled after the West Point cadet uniform and wore the United States Military Academy insignia on her hat. She may have been copying cavalry wives who liked to wear their husbands' forage caps or dress helmets on hunting expeditions.

Despite her "delicate" health, Ellen Biddle was anything but fragile in the saddle. When her husband, James, bought her a spirited sorrel mare, it was Ellen who chomped at the bit for three days while heavy rains prevented her from riding the new animal. When the sun finally came out, she sent orders for the mare to be saddled. A sergeant at the stables warned Colonel Biddle that the horse was extremely fractious. As soon as Ellen mounted, the animal reared and broke away from the men trying to control it. The officer's wife quickly realized she was going to have to jump off, a risky maneuver at any time but especially while mounted side saddle and wearing a long riding habit. If her skirt caught on the saddle horn, a woman could be dragged or possibly trampled to death by a rearing horse. Ellen might faint theatrically at the sound of the retreat gun or when she heard that a lion had escaped from a nearby circus tent, but this time she rolled in the dirt and got up, commenting that the mare must be keyed up due to overfeeding and lack of exercise. When she went to the stables the next day, determined to try again, the animal was gone. James Biddle, knowing his wife would not give up, had sold the horse without telling her in order to avoid the danger. Ellen, whose pride in her riding skill was equal to Frances Roe's, undoubtedly "rode" her husband for some time about such highhanded behavior.

Seventh Cavalry officers boasted to everyone that no other army wives rode as well as their's. Autie Custer bragged to Libbie's family that she was "now an expert horse-woman, so fearless she thinks nothing of mounting a girthless saddle on a strange horse. You should see her ride across these Texas prairies at such a gait that even some of the staff officers are left behind."[10] Riding at a gallop across the plains presented special risks from such things as prairie dog holes and alkali bogs. Faye Roe had to rescue Frances and her horse when they were trapped in a quicksand-like bog. Despite those potential dangers, Libbie was primarily concerned about the wind, which might blow her skirts up, threatening her modesty rather than her life. For that reason, she had the hem of her riding habit weighted until it was so heavy that she could barely lift it over her head to take it off without help.

Alice Baldwin was also more worried about her modesty than her safety when she was chased by Indians soon after her arrival in the

West. As she and her officer escort fled, her saddle girth broke, and the lieutenant ordered her to ride bareback and astride. Alice protested that it would reveal a great deal of her lower anatomy. The officer responded, "Damn your legs! . . . I've got to get you home."[11] Alice arrived safely back at the post but was covered with embarrassment—and saddlesores.

Libbie and Autie Custer felt very secure when they escorted some visiting personnel on a tour of the Kansas countryside. The twenty officers, three wives, and some enlisted personnel sang songs as they followed a meandering creek on a sixteen-mile ride. Fortunately this sightseeing group missed a body of Indians traveling the same route at about the same time. Next day the Custers learned that the natives had attacked a nearby stage depot and killed the people working there.

Two ominous-looking men approached Fannie and Orsemus Boyd when they were out riding near Fort Union but left them alone when Boyd made it clear to them that he was armed. The officer and his wife later discovered that the men had apparently murdered, only fifteen hundred yards from the fort, the trooper who carried the mail. Pursuers quickly tracked down the killers and brought them back to be held in the guardhouse. That night civil authorities arrived and demanded that the murderers be handed over. Despite pleas from the prisoners, the commander delivered the men to the sheriff and posse. The instant that the group was off the military reservation, the sheriff was "overpowered" and the two killers were hanged from the nearest telegraph poles. (There wasn't enough wood in the neighborhood to hang them from a tree.) Women going horseback riding had to avoid the area for several days or be forcibly reminded of the immediacy of frontier justice.

The second question most wives were asked when they arrived in the West was, "Do you shoot?" Frances Roe's husband, Faye, considered it essential in Indian country that she learn how to handle a gun, and he made her practice with a Spencer carbine until she could hit a four-inch bull's eye seventy-five yards away. When he suggested that she try a heavy Springfield rifle, the recoil kicked her flat on her back, and the noise nearly deafened her. Seventh Cavalry officers liked to say that Mrs. "Fresh" (Algernon E.?) Smith had learned how to shoot and "hit something, too." Libbie Custer said the "dullest" of the other wives understood from that comment that the men "thought it an impossibility for the rest of us to ever have an accurate aim."[12] Grace Paulding's husband, William, was certainly concerned about what she would hit. Grace hadn't taken lessons but insisted on sleeping with William's army revolver under her pillow while he was away on duty. Mrs. Paulding believed that she was "behaving in the best western tradition," but undoubtedly would have questioned her persona as a strong frontier woman had she known that Captain Paulding had unloaded the weapon, afraid that she would shoot herself.[13]

Katie Garrett admitted to Autie Custer that she knew nothing about horses and guns, was afraid of both, and felt "like a fool, not being able to do anything that others do out here."[14] The next morning Custer and his brother, Tom, began giving her lessons, driving the girl "like a galley slave" until she developed into a proficient rider and excellent shot. They had promised Katie that if she attained sufficient skill they would allow her to attend a buffalo hunt. She would not be permitted to participate, however, but would have to stay at a safe distance with the wives. When a herd was discovered nearby, the garrison turned out, with most of the women traveling by ambulance. Libbie Custer watched the hunt with opera glasses kept in a velvet case. Katie and Mollie chose to ride horseback, and Frank Gibson, Katie's fiancé, was mounted on a horse called Comanche. (The animal would later be the only cavalry survivor at the Battle of the Little Big Horn.) As the men charged into the herd, the sisters followed a parallel course on a nearby hill. Mollie's horse suddenly went lame with a stone in its shoe, and she slid off the animal to try to dislodge it. As she concentrated on the task, Mollie was unaware that a buffalo had separated from the herd and was bearing down on her. Knowing that the kneeling woman could not get away on a lame horse, Katie took action. "Leaning way over in my saddle, I aimed . . . and shot—once—twice. The beast whirled upon me, so close that I could almost feel the breath of his . . . nostrils, and plunged." Her horse shied, throwing Katie to the ground and knocking her unconscious. When she came to, the dead buffalo was nearby. The officers were gathered around Katie, concerned at first, but increasingly furious with the women for disobeying instructions to remain with the other ladies. A stern Custer lectured Katie but weakened it at the end when he added enthusiastically, "Holy Mackerel, am I proud of your marksmanship!"[15]

Hunting expeditions provided an exciting opportunity to both relieve boredom and obtain additional sources of food and clothing. During one hunt, officers and their wives brought back four bears, sixteen deer, eighteen elk, ten antelope, and an uncounted number of quail and pigeons.[16] The "bag" was divided between the officers and the enlisted mess while the furs and skins were used for clothes and household decorations. Alice Baldwin had an exchange arrangement with some bachelor officers. She would feed them if they would lend her a horse for a daily ride and provide a variety of game for the table. Everyone understood that an important additional benefit of hunting was that the men became familiar with terrain that they might have to fight on one day.

Racing was another popular diversion involving horses. At Fort Mason, Texas, twenty-four of the thirty-four officers in the Second Cavalry were from the South, where the sport was greatly loved.[17] The government authorized each officer to keep two horses. Many of the animals at frontier posts were thoroughbreds and cavalry officers were skilled and enthusiastic riders. Fort Davis, Fort Mason, and many other western military establishments had racetracks laid out, some with wooden stands for spectators. A special section was usually reserved for the ladies so that they could avoid the rowdier element attracted to the races from the surrounding countryside. At Fort Sill, officers formed a jockey club, and races were held on a one-mile course every Saturday afternoon. Officers at Fort Leavenworth had their own racing colors, which were reflected in the ribbons or scarves worn by their wives or sweethearts. Prizes included golden spurs and silver-mounted riding whips. Gambling was an inevitable aspect of the sport as officers wagered champagne and wives bet their gloves and handkerchiefs. Losing a wager on the frontier really meant something because the objects risked were often hard to replace.

Card parties sometimes involved gambling and were also popular, especially on long winter evenings at the snowbound northern posts. When Lt. and Mrs. John McBlain entertained with a card party at Fort Robinson, the forty-eight guests crammed into their quarters might have played casino, euchre, or keno.[18] Women at western posts were daring enough to enjoy a "ladies night" at the officers' club with gambling, liquor, and an occasional cigarette. Frances Roe and other wives at Fort Shaw played whist so late that they had to walk home through the darkest night they had ever seen. It was a lonely walk because the men were out campaigning, and the post was almost empty.

Some of the same wives who gambled on Saturdays managed to get up in time on Sunday mornings to lead church services. In 1850 the majority of active church members in the United States were women.[19] Worship services in the East had provided for both their religious and social needs. In the West, the military had only three chaplains for all the frontier garrisons.[20] When on the trail, Eveline Alexander reported that it distressed her "to travel on the Sabbath and to see the day so little regarded as it is in the army."[21] Since Uncle Sam did not see fit to provide spiritual support for its troops, women planned religious activities at most posts. Emily FitzGerald had ten participants in the Sunday school she organized for the laundresses' children at Fort Lapwai.[22] Elizabeth Burt and her sister, Kate, held similar classes for the soldiers' children at Fort Bridger. Women at Fort Snelling gathered for a prayer service every Sunday afternoon; the wives at Fort Union formed a choir and presented an Easter program for the garrison. Libbie Custer and other Seventh Cavalry wives were participating in a song service at Fort Abraham Lincoln at the very moment that many of their husbands were being killed at Little Big Horn.

Fort Shaw was fortunate enough to have a worship service every other Sunday night, but the Rev. Mr. Clark had to ride eighty-five miles from Helena to hold it. The post even had a choir with a star "barytone" who had come to the United States with a touring opera company. The military had gained his services when an attack of diptheria ruined his voice for the stage. When the Presbyterian minister assigned to Fort Davis finally arrived, he held services only on Sunday evenings, and it was predominantly a class for the children of the post. The chaplain also held a school to teach illiterate black soldiers how to read and write; the ladies felt that effort received much more attention than his ministerial duties. Mary Swanson at

*Elizabeth Reynolds Burt
(Courtesy U.S. Army Military
History Institute)*

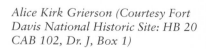

*Frances Anne Mullen Boyd
(Courtesy University of
Nebraska Press)*

*Alice Kirk Grierson (Courtesy Fort
Davis National Historic Site: HB 20
CAB 102, Dr. J, Box 1)*

Helen Grierson Fuller (Courtesy Fort Davis National Historic Site: BA-6)

Frances Mack Roe (Courtesy University of Nebraska Press)

*Martha Dunham Summerhayes (*Vanished Arizona, *1911 edition)*

Nannie Mills in native costume. The blond Mrs. Mills (also pictured on the cover) apparently donned a wig and stained her skin to get an authentic appearance. (Courtesy U.S. Army Military History Institute)

Mrs. Henry J. Goldman riding astride and wearing some form of pants, Fort Apache, Arizona, c. 1880. (Courtesy U.S. Army Military History Institute)

Elizabeth Bacon Custer
(on the right) and her sister-
in-law, Margaret Custer
Calhoun (Courtesy U.S.
Army Military History
Institute)

Jennie Platt Barnitz (Courtesy U.S.
Army Military History Institute)

People in front of tents at Fort Duchesne, Utah. Woman in the center of front row is Mrs. Frederick Benteen; man at right end of back row is her husband, Maj. Benteen. (Courtesy National Archives and Records Administration: 111-SC-103528)

Ada Adams Vogdes (on the left) holding a small child and sitting with an unidentified woman companion at San Diego, California, 1892. (Courtesy The Huntington Library: HM 29204)

Bowen, the Summerhayes' "faithful soldier-cook" (Vanished Arizona, 1911 edition)

The Summerhayes' quarters at Ehrenberg, Arizona (Vanished Arizona, 1911 edition)

Sutler's store at Fort McPherson, Nebraska, 1873 (Courtesy Western History Collections, University of Oklahoma Library, No. 1250, Rose Collection)

Rustic hotel, Fort Laramie, Wyoming, 1883 (Courtesy American Heritage Center, University of Wyoming, Mrs. Ray M. Littler Collection: 6363)

Post hospital (center building) at Fort Douglas, Utah, 1880s (Courtesy U.S. Army Military History Institute)

Wives and daughters of officers stationed at Fort Keogh, Montana, 1890s. Although the picture may have been staged, many army wives on the frontier did drink, smoke, and gamble. (Courtesy Christian Barthelmess Collection, Miles City, Montana)

Military couples dance on canvas spread on the banks of the Yellowstone River, Fort Keogh, Montana, 1892 (Courtesy Montana Historical Society, Christian Barthelmess Collection: C-347)

Officers and wives dressed for a masquerade ball, Fort Assiniboine, Montana, 1891 (Courtesy American Heritage Center, University of Wyoming, F775-A, Ed Nolan Collection: 3371)

Officers and their families in the hills above Fort Davis, Texas (Courtesy Fort Davis National Historic Site: FODA HG-25)

A "mounted troop" of wives and children at Fort Laramie, Wyoming, 1888 (Courtesy Fort Laramie National Historic Site)

Army family on the porch of their quarters at Fort Elliott, Texas, 1881. The servant on the left is apparently considered enough a part of the family to be included in the picture. (Courtesy U.S. Army Military History Institute)

Apache warrior Geronimo at the wheel of a touring sedan, 1905 (Courtesy National Archives and Records Administration: 075-IC-1A)

Army family visiting Sioux chief Sitting Bull and his family in 1882, only six years after the Battle of the Little Big Horn (Courtesy National Archives and Records Administration: 111-SC-83744)

Tenth Cavalry escort in Gen. Wesley Merritt's party at lunch, St. Mary's, Montana, 1894 (Courtesy Montana Historical Society, Helena)

The first lady voters in Guthrie, Oklahoma Territory, June 5, 1889 (Courtesy Western History Collections, University of Oklahoma Library, No. 108, Swearingen Collection)

Concord Stage used on the Overland Trail by the U.S. Express Co. African-American troops are riding on top. (Courtesy Western History Collections, University of Oklahoma Library, No. 1689, Campbell Collection)

Water wagon at Fort Keogh, Montana (Courtesy National Archives and Records Administration: 111-SC-97438)

U.S. Army ambulance used to transport wives and children of army personnel (Courtesy Western History Collections, University of Oklahoma Library, No. 1693, Campbell Collection)

Military families skating at Fort Keogh, Montana, in the late 1880s (Courtesy National Archives and Records Administration: 111-SC-97955)

Winter at Fort Yates, North Dakota, c. 1890 (Courtesy U.S. Army Military History Institute)

Fourth Cavalry band, Fort Huachuca, Arizona, mid-1880s (Courtesy National Archives and Records Administration: 111-SC-87372)

Water supply for the post in the hills above Fort Huachuca, Arizona. (Courtesy National Archives and Records Administration: 111-SC-87834)

Amusement hall, Fort Custer, Montana (Courtesy National Archives and Records Administration: 092-F-17-21)

Officers' quarters, Fort Leavenworth, Kansas, c. 1880 (Courtesy National Archives and Records Administration: 092-F-33-9)

Fort Davis wrote to another officer's wife, Grace Maxon, that she was homesick for church services.

Many of the women had been strongly religious when they left the East, but their extended time on the frontier away from regular worship possibly left some of them less attached to organized religion. Mattie Summerhayes believed that people on the frontier "almost forgot that such organizations as churches existed."[23] Although the majority of the women came from conservative denominations that strongly condemned divorce, some officers' wives separated from their husbands after they returned east. The fact that divorce was very common in the West and that the U.S. divorce rate doubled between the end of the Civil War and the beginning of World War I may have influenced the women. However, such independent action also suggests that the wives may have been less influenced by traditional religious values during their time on the frontier.[24]

Although military garrisons didn't always have chaplains, most had a large building that served as a combination ballroom, theater, and chapel. It was seldom a chapel and only occasionally a theater—but constantly a ballroom. The army loved to dance. Ellen Biddle said that military wives were able to keep their youthful figures because of regular exercise at the weekly dances, or hops, that women organized at each post.[25] When there weren't enough officers' wives at Fort Stanton to have separate dances each week, the women attended those given by the soldiers. However, when an enlisted man in dress uniform arrived uninvited at an officers' dance at Fort Supply, he was escorted out. At Fort Custer, Montana Territory, officers danced with laundresses and wives with enlisted personnel at a St. Patrick's Day ball given by a predominantly Irish unit. James Biddle almost turned down an invitation to a dance near Fort Lyon that was being held to celebrate the marriage of Kit Carson's son. Mexicans would be present, and he didn't want Ellen to hurt their feelings by refusing to dance with them. To his surprise, she not only danced with the Mexican neighbors but performed the schottische with a short, fat, Dutch baker. The enlisted men of the Seventh Cavalry took turns giving formal balls in their barracks during the winter at Fort Abraham Lincoln. Women from nearby Bismarck, a few female servants, and the laundresses partnered the enlisted men. The first sergeant opened the dancing; the officers and their wives formed a set at one end of the room. The Custers's only concern was that none of the officers' wives make fun of the unorthodox outfits worn by servants, laundresses, or women from town.

Dress became a special problem when the dance was a masquerade ball. Fannie Boyd found it a real challenge to conceal her identity among the limited number of people at a frontier post. However, Frances Roe was quite successful at disguising herself at a masked ball given in Helena. The regimental colonel, apparently thinking she was someone else, followed her all evening. Since the senior officer had not tried hard to disguise his identity, Frances lost out in both partners and fun as the junior personnel were not inclined to interrupt the colonel's pursuit of the woman. At the unmasking the officer was horrified to discover that he had been chasing and flirting with the wife of one of his second lieutenants. Her husband, Faye, was even less amused.

When Roe organized a masked ball at Fort Lyon, Colorado, it was held in the medical facility's new ward, which had not yet been opened. The offices were decorated as ladies' dressing rooms, and supper was served in the hospital's dining area. Attendees from as far away as Forts Leavenworth, Riley, Dodge, and Wallace, Kansas, crowded every corner of the post. Almost everyone was in costume. One officer was dressed as a skeleton, wearing a tightly fitted brown suit on which some student of anatomy had painted every bone in the human body. Two of the infantry officers somehow managed to come dressed as sailors. Dancing began at 9:00 P.M., supper and the unmasking occurred at midnight, then more dancing took place until 5:00 A.M. The women had worked hard to create a fairy-tale setting for the party, and Frances bemoaned the fact that only a few days later the new ward would be "filled with iron cots and sick soldiers, and instead of delicate perfumes, the odor of nauseous drugs will pervade every place."[26]

A bugler sounding "Assembly" gave Ellen Biddle a similar moment of reality in the middle of a hop at Fort Whipple. One minute the men were wearing dancing shoes, the next it was "boots and saddles" as they were off to chase renegade Apaches.

Music for such dancing was usually provided by elements of the regimental band. Legislation in 1866 had severely limited the number of musicians in infantry and artillery bands and for a short time permitted the cavalry only twenty-four trumpeters. Recognizing the importance of martial music, most commanders levied an assessment on the men of their regiment to support a band. Col. Benjamin Grierson, a former music teacher, asked every white officer of the Tenth Cavalry to donate fifty dollars and each black enlisted man to give fifty cents to purchase instruments and buy sheet music. The Seventh Cavalry collected $959.00 with its assessment.[27] The Twenty-Fourth infantry used the funds it gathered to purchase a musical library eventually valued at over six thousand dollars.[28]

Most commanders preferred to have German or Italian musicians to play this music. Lt. Col. George Crook felt so strongly about this that he recommended someone be sent to the entry point in New York to recruit army bandsmen from the arriving immigrants. The Eighth Infantry band had so many foreigners that Mattie Summerhayes said it was imported "direct from Italy."[29] Custer's trumpeter in the Seventh Cavalry, Giovanni Martini, had served as a drummer boy with Garibaldi, and the Eleventh Infantry bandmaster at Fort Huachuca, Arizona, was Achilles LaGuardia. (His son, Fiorello, would move east and become the flamboyant mayor of New York City.) When the regimental band appeared on the lawn to welcome the arrival of the Kimballs at their new assignment, Maria was surprised to discover that the bandmaster, a German named Daleiden, was a graduate of the University of Gottingen.

As adjutant at Fort Shaw, Faye Roe worked hard to reorganize the regimental band, getting them nicer uniforms and receiving some new instrumentation from the director of the Marine band, John Phillip Sousa. Sousa had been "most kind and interested" in Roe's efforts and even dedicated "The March Past of the Rifle Regiment" to his unit. The band played at guard mount every morning and presented a concert each Friday evening. It did so well that the post commander decided that some of the bandsmen, along with a group of enlisted singers, should provide music at church services when the Rev. Mr. Clark came from Helena to preach. Since it was a religious exercise that obviously needed a woman's touch, the senior officer ordered Frances Roe to take command. After arguing perfunctorily against the idea, Frances gave in, admitting that she "did not want some one else to take charge!"[30] Roe selected the music, rehearsed the singers and six musicians assigned to the duty, and nervously arrived for the chapel service, aware that failure of this innovation would bring severe criticism. She sat as quietly as she could because every time she turned her head or brushed flies away from her face, the musicians grabbed for their instruments. It was a very successful performance. Later, to show her appreciation for the hard work and "their obedience to my slightest request," Roe sent them a cake and fresh eggs as a thank-you gift.[31]

In addition to supporting the band, part of the assessment money went to buy books and newspapers for post libraries. The one at Fort McPherson, Nebraska, contained 362 books while the library at Fort Sully, South Dakoka, had 800.[32] In 1849 the Council of Administration at Fort Gibson appropriated $49.91 for newspaper subscriptions to the *Daily Herald, New York Intelligencer,* and others.[33] The library at Fort Robinson included the *Army and Navy Register,* three daily newspapers, and four periodicals, including *Harper's, Puck,* and a black weekly paper from New York called *The Freeman.* A few years later it added the *Atlantic Monthly, Scribner's,* and *Century.*[34]

Fannie Boyd considered reading the only luxury at Camp Halleck and looked forward with "great delight" to mail deliveries that brought the serialized stories she was following in various periodicals. After she empathized deeply with one story that had a heroine cast ashore on a desert island far from civilization, the mail failed to deliver the next five installments. Fannie and Orsemus were left to fill in the gaps with their imaginations.

Until expansion of the railroad system, mail with its touch of the outside world came only once a month to many frontier posts. If a letter from the East made a certain contact point for transport via railroad, riverboat, or stage, it usually could be delivered to the recipient within thirty days. If it missed that scheduled departure, however, it might be delayed more than two months. When the mail was late, Fannie Boyd wrote that "nothing else could be thought of or talked of" until it arrived.[35] Helen Chapman and another army wife were so eager for news from home that they rode alone across eight miles of desolate prairie just to pick up the mail at Brazos, Texas. Lydia Lane described how everyone at Fort Stanton eagerly watched a certain hill around which the mail carrier had to come—if the

Indians hadn't gotten him. When the courier was killed, loss of this brief contact with civilization was usually bemoaned as greatly as was loss of the man.

Arrival of the mail was such an exciting time that the commanding officer at Fort C. F. Smith allowed the three officers' wives to attend its distribution. Elizabeth Burt impatiently watched the growth of her own stack of mail and "afterward devoured the month old letters and papers."[36] One army wife doled out the newspapers to her husband each morning, laying one on the breakfast table as if the paper boy had just traveled a thousand miles to deliver it to their front door. Papers and periodicals were passed from person to person until the paper literally disintegrated in the reader's hands. One officer who was at the end of the chain was disgusted to find that the last five pages of an intriguing story had apparently fallen apart with repeated handling. Dr. McKay said that only magazines and the mail helped make assignment to the very isolated Fort McRae "better than being in a penitentiary."[37]

Sometimes travelers arriving at western posts provided news and moments of excitement. In 1877 Fort Omaha welcomed President and Mrs. Rutherford B. Hayes as well as former President and Mrs. Ulysses S. Grant. Mark Twain was a guest of Andrew and Elizabeth Burt at Fort Missoula, Montana, while Frederic Remington painted at several frontier locations. Eveline Alexander was the hostess and only woman at a dinner for Lt. Gen. William Sherman given in a tent at Fort Stevens, Colorado. She managed to obtain a saddle of mutton and various vegetables for the meal, but the general had to eat it while seated on a trunk. Eveline told him the only luxury she could offer him was what he regretted most about leaving camp life—he could throw his coffee grounds on the floor.[38] The twenty-two-year-old Grand Duke Alexis of Russia decided to hunt buffalo when he toured the United States in 1872. Maj. Gen. Philip Sheridan ordered the officers of the Military Division of the Missouri to report on locations and movements of buffalo herds; Christmas furloughs were canceled as Second Cavalry personnel worked to construct a special campsite. The scout for the hunt was Buffalo Bill Cody; another participant was Autie Custer. In July 1884 officers and their wives at Fort Ellis had to prepare for a visit by the president of the United

States, the lieutenant general of the army, and the governor of Montana, who were all coming to "inspect" Yellowstone Park. The fact that the park was finally accessible by railroad gave congressmen, generals, and judges what Frances Roe called "a fine excuse for an outing at Uncle Sam's expense."[39] Ellen Biddle was delighted when General Schofield arrived at Camp Halleck because, "had it not been for these occasional visits, life would have been very dreary."[40]

Visitors to a frontier garrison often were given a guided tour of the local "zoo" kept by military personnel. Teresa Viele gathered a fawn, two goats, a flock of doves, chickens, a parrot, four dogs, some mockingbirds, orioles, and a mountain lion cub. Seventh Cavalry officers and their wives had a wolf, prairie dogs, raccoons, porcupines, turkey, badgers, antelope, and buffalo as pets. Frances Roe had a gray squirrel that she led around by a tiny "picket rope" made of ribbon; another wife kept a horned toad in her pocket.

Soldiers and civilians knew that the Custers loved animals and thus sent them four-legged gifts that became "members of our family."[41] One mare was a great favorite. When a cold storm came up while the Seventh was in the field, Autie brought the animal from the picket line and placed her under the tent fly. Reaching through the tapes that closed the tent opening to give the mare some sugar, Libbie could feel the animal shivering with cold. When Autie asked if she minded the horse being so close, his wife reassured him but added that it was providential that horses didn't usually lie down or she would be "wheedled" into giving up her bed.

Libbie rebelled only when one donor delivered a mountain lion. It had to be kept in the cellar, which made the cook somewhat hesitant to go down for supplies of food. Custer yielded to Libbie's fears and arranged to send the mountain lion east to a zoo in the "States." When the time came to box it for transport, they had to chloroform the animal. Regaining consciousness in the baggage room at the railroad station, the lion was furious and somehow managed to escape. In a massive understatement, Libbie wrote, "The freight agent spent a wretched day."[42]

Tom Custer kept a collection of rattlesnakes and was never able to resist adding a snake with more than seven rattles to his herpetorium. He would use the butt of a rifle to pinion the snake near the head, then seize it by the back of its "neck" and drop it down the sleeve of his orderly's coat, which had been tied at the wrist. Periodically he would mischievously demand that a less-than-enthusiastic Libbie admire his collection, which he kept in hardtack boxes. She tried to avoid this "entertainment" but "might as well have argued with the snakes themselves for all the good accomplished."[43] While he lifted the reptiles out of the boxes to exhibit them, his sister-in-law stood on his campbed, her toes trembling in the covers. When the "show" was finally over, Libbie went home "almost frisking with joy" at her escape from the ordeal—until the next time.[44]

Flora Cooper's daughter Forrestine raised five baby mice, keeping them alive by feeding them from the tip of a twisted cloth that had been dipped in a mixture of milk, warm water, and sugar. Since Flora was afraid of mice, Forrestine was required to keep them outside. However, when the temperature dropped, the child sneaked the rodents into the house to keep them from freezing to death. Looking for someplace warm to hide them that night, Forrestine placed a tiny mouse in each of the fingers of Flora's fur-lined riding gloves. She intended to remove them before her mother awakened. The next morning, as her child peacefully overslept, Flora decided on an early morning ride. In her hurry she must have forgotten a primary rule of the frontier: to shake one's shoes, socks, or gloves before putting them on to see if anything has taken up residence. Grabbing her gloves and shoving them onto her fingers, she almost died—and the mice did. Forrestine and her father had a military funeral in the backyard for the pets, but the child was brokenhearted when her father refused to fire a salute over the rodents' grave.

Making children happy was often a challenge on the frontier, especially during the holidays. Instead of the arrival of Santa Claus, children at Fort Phil Kearny expected an Indian attack after some of their fathers were killed in the Fetterman Massacre on December 21, 1866. Fort Robinson's children were afraid even Santa couldn't make it through a blizzard surrounding the post, but Cpl. Martin Weber and a driver used six mules instead of eight reindeer to deliver their holiday gifts on time. When the men arrived at the post, the excited children ran out to meet them chanting, "The Christmas wagon has come."[45] Mrs. Perry erected a Christmas tree and gathered presents for the laundresses' children at Fort Lapwai, but Frances Roe wasn't as fortunate at Fort Lyon. They couldn't find any evergreen trees near the post. Neither could Alice Grierson at Fort Davis; she rigged "the best tree she could" with artificial flowers, ribbons, and Chinese lanterns.[46]

Alice did even better for New Year's Day. As the commanding officer and his wife, the Griersons were expected to give a large reception for the garrison each January 1. At Fort Concho, they served their holiday guests eight turkeys, a ham, a goose, some venison, three fruit cakes, three marble cakes, two jelly cakes, and two white-cakes, with citron, pickles, canned pears, preserved quinces, apples, and raisins.[47] This escape from the usual diet of roast beef, beef steak, ground beef, and beef stew made the Christmas season especially exciting. The post trader at Fort Lyon sent all the way to St. Louis for turkeys, canned oysters, and celery to offer variety during the holidays. Normally the post only had potatoes—and beef.

Fannie Boyd had her monotony relieved when the Eighthth Cavalry celebrated Christmas at Mesilla and Las Cruces, New Mexico, on their way from Fort Bayard to Fort Clark, Texas, in 1875. While the officers and their wives danced at a party in their honor, enlisted personnel toasted the season too liberally and got into a "perfect battle" outside the party.[48] The officer in charge ordered the units to break camp and resume the march eastward, dragging the inebriated men away from the celebration. The officers and their wives were forced to catch up to the column as best they could after the holiday.

Conversely, the enlisted personnel at Fort Lyon had every button shining when the officers and their wives visited the barracks on Christmas 1871. The men were so perfect that Frances Roe had to struggle to resist the temptation to tell the general's little boy to pinch one and make him jump. The first sergeant displayed the tables loaded with food, including the plum cake that tradition required an officer's wife to provide for her husband's company each Christmas. Faye Roe had almost devoured the rare treat before he discovered that it was to be delivered to the enlisted men in the barracks.

Food was also a significant part of celebrations for the Fourth of July, another important holiday for the military. The sutler hosted a picnic for the personnel at Fort Fetterman in 1869, providing wine, champagne, brandy, cakes, nuts, and other delicacies to his guests. The 1879 celebration at Fort Yates, North Dakota, included a rifle match and baseball game between officers and enlisted personnel, a hundred-yard footrace, wheelbarrow races, a greased pig catch, a fireworks display, a band concert, and a grand ball given by the officers and their wives.[49] Fort Robinson and the nearby town of Crawford, Nebraska, celebrated together, with Indian dances, horseraces, parades, baseball games, and a giant tug-of-war between civilians and military. One year more than four thousand people attended the events.[50] A long-overdue payday was treated like a holiday at Fort Phil Kearny on October 31, 1866. Poems were read, speeches were made, the new flagstaff was dedicated, the regimental band played, and cannons were fired. After an unexpected Indian attack in the afternoon, a dance was held that night. A St. Patrick's Day celebration at Fort Concho in 1876 pitted Irish personnel against black enlisted men in various types of races as well as a competition to climb a greased pole. Often the events were military contests, between teams, to see who could pitch a tent or pack a mule the fastest.

The baseball diamond often provided a nonthreatening meeting ground between black enlisted personnel and white military units or civilians. The Sixth Cavalry at Fort Lowell, Arizona, challenged a team from nearby Tucson, and a group of soldiers stationed near the Mexican border wagered two barrels of Milwaukee beer on the outcome of a baseball game with some local cowboys. Only a few of the officers were considered proficient enough to play on their unit teams, but many coached and their wives were vocal cheerleaders.

Although most sports were designed primarily for men, women increasingly participated in athletics after the Civil War. In addition to riding, shooting, and skating, army wives in the West played tennis, though it wasn't deemed suitable for them to actually break into a sweat or be too competitive at the game. Croquet was considered more appropriate for ladies since "it required considerable skill but not too much strength or technique."[51] At Fort Robinson, Capt. August Corliss taught his wife and Col. Edward Hatch's daughter, Bessie, how to fence. Women at Fort Davis who liked to swim went to Phantom Lake, about thirty miles north of the post, where officers and wives played in the water that ran out of a mountain cave. On

these outings, the women swam easily in lighter, less-concealing garments than they could have worn in the East, where layered beach-
wear made swimming practically impossible.

Phantom Lake was also a popular place for fishing, a sport that attracted many army wives. Alice Grierson enjoyed a fishing trip at
Fort Concho that included forty-seven men, women, and children.
The black members of the band served as an escort and performed in
the evening after dinner. Several soldiers and the post doctor apparently tap danced on a board that had served earlier as the food table
at the campsite. Alice was an eager fisherwoman and wrote her son
proudly that she "got as fine a bass as was caught."[52]

Despite the fact that a nearby officer was using a fancy new rod
and reel, it was Frances Roe who had similar luck on a fishing trip in
Montana. A magnificent trout was hungry for the grasshopper she
had attached to the hook on her common willow pole. Frances had
no reel but was determined not to lose the fish, which was struggling
frantically. The army wife marched resolutely away from the stream
and scrambled up the four- to five-foot-high bank until the flopping
fish was dragged out of the water. The three and-one-half pound
trout provided that night's dinner. When she later went fishing with
Gen. George Crook, Frances, in two hours, caught sixteen trout
weighing a total of twenty-five pounds.[53] She would "tuck up" her
skirts, despite the presence of an enlisted escort, and wade into the
"foamy, roaring torrent" to get at the fish.

While the East offered women a wide variety of passive entertainment such as plays, symphony concerts, and lyceum lectures, most of
the diversions on the frontier, such as amateur theatricals, riding,
shooting, dancing, and the fishing that Frances Roe enjoyed so much
required their active participation. The more tolerant, family atmosphere at frontier posts offered less risk of censure to army wives for
mixed swimming, dancing with enlisted men, or leading a squirrel
around on a leash. Unacceptable by eastern standards, such behavior
reflected the women's adaptability to the simpler, often more rugged
pleasures of the West. The development of new skills and their involvement and even leadership in social activities, as when Frances
Roe took command of the orchestra for church services, not only kept
the women busy but also became a source of personal satisfaction and

self-discovery. Roe wrote that there were those who "yawn and complain of the monotony of frontier life, but these are the stay-at-homes
who sit by their own fires day after day and let cobwebs gather in
brain and lungs. . . . These, too, are the ones who have time to discover so many faults in others, and become our garrison gossips! If
they would take brisk rides on spirited horses in this wonderful air,
and learn to shoot all sorts of guns in all sorts of positions, they would
soon discover that a frontier post can furnish plenty of excitement."[54]
If so, the women planned and provided much of it themselves.

Cholera and Creosote

BEFORE THEY WENT west, army wives had undoubtedly read articles and promotional material that described the active, outdoor life on the frontier as healthy and invigorating. Many of the women looked forward to raising their children in clean, crisp air and wide-open spaces, far from the epidemics that periodically spread from the slums of overpopulated, tightly packed, eastern cities. However, they quickly discovered that the benefits of life in this pristine environment were often counteracted by diseases caused by the military's marginal diet, substandard quarters, and lack of adequate medical care. Isolation from civilization, the constant threat of Indian attack, and long periods of separation from husbands and fathers also drained the emotional health of army wives and children in the West.

Potential danger from man and animals was always present. In 1868 Albert Barnitz wrote his wife, Jennie, that a gray wolf that was rabid had attacked personnel at Fort Larned, Kansas. The animal had careened through the post, biting a guard, a man already in the hospital, and a lieutenant sitting on his porch, and chomping down on one soldier in a tent so tightly that he was dragged out of his bed. The wolf had fortunately missed when it lunged at several women. Since rabies serum was not developed until 1899, those who were bitten at Fort Larned must have suffered an agonizing death.[1]

Nature could attack just as unexpectedly. The Burt's eleven-year-old son begged to accompany his father on a government expedition to confirm the discovery of gold in the Black Hills. Although Ellen Burt was concerned about Indians, it was a violent thunderstorm that injured the child. Leaving his horse to seek shelter with some soldiers under a tree, the boy had huddled beside the trunk; next to him was a rifle leaning against the bark. Lightning struck, traveled down the

tree, and was deflected by the metal barrel of the gun. The bolt killed
a horse nearby and ran through the length of the child, leaving one
mark on his cheek where it entered and a hole the size of a dime in
his shoe where it exited. Andrew Burt and the doctor worked an
hour to save the boy's life.[2]

The 1890 report of the secretary of war informed the president that
the army had suffered 9,473 such accidents, wounds, and injuries
among its troops that year.[3] To help those who were hurt at frontier
posts, there were only 147 military doctors west of the Mississippi
River. They had to provide care for more than twenty-thousand men
as well as the entire population of wives, children, and laundresses.[4]
Although Congress had authorized a much larger medical corps, by
1873 the service had sixty-four vacancies. To address the shortage,
Washington approved the use of civilian physicians but in 1874 limited the number who could be hired to seventy-five.[5] Few of these
"contract doctors" were anxious to work on the Indian frontier or
travel to isolated posts.

Although the number of military doctors was limited, most of
them were highly qualified. An eminent physician in New York assured Ellen Biddle that the Army Medical Board examination was
extremely difficult. Those who passed would do very well in a civilian practice, and both wondered why such physicians would settle
for the small compensation and hard life provided by the army.[6] Walter Reed, who proved in 1900 that mosquitoes transmitted yellow
fever, was one who did. With two medical degrees, one from the University of Virginia and another from Bellevue Medical College in
New York City, Reed entered the army in 1875 and served at various
frontier locations. During his time at Fort Lowell, Arizona, Reed decided that malaria was caused by the vast temperature span between
the hours of daylight and dark. The soldiers must have been delighted when the doctor convinced the post commander to delay
reveille until after sunrise to lower exposure to the disease. Since
mosquitoes didn't work by the clock, however, the outbreak apparently continued. R. H. McKay, a former Civil War doctor from Iowa,
was another who passed the Army Medical Boards. He was sworn in
as an acting assistant surgeon on January 29, 1869. When Dr.
McKay arrived at Fort McRae to begin his tour, his predecessor, Dr.

Lyons, was eating dinner. The meal occupied one end of the table; a human skull and dissecting instruments were at the other. McKay wrote that it was needless to say that Lyons was a bachelor, for "no woman would stand for that sort of table decoration."[7] Dr. McKay found an entire skeleton buried on the parade ground at Fort Selden. Looking down, he noticed the top of the skull protruding from the dirt. The tramping of feet during constant periods of drill had unearthed the bones.

Although the accounts by officers' wives don't mention that Reed and McKay did so, army doctors were permitted to augment their income by treating civilians. The military doctor at Camp Halleck assisted Chinese laborers and others who were hurt while working on the nearby Union Pacific Railroad. Since the patients were housed in a hospital tent at the post, Fannie Boyd could easily hear the screams of the injured men who were being treated. Caroline Frey Winne's second husband, Charles, was assigned to Sidney Barracks, Nebraska, and was the only physician in that part of the state. Caroline bragged to her brother that Charles had made $163.00 from outside patients in a little over a month, doubling his income. She told how a seventy-year-old man had fallen out of a cart the previous week and broken five ribs. Despite the medical attention he received from Charles, Caroline reported that, "The old man died, but his brother is good for $40."[8] The doctor at Fort Abraham Lincoln received two large sacks of onions for amputating a rancher's gangrenous leg and considered the gift of the vegetables better than money.

In addition to caring for the sick, an army doctor also administered the military hospital and pharmacy, acted as coroner, supervised the post cemetery, and served as public health officer, inspecting military buildings, grounds, and foodstuffs for sanitation problems. There were plenty to find. In 1874 the post surgeon at Fort Laramie reported "peaks of manure from the cavalry stables and the filth and rubbish from the post . . . has been deposited for many years on the north side and immediately contiguous to the post." He later added, unnecessarily, "The stench is at times almost unendurable."[9] The yards behind the quarters at Fort Robinson were "honeycombed with privy vaults," and the grounds were "saturated with kitchen and laundry slops."[10] Packs of dogs, who probably fought over the garbage, frightened the horses until Col. Guy V. Henry threatened to shoot the canines.

Obtaining pure water was a constant problem on the frontier. Most garrisons collected their raw sewage in barrels, then dumped it into nearby streams. As summer heat left stagnant pools or as heavy rains or melting snow flooded creeks and rivers, the drinking water was often contaminated, resulting in cases of typhoid and outbreaks of cholera. Dr. McKay's little girl became ill with typhoid fever after attending an entertainment given by the enlisted men at Fort McRae. When she died, the soldiers helped to bury the child in a coffin built by the quartermaster. Alice and Benjamin Griersons' thirteen-year-old daughter, Edith, died of typhoid at Fort Concho in 1878 and was buried "like a soldier girl."[11] That same year the disease was so prevalent in Helena, Montana, that the army doctor ordered Frances Roe and other military wives to leave the area.

Cholera was a constant concern to frontier physicians. The pain experienced was so excruciating that the disease was known in France as *mort-de-chien,* a dog's death. Vomiting and severe diarrhea brought dehydration until the patient's features became a "shrunken caricature" of their former self.[12] Paralysis of the tongue often made it difficult to swallow one of the recommended remedies, two drops of creosote in cinnamon water mixed with half an ounce of thick mucilage. Although one of the treatments, drinking a mixture of salt and vinegar in hot water, actually helped by replenishing the body's needed minerals, the majority of people who contracted the disease died—after sharing the infection with others.

Helen Chapman became ill during a cholera epidemic in Texas in 1849. Out of a population of six hundred at Brownsville, there were ten to twelve deaths every day for a period of thirty days. The disease was sometimes fatal after only five or six hours of illness. Medical care was scarce because two of the three doctors had died, and the last also become ill. Since no physician was available, Helen's husband, William, cared for her and ended up providing medical advice for most of the other people in town. The army wife eventually survived but weighed only eighty-six pounds as she began her recovery.

Fleeing to avoid the disease, people simply spread it to a wider area. Whole towns in the Rio Grande valley were almost wiped out.

Over 25 percent of the command at Fort McIntosh became ill and 75 percent of those stricken didn't recover. Brownsville and the military at Fort Brown suffered repeatedly: from the 1849 cholera outbreak; a siege of dengue fever in 1850–1851; and yellow fever epidemics in 1841, 1845, and 1853.[13] Army wives at the post were fortunate in one respect—at least dengue fever didn't seem to attack women and children as often as it did men.

Some of the officers' wives at Fort Harker, Kansas, weren't as fortunate as Helen Chapman. Two of them died in the 1867 cholera outbreak at the fort and the third departed. Alice Baldwin was the only officer's wife who remained. Nuns from the Sisters of Mercy near Fort Leavenworth came to help care for the victims. At the height of the epidemic Libbie Custer arrived at the post but was later ordered away to Fort Riley. Perhaps in an effort to reach her, Autie Custer left his command without authority and rode more than two hundred miles across the Kansas countryside to reach Fort Harker. Finding Libbie gone, he pursued her to Fort Riley. If the unauthorized trip was due to devotion, it earned him a court-martial and suspension of rank and pay for a year.

The mortality rate at Fort Harker was so high that it was finally decided not to make public the number of dead. Its hospital was considered to be one of the best on the plains, and it needed to be. The command there was just beginning to recover from the estimated two hundred deaths in the vicinity when a unit passing through brought smallpox to the post.[14]

Flora Cooper was on her way back to Fort Concho in 1874 from a visit to her family in Philadelphia when outbreaks of cholera and yellow fever left her quarantined with her children at Navasota, Texas. Flora was fortunate that another individual stranded with her was Maude Jeanne Young, a school principal who also happened to be the daughter of an official with the Houston and Texas Central Railroad. Despite the quarantine, mail was still going through and Young's father arranged to have a Pullman car attached to the back of the mail train. Maude, Flora, and the children traveled from the contagion area despite the objections of many residents in towns along the way. Hunger finally forced them to leave the train briefly in an unsuccessful search for food. One woman with a gun, terrified of the epidemic, ordered them, "Git or I'll shoot."[15] After twenty-four hours the women finally succeeded in getting some beer and pretzels, which everyone devoured, including the children. Finally reaching her goal, Flora decided that it had all happened because she had started her trip on Friday the Thirteenth.

Yellow fever and malaria were two of the most common diseases faced by army wives in the Southwest. The military learned by experience that troops and families sent to Texas had to arrive in early December if possible, after the first frost of the season had killed all the mosquitoes. In the outbreak of yellow fever at Fort Brown in 1853, medical personnel tried quinine, calomel, mustard baths, and even blood-letting, but 50 of the 245 victims died.[16] Malaria or "intermittent fever" struck every man, woman, and child at Fort Merrill, Texas, during a two-month period in 1854. That same year there were twenty-seven cases of malaria among the fifty-two women and children at Ringgold Barracks.[17] When the military ran out of quinine, it used a combination of nitric acid and arsenic to treat the victims.

Circular No. 4, a report by the surgeon general's office issued on December 5, 1870, categorized the diseases affecting the army as typhoid fever, malarial fevers, diarrhea and dysentery, tonsillitis, epidemic catarrh (upper-respiratory infection), venereal diseases, rheumatism, and phthisis (consumption).[18] It described how the men (but almost never the women) on the frontier were cared for at hospitals that ranged from the two-story, 128-foot-long sandstone building with radiating wings at Fort Richardson, Texas, to the one-story adobe hut with sod roof and dirt floor at Fort Selden, New Mexico. The hospital at Fort D. A. Russell, Wyoming, was considered "convenient" and would have been "comfortable" had not "the shingles on the roof . . . warped so that the snow blows in to some extent in winter."[19] Individuals who were ill at Fort Fred Steele, Wyoming, were treated in hospital tents while the temperature outside ranged from 90 degrees to minus twenty-one degrees. Eventually a log building was converted into a temporary hospital, but the mud chinking between the logs had fallen out until "daylight could be seen in any direction through the crevices in the walls and roof of the ward."[20]

The hospital at Fort Laramie had so many patients that some of the sick also were forced to remain in tents all winter. Severe storms repeatedly blew down the tents on top of the patients until by spring the canvas had been torn to shreds. The following summer, in 1867, the army added to the old medical facility and constructed around it "an adobe wall 10 feet high and 2 feet thick . . . [with] strong bastions at two diagonal corners . . . [that would] serve as a stronghold in case of an attack by Indians."[21] The men may have considered it an omen in 1874 when the military built the new Fort Laramie hospital on Cemetery Hill.

When the government didn't erect a hospital at Fort Davis in 1867, the army doctor assigned to the post made a deal to provide civilian workers with medical care if they would construct the hospital. When the army finally did build a twelve-bed medical facility in 1874, it cost $7,500.00, almost as much as the rest of the post put together. The military hated to expend so much money on hospitals that were only intended to last a maximum of ten years. Scientists believed that the components of such buildings absorbed germs and that their use for a longer period of time would increase the spread of disease.

While Circular 4 described varying levels of medical care in frontier hospitals, it is unlikely that any of the staff or facilities had provisions for patients with psychological problems. An insane soldier being taken to Bismarck for care was one of the party of six when Katie Garrett and Mollie McIntosh were escorted from Fort Rice to Fort Abraham Lincoln to prepare for Katie's wedding. During the journey, the huge patient complained bitterly to the women that his brother-in-law was torturing him by putting snails all over his bed until he couldn't sleep. When he decided that Mollie was his sister, Jennie, the man begged her repeatedly to make her husband stop tormenting him. The extreme heat, hordes of grasshoppers, and their traveling companion "made the trip fantastic." Manic activities by the huge patient nearly capsized their boat as they crossed the Little Heart River, a source of some concern to the women since neither could swim. After months without rain, a ferocious storm rocked the ambulance in which they traveled, and hail the size of hen's eggs pounded the canvas cover. Upset by the storm, the patient, who was manacled to a burly enlisted man, "stood erect, almost jerking his guard off the seat, and lunged for the door. Instantly his powerful bodyguard dragged him back, trying to calm him, but in vain." As the two large men struggled within the close confines of the ambulance, Mollie worked her way around them until she was beside the patient, put a hand gently on his arm, and stated, "Jennie's here." Instantly the man relaxed and sank down on the seat beside her. "Oh, Jennie," he mumbled, "you've come to save me from the snails." Throughout the chaotic storm and the long, cold night that followed, Mollie McIntosh sat holding the sick man's hand, reassuring him that his sister Jennie was protecting him.[22]

A long period of extreme isolation and constant danger from Indian attacks caused two men, one of whom was the post doctor, to go insane at Fort C. F. Smith. The pressure of leaving family and friends in the West to return to the formal and highly structured lifestyle at eastern schools undoubtedly contributed to the nervous breakdowns suffered by two of the Grierson sons, Charles and Robert. Mattie Summerhayes had to be sent away from Arizona when she began to see specters of death in the dirt and isolation at Ehrenberg. It took eight months of trees, flowers, and good food on Nantucket before Mattie decided to rejoin her husband at their new home at Camp McDowell. Sending her baggage west by boat, Mattie's depression may have returned when the ship carrying her belongings burned. She was left with only a ballgown and the clothes she was wearing. It was two months before she was able to get new outfits from the East.

Special care was also needed for those with venereal diseases and alcoholism, which were very prevalent in the army during this period. A study in 1880 indicated that 8 percent of the officers and enlisted men had venereal diseases, which they undoubtedly shared with their wives and "friends."[23] When an army doctor reported that there were no cases of syphilis at Ringgold Barracks, it was listed as a fact without precedent. During the same period 4 percent of the army was hospitalized as alcoholics.[24] This category indicated that the individuals were already experiencing advanced delirium tremens. A writer and former officer, Duane Merritt Green, considered whiskey and wives the most corrupting influences at western posts, although not necessarily in that order.[25] In 1877 a captain on the northern plains was found strangled to death, his neck caught between two pickets of a fence. The post surgeon speculated that the captain, who had been drinking excessively the night before, had been walking home when he had become nauseated. Leaning over to vomit, the officer had lost consciousness and toppled onto the fence, where he died. One of Autie Custer's officers, who had just reported to the Seventh Cavalry, arrived at Libbie's door to make his obligatory call upon the commanding officer's wife. The newcomer was so drunk that when Libbie went to greet him, he collapsed across the threshold at her feet.

Officers' wives themselves frequently used alcohol although some of them probably didn't realize it. The tremendously popular Lydia Pinkham's vegetable compound, regularly advertised in *Godey's Ladies Book,* was 15 percent alcohol.[26] Sometimes the liquor was in a prescription, as when one army doctor gave officers' wives his "Magic Relief," made of sassafras, cloves, cinnamon, sulphur, opium, myrrh, ammonia, and a gallon of alcohol.[27] Emily FitzGerald, wife of Dr. John FitzGerald, the post surgeon at Fort Lapwai, consumed a case of stout in an effort to gain weight after she had been ill. Emily wrote to her mother that, "I am afraid you won't let me into such a respectable family as yours when I come home with my failing for 'Porter.'"[28] Mattie Summerhayes was introduced to the "real old-fashioned army toddy," a new experience for a woman brought up to believe "wine-bibbing and whiskey drinking . . . as belonging only to the lowest classes." Before, when her father had two fingers of fine cognac each night before dinner, Mattie "considered that a sort of medicine for a man advanced in years."[29] When a sergeant participating in a buffalo hunt was thrown from his horse and broke his arm, none of the surrounding officers had any liquor to give him while it was being set. An orderly explained the situation to four officers' wives in a nearby ambulance, and one of them reached under the seat, pulling a flask out of her belongings. Those watching were surprised. Libbie Custer explained why by saying that the woman who had the flask was the only wife in the ambulance who was not known to drink.[30]

Gen. John Gibbon presented a bottle of gin to Andrew and Elizabeth Burt when their baby was born at Fort Sanders in 1867. He recommended that it be given to the child if it developed colic. When Elizabeth responded that she had never used gin, Gibbon replied,

"Then you don't know what a blessing it will prove. I have raised a large family out here in the West and know."[31] The Burts put the bottle away, but the baby had no colic and so it wasn't needed. Much later it was discovered that the gin had disappeared, presumably not consumed for medicinal purposes.

As with the "Magic Relief," many of the medications the women used contained drugs as well as alcohol. Morphine, cocaine, heroin, and opium were available across the counter. Paregoric (camphorated tincture of opium) was present in almost all medicine chests, and cocaine was especially popular for treating sinusitis and hay fever. In fact, Coca-Cola used cocaine in its recipe until 1903, when they replaced it with caffeine.[32]

When doctors were away for long periods of time on patrols or expeditions with the troops, it was up to army wives to provide medical care for themselves and their families. Many of the home remedies the women concocted contained various kinds of drugs. A mixture of olive oil, ammonia, turpentine, and tincture of opium was spread on insect bites, while ingrown toenails were treated with a combination of the deadly muriatic acid, nitric acid, and zinc chloride. Zinc chloride by itself was touted as a sure "cure" for cancer. Tannin, a vegetable compound used to prepare leather, could either toughen a woman's nipples for breast feeding or smooth out the wrinkles on her face. Chloroform was rubbed on toothaches, gunpowder was applied to warts, and liniments were prepared with a base of goose grease or skunk oil. Asthma patients rolled and smoked daisies or honeysuckle while patients with heart problems drank a tea made of purple foxglove (which would later form the basis for digitalis). Turpentine was a popular medication. It could treat snakebite, moisten a teaspoonful of sugar to be taken by those suffering from a sore throat, or be rubbed on hemorrhoids, an affliction that caused severe problems for people who were frequently in the saddle. A colonel who recommended it to an individual suffering from a case of piles noted that the turpentine "would make him prance around a little while."[33]

Recipes for such "cure-alls" were listed in popular health journals of the period, but women on the frontier also learned about new medications and techniques from Indians, who introduced fifty-nine valuable drugs to modern science.[34] Wads of cobwebs, readily available at frontier posts, could be stuffed into wounds to stop bleeding. Poultices of cooked onions were spread on the chests of bronchitis sufferers; garlic tea was used to treat rheumatism. When Alice Baldwin's baby daughter, Juanita, was teething, an Indian medicine man went outside and gathered some rattlesnake rattles. Shaking them and chanting softly, the medicine man quickly put the child to sleep. The Custer's servant, Burkeman, presented the mother of a new baby with the vertebrae of a rattlesnake he had killed because he had heard that it was good for a teething child to chew on.

There was no dependable "cure" for one of the greatest killers of the nineteenth century—childbirth. *Godey's Lady's Book* stressed that motherhood was the "fulfillment of a woman's physiological and moral destiny,"[35] and a medical book suggested that she "should be able to bear a healthy child every twenty months."[36] The fact was that only 23 percent of American women born in 1850 lived to see their children grown, primarily due to the complications and dangers of giving birth.[37] For army wives on the frontier, where tensions were high and living conditions harsh, the risks were even greater. The physician at Fort McKavett in 1853 listed five births during the year; two of the deliveries were breech but all of them were difficult. In 1870 Assistant Surgeon E. McClellan at Fort Garland, Colorado, informed the surgeon general that he had delivered nineteen babies in a little over a year, with fourteen of the mothers suffering postpartum hemorrhaging.[38]

It was not unusual for a pregnant woman to be traveling with a military unit, and bouncing about in an unsprung wagon frequently brought on premature labor. Before his marriage to Katie Garrett, Frank Gibson had to act as midwife for a woman traveling with his column from Fort Riley to Fort Leavenworth. Taking the army wife out of the ambulance, the men laid her on some gunny sacks that had been spread on the ground under a blazing sun. Using a penknife and handkerchiefs, the recent West Point graduate delivered "a wee, very premature recruit."[39] Taking off his dirty uniform blouse, the officer wrapped the baby in it, then placed his forage cap over the child's eyes to protect them from the glare. Both mother and baby were placed back in the ambulance, and the group proceeded slowly toward their destination. The premature infant miraculously survived, but the mother's fate is unknown.

Fannie Boyd wrote that she had delivered ten babies during her years on the frontier, but she had also prepared an equal number of women for burial.[40] Watching family members and friends die in childbirth or as the result of postpartum infections, many women were desperate for some way to avoid pregnancy. Although new methods of birth control, such as the rubber condom and the rhythm method, were developed in the 1870s, books and pamphlets about contraception were considered obscene, and many writers went to jail. In 1873, a publisher who issued an illustrated version of an 1833 volume on douching was sentenced to two years of hard labor for distributing obscenity to the 277,000 readers who bought his book.[41] Since authorities did their best to control access to such advice, word was often passed from woman to woman. Army wives at isolated frontier locations were among the last to hear the limited information. Emily FitzGerald and other women at Sitka, Alaska, in 1875 had "meetings of horror" on the topic of birth control.[42] When she and Dr. FitzGerald were transferred to Fort Lapwai, Emily discovered that none of the army wives there had children but wanted them. "It does seem too funny to me. I and my whole set of intimate friends [in Alaska] have been engaged in wondering how to prevent any more babies coming. Now I get among these people who would give their heads to have a baby and are just as busily engaged trying all sorts of means so as to have one."[43] She wished she could show off her two children to her family in the East but also stated firmly, "I don't want any more." Libbie Custer, who longed for children, described in a letter to Autie a visit to an acquaintance in Illinois who was suffering with childbirth illness. The woman told Libbie, "Just think . . . in ten years I have had seven children—and you not one." Libbie followed the story with the comment, "And she seemed to envy me."[44]

Army wives who were not happy to find themselves in a "delicate condition" were already well acquainted with one solution to the problem. In eastern cities advertisements for abortion doctors and treatments were thrust into women's hands as they went about their daily activities. The cost estimate was ten dollars.[45] Powerful abortifacients such as cottonroot, snakeroot, and savin, which was extracted from juniper bushes, were advertised in eastern papers under such names as "Madame Restell's Female Monthly Pills" or "Dr. Monroe's French Periodical Pills."[46] When men came home from the Civil War, the sale of cottonroot alone increased 400 percent. One physician in Syracuse, New York, estimated that nine thousand such tablets were used annually in his city, which had a population of fifty thousand women. A doctor in Chicago believed that 25 percent of the pregnancies there ended with intentional abortions; the estimate for New York City was 20 percent.[47] A poison register for a western store repeatedly lists purchases of abortifacients such as oil of tansy and pennyroyal for treatment of "problems with menses."[48] Those women at remote posts who couldn't obtain drugs prepared post-coital douches made with vinegar or baking soda; others hoped to induce abortions by inserting goose quills in an effort to dilate their own cervixes. Alice Grierson told her husband that she "would rather die, than have another child," but acknowledged that she had not really been tempted to commit suicide or resort to "the fearfully frequent National crime of abortion."[49]

Women who tried to avoid motherhood were going against the medical and moral stereotypes of the nineteenth century. *Ethics of Marriage,* written by H. S. Pomeroy in 1888, suggested that a woman with no children "faced a greater chance of disease than did mothers."[50] Gilbert Holland, one of the most popular advice writers in the Victorian era, taught that bearing children "made women healthier" and helped them avoid complications in menopause. In his highly acclaimed tract, "Sex in Education, or a Fair Chance for the Girls," Dr. Edward H. Clark suggested that the various parts of the female body competed for the resources that made it operate effectively.[51] For that reason it was believed that a woman's system could not simultaneously handle two things well. Young women were advised to avoid education or intellectual activity because the increased amount of blood required by the brain for such efforts would lessen the flow to the reproductive organs, lowering their ability to have children or a healthy sex life. Medical writer S. Weir Mitchell contended that a girl's "future womanly usefulness was endangered by steady use of her brain."[52] A lecture to the students at the Philadelphia College of Medicine stated, "Woman's reproductive organs are pre-eminent. They exercise a controlling influence upon her entire system, and entail upon her many painful and dangerous diseases. They are the source of her peculiarities, the center of her sympathies, and the seat of her diseases. Everything that is peculiar to her springs from her sexual organization."[53]

Many such medical specialists considered it a natural state for a refined woman to be delicate or even sickly. Writers such as Alexandre Dumas had popularized the fragile heroine, and robust young women struggled to project the proper frail and ethereal image required for "true" womanhood. Army wife Ellen Biddle, who had jumped off a rearing horse, wrote repeatedly of her delicate health. She was famous among officers' wives for her ability to "faint" on cue. While traveling east by railroad, she described how she had to lie down for days on end "while my friends did everything . . . for me."[54] When her son got a rash from poison oak, she fainted whenever the doctor came to change the dressing, "knowing the child suffered."[55] She convinced everyone she was going to die after she experienced a miscarriage at Camp Halleck. For three months "the doctor rarely left my bedside, as I required constant watching."[56] She engaged a private Pullman car to transport her, a hired nurse, and the doctor to San Francisco, where she recovered at the beach.

This same delicate creature was on an outing in the country near Galveston, Texas, when the man driving her carriage apparently lost control of the horses. Ordering her small sons to lie down on the floor, Ellen wiggled through the window, climbed up on the driver's seat, grabbed the reins, and gained control of the runaway team. She drove them all the way back to the post, where the driver was sent to the guardhouse—and Ellen fainted. During a visit to New York City, Ellen helped form a bucket brigade to fight a fire in the house where she was staying. Her violet silk gown apparently didn't get too wet because, after the exertions of putting out the fire, she left with friends to attend the opera. After four years of living in the East, her husband was ordered to return to the West, but Ellen decided she was not strong enough to make the trip with him. She settled in Berkeley Springs, West Virginia, decided to build a new home, and went every day to the construction site to supervise the work.

Many women in the West didn't have to "struggle" to be delicate; life and their experiences produced that result. Three ladies were thrown to the ground when Col. Edward Hatch upset his four-horse carriage while driving them around Fort Robinson, Nebraska. Delia Thornton Casey was extremely fragile after her ambulance overturned on the way to Fort Union, New Mexico, in 1866. Casey fractured her ribs and injured her back, and had to use crutches for several months.

Wives suffered through the deaths of their husbands and small children. Alice Grierson herself died in the West, and Annie Yates, Frances Grummond, Mollie McIntosh, Emily FitzGerald, Fannie Boyd, Caroline Frey Giddings Winne, and Libbie Custer and her sister-in-law, Margaret Calhoun, all lost their spouses to warfare or disease on the frontier. At the Little Big Horn, Libbie lost her husband, two brothers-in-law, and a nephew, yet when word came of the destruction of the Seventh Cavalry, she made it her duty to accompany the post surgeon, J.V.D. Middleton, and Lt. C. L. Gurley to tell the other wives at the post that their husbands were dead.

Mrs. Hans Gasman's husband was in the field over the period of days when her child was born, died, and buried at Fort Concho; Dr. and Mrs. McKay lost their small son when he fell into a pot of boiling water that a servant had just removed from the stove at Fort McRae; and Katie Gibson cut up her wedding dress to line the pine box that was used as a casket for the Frederick Benteens' little girl. Teresa Viele visited the cemetery at Ringgold Barracks many times and discovered the grave of a small child among the ranks of soldiers. She "felt the deepest sympathy for the mother far away, who had been forced to go and leave her baby in this wretched place."[57] Yet when the Vieles departed, the cemetery contained another tiny grave, occupied by their six-month-old baby. Helen Chapman, mourning the loss of a child in Texas, was struck by the fact that in Mexico the death of a small child was a time for rejoicing. Lively music was played at the funeral, and the family shot off sky rockets. The Mexican women explained to the grieving American wife that they were celebrating the fact that the little one was happy in heaven. If they mourned, they believed that it would make God angry.

Mrs. Verling Hart made regular trips to visit her child's grave in the cemetery at Fort Rice and sometimes was accompanied by children from the post. One day when they were occupied with weeding the area and planting flowers on the small mound, an Indian in full war paint appeared from behind a tombstone. Knowing that it would be fruitless to scream since the group was too far away from the fort to be heard, Mrs. Hart ignored the warrior and warned the children not to show any fear. When the Indian approached and asked if the "papoose" in the grave was her's, Hart nodded and got to her feet. With the children trailing behind her, she started for the fort, but the sympathetic Indian walked with her through the gate, into the stockade, and up to her very quarters. He remained peacefully on the porch while she went into the dining room and gathered a plate of food from the lunch waiting on the table. After taking him the meal, the army wife walked back inside the house and collapsed from the danger presented by visiting her child's grave.[58]

When Katie Gibson became lonely during the long winter at Fort Rice, she would take out her family album and look at pictures of her loved ones, who were far away in the East. One day when she was doing so, two children from the garrison came for a visit. Examining the photographs, the children were struck by a picture of an elderly man and asked Katie who it was and where he was. She replied that it was her father and he was dead. The little boy asked, "Who killed him?" Katie considered it a reasonable question, "for no one died a natural death out there, but was killed either by Indians, or in barroom brawls, or frozen to death."[59] When she responded that no one had killed him, the children were puzzled by the novel idea that someone could die of old age. The little girl finally realized, "Nobody killed him . . . he just died his own self." In a land where the post cemetery at Camp Date Creek in 1869 had not one occupant over twenty-three years of age, none of whom had died a natural death, the children's confusion is easily understood.[60] The boy and girl looking at the picture of Katie's elderly father seldom had met civilians, rarely had seen an old person, and never had experienced a death that did not come without violence or disease.

In the West, army families lived with the immediacy of death as fathers and friends who left for work in the morning sometimes didn't return at night. Unity in the close confines of an isolated garrison made the losses from attacks, disease, or childbirth sting in a more personal way than they might have in eastern society, where people were insulated by ritualistic sympathy calls, black dress, two years of mourning, and calling cards with one-quarter-inch-wide sable borders. Such formality bred a remoteness that helped protect individuals from the reality of the experience. On the frontier, however, where personnel were rolled to the grave in a barrel or buried in cases that proclaimed the contents as cavalry trousers, there was no sanctuary from the risks and harsh realities of life—and death.

Mollie McIntosh, described by her sister, Katie, as "physically strong and fearless," believed that this living on the edge was a "hazard of existence . . . [that] tempted adventurous souls and lured them" to the West.[61] While most army wives had traveled there out of a sense of duty and devotion to their husbands, many who remained undoubtedly shared Mollie's sentiment. Certainly the element of danger, as in times of war, intensified emotions and relationships on the frontier. Helen Chapman wrote her mother, "In my last letter, I told you of Dr. Levely's death, and my feeling that in the future, I must avoid such scenes. But in frontier life, this seems to be impossible and the few collected together in such distant places, cannot shelter themselves under the plea of delicate nerves."[62] The sight of mutilated bodies, scalped and full of arrows, or the stacks of epidemic victims ready for burial brought to military wives a heightened awareness of their own vulnerability as well as that of their loved ones and their extended family, the military community. With this increased realization of the immediate dangers and the possibility of dying, these women developed a new appreciation of what was truly meaningful in living.

> To those who fight for it,
> Life has a flavor
> the protected will never know.
>
> **Anonymous**

An Itch for Epaulets

WHILE LIFE IN the West presented officers' wives with many hardships and shortages, frontier outposts did provide them an abundance of energetic young men eager for feminine companionship. Infantrymen and gallant cavalry officers such as Robert E. Lee, J.E.B. Stuart, and George Armstrong Custer offered good looks and charm in a land where one post with 168 military personnel had just 11 women.[1] Teresa Viele, the only "lady" at Ringgold Barracks during her husband's assignment there, wrote, "Wall-flowers are an unknown shrub in this part of the country; the men have too much gallantry to allow them to flourish."[2] Mattie Summerhayes believed that women in the West were able to fool themselves about their looks and figures because there were lots of men ready to proclaim their beauty—and few long mirrors. One wife commented that she had never had to do anything for herself while in the company of military personnel at frontier garrisons. When Ellen Biddle's path across the parade ground was barred by a mudpuddle, a colonel ostentatiously threw down a military cape and led her across it, saying, "Sir Walter Raleigh outdone."[3] The colonel's grand gesture cost him little—the cape belonged to someone else.

Helen Chapman had two guests from New York and found it amusing "how ladies love to visit in a garrison. No matter how rude the accommodations, it is all the same. The gallantry of military men supplies every deficiency."[4] Frances Roe described a dance at a frontier post by saying, "The girls East may have better music to dance by, and polished wax floors to slip down upon, but they cannot have the excellent partners one has at an army post, and I choose the partners! The officers are all excellent dancers . . . and when you are gliding around, your chin, or perhaps your nose, getting a scratch now and then from a gorgeous gold epaulet, you feel as light as a feather, and imagine yourself with a fairy prince. . . . I know what I am talking about, scratches and all."[5]

Ladies with single relatives sent letters east inviting them to visit what became a frontier marriage mart. At a time when society considered it "both economically and socially desirable for dependent young ladies to be hustled under the protecting roof of someone," many women in the East were condemned to spinsterhood by the high mortality rate of men fighting in the Civil War.[6] However, the scarcity of women at western outposts greatly improved matrimonial prospects. A correspondent at Fort Davis suggested in an 1882 *Army and Navy Journal* that if "Eastern mamas" sent their daughters to a frontier garrison, "none of them [would] languish for the addresses of chivalrous young men."[7] When Gen. and Mrs. Charles King had a "charming girl" visiting them at Fort D. A. Russell, "all the bachelors at the post were paying her devoted attention. There was not an hour from guard mounting to midnight that some of them were not infesting the premises, and Mrs. [King] not infrequently had to order the laughing crowd out of the house when midnight came, declaring that her friend and guest must be allowed a few hours between visits."[8] One regimental commander believed that "a few young ladies coming from civilization have a wonderful effect on brightening up everything. . . . They are always a valuable acquisition."[9]

Alice Grierson invited her cousin, Olive McFarland, and her husband's nieces, Helen and Grace Fuller, to stay with her family in Texas. The girls helped her and served as teachers for the Grierson children while husband-hunting. After several months, Helen chose Lt. William Davis, and Grace selected Lt. Mason Maxon. These new army brides then continued the matchmaking tradition as Helen invited Davis's spinster sister, Ida, for a visit, and both Helen and Grace tried to find a husband for their younger sister, Louisa. Olive McFarland, the only one of the original Grierson three who departed still single, may have been too particular because she wrote to relatives in the East that "nice young officers are not very plent[iful] here at present."[10] After studying the candidates carefully, the major that Olive finally selected for a husband turned out to be a dedicated bachelor who refused to "choose" her in return. When a woman turned down a proposal, she was said to have given her suitor "a mitten." Apparently a man rejecting the opportunity for matrimony was so rare in the West that there was no term for Olive's situation.

Even Autie Custer occasionally played matchmaker, encouraging Libbie, who was visiting family in Monroe, Michigan, to bring a single woman back west with her. He wrote, "Have you invited some young lady to stay with us next winter? Do not let it be of a past generation. Moral worth is superior to beauty, but a young lady visiting a garrison should be possessed of both, else young officers might regard escorting [the women] as fatigue duty."[11] Marion T. Brown must have met Custer's requirements because she had thirteen officers pursuing her during a stay at Fort Sill.

When Laura and Emily Mason arrived at Fort Gibson, officers competed hotly for these daughters of an Indian commissioner, nieces of the postmaster general, sisters-in-law of the governor of Michigan, and cousins of the commanding officer at the post, Richard Barnes Mason. Emily was twenty-nine and an acknowledged spinster when she wrote to her sister, Catherine (Kate) Mason Rowland, an army wife living in Detroit, that "the beaux give us no time, not one moment to ourselves. . . . We have been dancing all the week—every night."[12] She described how three men were sitting in the room while she wrote, waiting for her to finish. Even the officers stationed about fifty miles away at Fort Smith, Arkansas, entered the competition. Emily told Kate that she had to prepare "20 valentines all my poetry (original!)—and such doggrel [sic] for the officers at Fort Smith."[13]

When Laura became ill, Emily believed that it was because she had experienced "too much excitement—too many lovers (four in five weeks—and all in *earnest too*.)"[14] Laura herself acknowledged that "Washington . . . cannot boast of more visiting, more delights and more amusements than this garrison. . . . The officers are so attentive, so gallant and kind that I am perfectly enraptured with them all. . . . I should not be surprised if I should be pressed into the service [marry a military man]."[15] One of her suitors was the post's wealthy young doctor from Maryland, "the youngest surgeon of such high rank in the army." Laura assured Kate that she had "inquired into all his affairs. He has plenty of money, a carriage and horses, and could make quite a dash."[16] However, the girl was not enthusiastic about the match because the officer was ugly and his height was much shorter than his rank. Richard Mason's wife, Margaret, promised Kate that she had preached to Laura every day about "the horrors of poverty," encouraging her to marry the wealthy but diminutive young doctor. When "Laura says, Oh Cousin Margaret, but he is so ugly! I tell her never to mind that, unless she is sitting, she could never catch a glimpse of his face."[17] The prospect Laura favored was an officer from Virginia, "a very fascinating character . . . so clever and so handsome," who turned out to be a cousin of the girls.[18] Face apparently overcame fortune because Emily later wrote to Detroit that the young Virginian had asked for a leave of absence to visit the family in Washington the following May, presumably to propose. If he was accepted, one can be sure their engagement was not announced on a Friday. That was considered extremely unlucky.

Ellen Biddle frequently entertained family and friends from the East who were husband-shopping. When four ladies visiting at Fort Lyon wanted to accompany a troop on the first day's march of a long patrol, Ellen and another wife went along as chaperons. By nightfall, a dust storm of hurricane strength began to give the visitors a real taste of life on the plains. As the six ladies huddled in a tent, with veils over their faces to keep out the dirt, officers and soldiers spent the hours outside, holding the tent in place to keep it from being blown away. At Hot Springs, South Dakota, Ellen took a group of officers and visiting ladies for a swimming party. This time one of the lieutenants had a heart attack and died on the outing for want of readily available medical care. Incidents such as these and the fire that destroyed all the visitors' clothes at Fort Abraham Lincoln left ladies who went west before they were married with few illusions about what life would be like with the frontier army.

Grace Bunce, a student at Wells College, was invited by her roommate, the daughter of an army major with the Third Cavalry, to visit her family at Fort Sill. Although Grace had two "perfectly good beaus" at home and did not need to hunt for a husband, she decided to go on a "spree" before she settled down with one of the men. Part of the adventure soon included falling in love with Capt. William Paulding, twenty years her senior and the father of three daughters. When he was "Officer of the Day," Paulding invited her to accompany him on his evening rounds of the post and took her to a nearby

Kiowa village. There she met Quanah Parker—or at least saw him talking to William. The Indian chief totally ignored her. When Grace departed from the post at the end of the summer, Paulding had convinced her to marry him. He had to travel to the Bunce's summer home at Martha's Vineyard to persuade her father to allow the marriage, which took place on October 22, 1896. In the spirit of the military wedding, the organist, a Civil War veteran, interspersed the ceremony with various bugle calls, the meanings of which he had apparently forgotten. The guests were tremendously impressed with the military airs, but Paulding and the fellow officer who served as his best man could barely restrain their amusement when the notes of "chow call" or "stable call" reverberated through the church at solemn moments in the ceremony.[19]

Libbie Custer strongly believed that young officers on the frontier should be married and constantly invited eligible young ladies to stay with her in the West. She felt that officers who were single might be tempted to relieve the boredom and loneliness with heavy drinking and public "dissipation" with prostitutes, some of whom were laundresses assigned to the garrisons. Autie Custer's sister, Margaret Calhoun, also an army wife, accused Libbie of greeting new officers arriving at the post with, "I am glad to see you; I hope you are engaged."[20] Lt. George F. Hamilton of the Ninth Cavalry was—he married Kate Chaffee, daughter of the future army chief of staff, Adna Chaffee. It took only seventeen days for Allie Bullock, who was visiting her sister and brother-in-law at Fort Concho, to win a proposal from Maj. George Schofield. The bride was described as bright but "not . . . prepossessing in appearance."[21] Lt. Hans Gasman eloped with the daughter of a wealthy Texan, carrying her off from her Ursuline Convent school in San Antonio to their new home at Fort Concho. The delightful but very immature Mrs. Gasman shared quarters there with Flora Cooper's family, and while the lieutenant was away, his bride decided to host a taffy pull in her room. Everyone was astounded when the teenage wife, as a prank, stuck candy in the hair of Gen. Wesley Merritt, commander at Fort Concho and future military governor of the Philippines.

When Katie Garrett and Frank Gibson informed the McIntoshes of their coming marriage, Mollie McIntosh, Katie's sister, responded, "I'm not surprised, because I planned all this before you came out."

When discussing the location for the wedding, Mollie recommended that the couple be married at Fort Abraham Lincoln rather than returning to the Garrett home in Washington, D.C., for the event. Mollie argued, "Most of the regiment will be present then, and, after all, these people are Frank's closest friends and will be yours. . . . Besides, you'll see practically nothing of your old friends from now on, anyway." The statement made Katie realize that "this frontier life exacted a toll of social isolation" from the existence she had known. In a commitment to Frank Gibson and the army, the girl agreed to hold the wedding at the frontier post. Mollie McIntosh and the other Seventh Cavalry wives, Libbie Custer, Margaret Calhoun, Annie Yates, and Charlotte Moylan, helped make the wedding dress as well as other preparations. Within less than two years, all of these women except Charlotte and Katie would be widows.[22]

James LaTourrette performed five marriages during his tenure as chaplain at Fort Union, two of them for his own daughters, who married military men. The post was busy preparing for the wedding of the preacher's daughter, Mary, when the bugler suddenly sounded assembly. The officers and men were ordered to leave immediately by train for Oklahoma to help police the opening of the Cherokee Strip. Soon only six enlisted men, two surgeons, and LaTourrette remained at the post. That afternoon the telegraph keys began to click, and the quartermaster's wife scurried around the fort, trying to find someone who could understand the code. The only telegrapher had left with the regiment. A nephew of LaTourrette, visiting for the wedding, was able to decipher that the troops had been halted at Raton, the army having decided that they wouldn't be needed after all in Oklahoma. At sundown, the soldiers marched back into Fort Union, and the wedding went ahead, although obviously not as scheduled.

Living together in such an uncertain existence either reinforced the marriage bond or resulted in extra stress that fractured it. It was not accidental that officers leaving for a patrol or long campaign marched out of the fort thinking of "The Girl I Left Behind Me." Libbie Custer described how waiting wives were "a prey to all the horrors of imagining what may be happening to one we love. You slowly eat your heart out with anxiety, and to endure such suspense is simply the hardest of all trials that come to the soldier's wife."[23]

Men were away months at a time, and officers returned so sun-burned and lean that their wives and children didn't recognize them. One officer who arrived home late at night after his family had gone to bed awoke next morning to find his small son beating on his chest and shouting, "You S.O.B., get out of my mother's bed."[24] Custer, Donald McIntosh, Frank Gibson, and other Seventh Cavalry officers returned to Fort Abraham Lincoln one morning at dawn after a two-month absence on the Black Hills Expedition. They had heavy beards, skin lined and leathery, clothes patched but still torn. Modesty and proper decorum were forgotten as women in robes and "flying hair" came tumbling out of their quarters to greet the returning troops. After the long separation, Libbie Custer was "wild with joy" to see her husband. At first she hid behind the door, "ashamed to be seen crying and laughing and dancing up and down with excitement." Finally her impatience propelled her outside into his arms, where she was "overwhelmed with confusion" when the watching soldiers cheered her welcome home.[25] Libbie wrote to her aunt, Eliza Sabin, "Autie is too necessary to my happiness for me not to miss him every hour he is away."[26] Custer reciprocated, writing to his wife of ten years when she was visiting family in Michigan, "My Precious Darling—Well, here we are at last, at the far-famed—and to you far distant—Yellowstone. How I have longed for you during our march in what seems a new world, a Wonderland."[27] On June 22, 1876, Libbie wrote to her husband, "Oh, Autie, how I feel about your going away so long without our hearing. . . . Your safety is ever in my mind. My thoughts, my dreams, my prayers, are all for you. God bless and keep my darling."[28] A few days later Libbie finally did receive news. George Armstrong Custer had died at the Little Big Horn without ever receiving her letter.

Capt. Frederick Benteen, also of the Seventh Cavalry, signed letters to his wife, "oceans of love."[29] When duty took him away from her for seven months, the forty-three-year-old officer graphically portrayed his desire by drawing a picture of his penis, commenting, "When this you see—remember me."[30] Kate Benteen apparently did remember because it was one letter she saved.

Alice Grierson wrote to her husband, Ben, from Illinois, "Wouldn't I love to kiss, hug, love, and almost devour you if I could only have you to myself today."[31] He responded, "I never was as lonely and miserable in all my life before, when separated from you."[32] Desperate to avoid another pregnancy, the couple may have felt safe in the emotional exchange, since over a thousand miles divided them at the time. Alice described to Ben articles she was reading in *Revolution,* a journal originally produced by women's rights campaigners Elizabeth Cady Stanton and Susan B. Anthony. She also sent him a copy of a biography of Victoria Woodhull, an advocate for marital relations based on mutual desire rather than a wife's "duty" to subjugate herself to her husband's demands. Concerned about his wife's extended absence and the new ideas she seemed to be absorbing, Ben was increasingly prepared to "negotiate" their personal relationship and her responsibilities as a commanding officer's wife.

Libbie Custer considered life together in an isolated army setting "a crucial test of the genuineness of the affection."[33] If so, even the Custers, with their obvious delight in one another, didn't always score well on the exam. When Autie visited New York City in 1871, he wrote to his wife, describing the beautiful women there who vied for his attention. Apparently expressing her opinion of this information, Libbie tore up the picture he sent her. Custer's response to her action was, "My girl should be grateful that, seeing so many people as I do, to me she stands all the higher by contrast."[34] He had assured her on an earlier trip to the city that when he and friends from West Point had "sported" with the "Nymphs du Pave," he had not forgotten her for a single moment.

Libbie, however, may have put him out of her mind briefly when he was away from Fort Hays in 1867 on a "scout" for Indians. He had warned her early in "their" army career that she could "dance, ride, walk, with whom you will, but never allow any one officer to feel himself your special cavalier."[35] Custer's dash across Kansas that eventually led to his court-martial may not have been motivated entirely by his concern about Libbie's exposure to cholera at Fort Harker. The event may have been a reaction, at least in part, to gossip that his wife had forgotten the rule and was involved in a relationship with another officer. Like Mattie Summerhayes, Libbie did appreciate a handsome male physique. When she met Wild Bill Hickok, she effusively described him as "a delight to look upon. Tall, lithe, and free in every motion, he rode and walked as if every muscle was perfection. . . . I do not recall anything finer in the way of physical perfection than Wild Bill when he swung himself lightly from his saddle."[36]

Women who traveled alone and lived in isolated areas, with their husbands gone for long periods of time, had many opportunities for such temptations. When an officer and his wife shared quarters with a bachelor and duty took the husband away, the army wife lived alone with the single man. Helen Chapman shared a house with a Major Anderson when her husband, William, was absent on duty. While Jack Summerhayes was on an Indian scout, Mattie asked the post commander for a soldier to sleep in her quarters. The officer was careful to send an elderly enlisted man named Needham to protect the army wife—and her reputation. Eveline Alexander enjoyed dinner alone with Kit Carson while her husband, Andrew, was sick. The frontiersman, army scout, and officer also took Eveline riding and escorted her on a visit to a Ute village.

While Alice Grierson was away from Fort Sill in 1871, her son, Robert, kept her informed of all the flirtations going on among the officers and wives at the post. The eleven-year-old boy described to his mother how Dr. Henry Kilbourne had taken Mrs. Steven Norvell in his arms and carried her across a muddy area of the parade ground, a trip the woman said she enjoyed very much. Robert also noticed that a drunk lieutenant had turned Mrs. Elizabeth Myers upside down while trying to lift her into a wagon. This same woman would later be accused of a "scandalous intimacy" at Fort Sill with Lt. Quincy O'Mahar Gillmore. Colonel Grierson was away during the reported adultery, but Gen. Philip Sheridan was infuriated at the candid way in which the acting commander, Lt. Col. John Davidson, handled the "public court" discussion of the affair. As a result, Gillmore was forced to resign from the army, and Sheridan decided to scatter the officers assigned to the Tenth Cavalry at Fort Sill. Because of this adulterous relationship between one of his lieutenants and another officer's wife, Grierson was exiled by Sheridan to Fort Concho, a post that Ben described to his brother as "the most God-forsaken part of Uncle Sam's Dominions."[37]

Autie Custer complained that the officers at Fort Dodge, Kansas, were "carrying on" with the laundresses, one of whom had accused an officer of fathering her child. Infidelities at the post included two officers' wives who were sleeping with other men. The situation had driven one of their husbands to drink. The post telegrapher at Fort Laramie, Oliver Unthank, wrote to his wife, Emma, in 1873 that two of the men there were publicly feuding over a woman.[38] Jules Ecoffey, perhaps the post trader, was attempting to get his wife to leave Fort Laramie, but a Colonel Ilges was trying to convince her to stay. When Jules challenged the colonel to a duel, Ilges refused. The officer threatened to horsewhip Ecoffey if he came to the billiard room at the sutler's store, but evidently one of the men became so drunk that the confrontation never did take place.

At Camp Bowie Lt. Duane Greene had been "messing" [taking his meals] with Dr. and Mrs. S. A. Freeman for about two months when Dr. Freeman discovered that he was sharing more than food with the lieutenant. When he came home early on a summer day in 1877 and found his wife and Greene in the bedroom, the doctor attacked the young officer. The post commander resolved the situation by exiling the Freemans and giving Greene the choice of a quiet resignation or public disclosure of the situation during a court-martial. Either way, the adultery effectively ended Duane Greene's military career.

Lt. Marcus Reno survived Little Big Horn, but his future was mortally wounded by his relationship with women. He was court-martialed in 1876 because he supposedly used his position as commanding officer at Fort Abercrombie to ruin Mrs. James Bell's reputation. While her husband was away in Pennsylvania taking care of his sick father, Reno had pursued this lieutenant's wife. On December 18, he had taken her hands in his and tried to draw her close; three days later he placed his arm around her waist. Mrs. Bell apparently repulsed these advances. When she gave a Christmas party, the commanding officer was furious over not being invited. He commented to the post trader, John Hazelhurst, "This means war! Mrs. Bell has thrown down the gauntlet, and I will take it up. . . . I will make it hot for her. I will drive her out of the regiment."[39] When Rev. Richard Wainwright arrived at the post, planning on staying with the Bells, Reno warned him not to because "Mrs. Bell's reputation is like a spoiled egg. . . . She is notorious in the regiment as a loose character."[40] Reno told the minister that his (Wainwright's) name had been connected to Mrs. Bell's in a "licentious" manner by officers in the club room at the post. The commanding officer also said that Capt. Frederick Benteen and Lt. George D. Wallace had requested him to order Mrs. Bell to leave Fort Abercrombie because of her improper conduct and sordid reputation. The entire garrison became involved in the controversy. The fact that Mrs. Bell's husband was away, leaving her defenseless in the eyes of the regiment, infuriated the other officers. At Reno's court-martial, Benteen and Wallace denied requesting that Mrs. Bell be expelled, and officers present in the club room refuted linking Wainwright's name to her's. When the defense was allowed to question the issue of Mrs. Bell's reputation, Benteen, Wallace, and Maj. Lewis Merrill all acknowledged that it was not good. However, in a presentation based on the responsibilities of an officer when dealing with innuendo and slander, the judge advocate concluded his case by saying that a man could be indifferent to scandal, "but a woman has no defence save that which may be found in the arm of some avenging friend." If the wife of a brother officer was so accused, it was the responsibility of other officers "to confute and resent that slander and not to aid in its circulation."[41] Reno was found guilty and dismissed from the army. President Rutherford B. Hayes later commuted the sentence to suspension from rank and pay for a period of two years.

In 1879, Reno, who had been back on active duty only six months, was court-martialed again for conduct unbecoming an officer. The major had peeped through a parlor window to look at Emma Sturgis, daughter of Col. S. D. Sturgis, commander of the Seventh Cavalry. Emma explained at the court-martial that she had been terrified at Reno's sudden appearance at the window because her father had recently placed the officer under arrest, and she feared some reprisal by the younger man. Reno testified that he was a great admirer of Miss Sturgis, and Frederick Benteen swore that the major "was dead in love with the young lady."[42] The court decided that admiration was not sufficient cause for his misconduct, and on April 1, 1880, thanks to his attentions to a woman, Marcus Reno was dismissed for the last time from the U.S. Army.

Seven years later Major Benteen himself was found guilty of conduct unbecoming an officer for remarking to one woman sitting in a wall tent with a group of others, "Your husband must have a hell of a time with you."[43] Asked what he meant, Benteen responded that any woman with eyes like her's would make it lively for a man. After rendering these judgments, Benteen had then walked about ten feet away, out of sight but not out of hearing of the women, and urinated against another tent. This indelicate action and the seemingly innocuous statements were considered inappropriate enough to earn a guilty verdict and dismissal from the service. General Sheridan appealed the decision to President Grover Cleveland, who lowered Benteen's penalty to a year's suspension on half pay.

One officer who by today's standards would be considered guilty of improper conduct was Capt. George Sokalski. George and his wife, Annie, were not very popular at Camp Cottonwood, Nebraska, because of her eccentric behavior and his disdain, as a regular army officer, for volunteers who outranked him. In a statement reminiscent of Benteen's comment, when he first saw Mrs. Sokalski in her wolfskin riding habit, Lt. Gen. William T. Sherman exclaimed, "What the devil of a creature is that? Wild woman, Pawnee, Sioux or what?"[44] When Lt. Seneca Norton arrived at Camp Cottonwood, apparently to investigate irregularities discovered in the post's monthly reports, Sokalski suspected that Norton had actually been sent to gather evidence against him. This impression was seemingly confirmed when the lieutenant asked two strikers who had worked for the Sokalskis whether it was true that the captain beat his wife. If so, it would form the basis for a charge of misconduct. Discovering Norton's interrogation of the enlisted men, Annie Sokalski did not consider it an effort to protect her. She resented this outside interference in her marriage and charged into Norton's office, calling him a "dammed dirty little peep."[45] Her husband had to intervene, perhaps to protect the lieutenant from the "defenseless" woman's rage. Annie was prepared to testify in her husband's behalf at the eventual court-martial, despite the fact that George actually had both physically and verbally abused her. However, the judge advocate ruled that she was incompetent to testify, possibly as a result of her eccentricities and somewhat wild nature. George Sokalski was found guilty, but the ruling was soon set aside, perhaps because of his poor health. He died a few days later. Annie took her wolfskin riding habit, thirteen dogs, and free spirit back east, where she was undoubtedly considered even more of an eccentric.

Due to the scarcity of women in the West, men fought over them, and sometimes with them. A Tenth Cavalry blacksmith at Fort Davis was fined ten dollars for beating Mrs. Price, a laundress; the punishment was higher when Sgt. Lewis Taylor of the Twenty-Fifth Infantry was court-martialed for assaulting laundress Louise Hale. Taylor's stiff sentence—thirty days confinement at hard labor, loss of a month's pay, and reduction to the lowest enlisted rank—all suggest that Hale was not a prostitute but rather a victim of rape. Even officers' wives were not immune from the threat of violence. On the night of April 20, 1874, Corporal Taliafero "attempted a forcible entry to the quarters of Mrs. Kendall, whose husband was away at the time on duty. Mrs. Kendall warned the man from the window but he persisted in his efforts. . . . Mrs. K. seized a revolver and just as the scoundrel had succeeded in getting his head through the window she fired, sending a bullet through his brain and killing him instantly."[46]

Mrs. Julia Young only succeeded in wounding the man she fired at on Christmas day, 1886. She shot at her officer husband while he was on horseback, the bullet passing through his leg and killing the horse he was riding. In a letter to Alice Grierson, Helen Fuller Davis greatly lamented the loss of the horse, wrote that Julia had been released on one thousand dollars bail, and mentioned, almost as an afterthought, that Lieutenant Young was recovering in the hospital.[47] Although the motive for the attack was never stated, Helen Davis obviously considered the loss of the horse more important than the assault on the man. The casualness demonstrated in the letter suggests that at least Davis and probably Alice Grierson knew the reason for the attempted murder and both may have considered the shooting justified. Such candor between two army wives on the western frontier might not have been exhibited had the letter been addressed to conservative relatives in the East.

The more violent lifestyle in the West, the availability of weapons, the officers' extended absences on patrol or campaign, and the wives' resulting self-reliance all contributed to an increased rejection of the cult of domesticity. Many women who had come west initially seeking the protection society insisted they have through marriage learned to take care of themselves. In shooting Corporal Taliafero, for example, Mrs. Kendall acted decisively in a situation that would probably have left most ladies in the East frozen both with temerity and a lack of any means of self-defense.

As men and women at western outposts tried to work together to meet the challenges of married life in a harsh and lonely environment, some husbands were not always as chivalrous and supportive as they had been as suitors. Many men became frustrated at the stagnant promotion rate; in 1877 it took thirty-seven years for a new second lieutenant to make colonel.[48] Helen Davis learned that the dashing lieutenant she married had a drinking problem, and Teresa Viele eventually divorced her husband for adultery. Even if an officer had a strong, positive bond with his wife, he still had to leave her to respond instantly to the call of a bugle. All army wives found themselves in a bigamous relationship—they had married not only a man but a military system that officially considered them nothing more than camp followers, second always to the mission and the "needs of the service." Children might be dying, epidemics might be raging in the garrison, but the officers automatically assumed that wives would willingly subordinate themselves to orders from the third party in their marriages—the United States Army.

As duty came first and frequently for husbands, military wives were increasingly forced to make decisions, purchases, and commitments that in the East were reserved for the "head of the house." The illness or sudden death of the family horse or cow required immediate replacement, if possible. A determination to send a child back east to school could not always wait six months for his father's return from pursuing renegade Indians. Just as they were expected to fulfill their husbands' family responsibilities, some officers' wives were required to exercise de facto military authority in the men's absences. When Lt. William Lane followed some Apache raiders, his wife, Lydia, was left in the charge of the post. She held and distributed the unit funds and wrote that she was ready to die to protect the money.[49] On another occasion, Libbie Custer sat guarding a fifty- to seventy-thousand dollar army payroll while her husband and the paymaster went to lunch.

Many frontier officers' wives became professional partners with their husbands, involved in their careers in a way not characteristic of eastern women. When Benjamin Grierson threatened to leave the army, it was Alice who persuaded him to stay. When Frank Baldwin considered transferring into the cavalry in 1869, Alice Baldwin responded, "My darling, do as you see best. . . . I want you to do well and be prosperous like Gen. Custer."[50] In 1876 Katie Gibson didn't share Baldwin's desire. Much to the disgust of her sister, Mollie, Katie persuaded her husband, Frank, not to accept a transfer to the Seventh Cavalry regimental headquarters at Fort Abraham Lincoln. She did so because of "a sudden chill . . . like the touch of cold, invisible fingers, and a curious foreboding."[51] Lt. James Sturgis, who accepted the transfer in Gibson's place, was later killed at the Little Big Horn.

Women who married into the frontier army came to realize that they were a valuable, if not officially valued, part of the military family. Libbie Custer said, "We Army women feel . . . we are making history with our men."[52] Military doctor R. H. McKay honored the frontier army wife when he wrote, "Just now, 1918, we hear a great deal about the army . . . but do we ever hear anything about officers' wives? They may not be of great importance now, but how was it forty or fifty years ago? . . . How about the wives of the army officers of that day, who shared with their husbands the dangers and hardships of frontier life? I wish here to pay my tribute to one who shared with me all of the sorrows, and most of the hardships herein related, and many others not considered of sufficient importance to mention. One who seldom complained; whose courage never faltered."[53]

After reading of Mattie Summerhayes's adventures as an army wife, family friend and noted artist Frederic Remington wrote to her, "Now suppose you had married a man who kept a drug store—see what you would have had and see what you would have missed."[54] And following a meeting with a former suitor who was now a successful lawyer in Michigan, Libbie Custer declared, "What a humdrum life I had escaped by not marrying him . . . so monotonous, so commonplace."[55]

A Touch of Class

WHILE THE WEST necessitated an obvious physical adaptation in lifestyles, the army wives also underwent subtle adjustments in their attitudes about race, culture, and class. Interdependencies in the isolated environment modified some of their preconceptions concerning both their own roles and the value of others. In her book, *Daughters of Joy, Sisters of Misery*, Anne M. Butler writes, "Garrison communities, assigned to the most remote, inhospitable regions of the West, attempted to transplant . . . military life and protocol as they knew it in the East. This proved an impossible task. . . . The frontier overpowered the traditions they sought to preserve and produced garrison communities where social conduct often defied traditional patterns."[1] Situations and people who could be ignored in the East had to be acknowledged in the close confines of western outposts. Even prostitution came to have a recognized face. Interactions with the "inferior classes" frequently increased officers' wives' awareness of common humanity and the needs of others. Nevertheless, when the women organized Sunday schools for black children or cared for laundresses who were ill, they were inspired as much by a sense of noblesse oblige as empathy. Acquaintances frequently developed from these interactions, but friendships rarely did. At frontier forts, necessity and expediency resulted in slightly more tolerant, and definitely more integrated, communities.

Whether officers' wives came from Carlisle, Pennsylvania, or Charleston, South Carolina, the vast majority of them reflected the nation's cultural prejudice against blacks. Many women from the North had seldom interacted with Negroes; it is likely that some had never even spoken to an African American. Those from the South, such as Katie Gibson, had known only slaves and found it difficult to conceive of blacks in a more positive light. Such lack of knowledge as well as the presence of preconceived notions presented problems since many officers served with black units, which were nicknamed by the Indians as "Buffalo Soldiers." Libbie Custer, Francis Roe, Eveline Alexander, Flora Cooper, Helen Davis, Grace Maxon, and Alice Grierson all lived for a period of time in military posts garrisoned by black troops. While promotion often came faster for white officers assigned to "colored" units, almost all the wives would have understood the following advertisement that appeared in the *Army and Navy Journal*:

> A first Lieutenant of Infantry (white) stationed at a very desirable post in the Department of the South desires a transfer with an officer of the same grade, on equal terms if in a white regiment; but if in a colored regiment, a reasonable bonus would be expected.[2]

Frances Roe, for one, thought she deserved something extra for living with black troops. Although from New York, Roe shared with others the presumption that the black man was naturally inferior and thus should remember his "place." This view helps explain why she was unwilling to acknowledge in front of several black troopers that she was unable to ride a fractious cavalry horse. She admired their riding skill but cheapened the compliment by saying that they "stuck on their horses like monkeys."[3] Daily mingling of the races at Camp Supply in 1872 offended her, especially if a black sergeant was in charge of white troops. Frances was especially infuriated when a white lieutenant ranking them out of their quarters used his black troops to move the furniture.

Libbie Custer took a great interest in the white enlisted men of her husband's regiment, asking about their health and the well-being of wives, sweethearts, and children. Moreover, she did not demand special privileges that would make extra work for the troops while the unit was on the move or in the field. In response, the men came to her with their troubles and asked her to write letters for them. This same woman, so caring and so revered by white soldiers, considered the "early days of soldiering [by blacks] . . . a reign of terror to us women in our lonely unprotected homes." She insisted that a Negro recruit on sentry duty had taken a shot at a group of officers' wives out for an evening promenade around the post.[4] Autie Custer may have turned down an opportunity to serve with the newly formed, all-black Ninth Cavalry regiment partially because of his wife's attitude toward African-American troops. It was apparently only black *men* that she feared because Libbie expressed tremendous respect for the ability and patience of Negro servants, such as Eliza Brown, the Custers' black cook.

Eveline Alexander went to the hospital every day to read to white soldiers who had been wounded in combat, and she treated all the noncommissioned officers at Fort Union to lunch, but she was more afraid of black troops than she was of Indians in warpaint. While her husband, Andrew, was pursuing renegades in Colorado, an additional group of warriors threatened Fort Stevens. The officer in charge offered to send Eveline to safety at Fort Garland, but the army wife refused to go. The men he had chosen to escort her were Negro troops from the Fifty-Seventh U.S. Regiment of Colored Infantry, and Eveline was terrified to be alone with the black soldiers.

Flora Cooper had more reason to fear the white troops escorting her on a move from Austin, Texas, to Fort Concho in 1874. Charles Cooper discovered that some supplies he had purchased for the trip had not been loaded, and the officer had to return for them, traveling overnight, leaving his wife and children alone in the camp. When the white soldiers began to get drunk, the Coopers' black striker, Pvt. George Clark, sat down in front of Flora's tent with his carbine in his lap. As the drunken group approached, the black trooper informed them that he would kill the first man who came near the tent. Flora's black protector sat there all night, keeping the white men who threatened her at bay.[5]

Presumably Francis Roe would never have expressed her negative feelings in front of Alice Grierson because their views were diametrically opposed. Alice was the only army wife whose writings indicate that she took a special interest in the well-being of black enlisted men. Her father, John Kirk, had been involved in the Underground Railroad assisting runaway slaves and had apparently instilled a degree of tolerance in Alice. Although not totally without prejudice, she was far more open-minded about blacks than other army wives. Marriage to Benjamin Grierson and living on the frontier with African Americans reinforced her father's efforts. Grierson was a supporter of abolition and fought strongly for the rights of the black troops he led.

During their service in the West, Negro units had proven themselves extremely brave and capable. Officers commented that they fought "like fiends," and their Indian foes had great respect for the courage of black troops. The Tenth Cavalry alone won nineteen congressional Medals of Honor.[6] Gen. Alfred Terry, the great Indian fighter, called it the best regiment in the Department of Texas.[7] If so, it was because Col. Benjamin Grierson set high standards for his unit and took great interest in his men. He wrote to Capt. L. H. Carpenter, who was recruiting in Philadelphia, "You will use the greatest care in your selection of recruits. . . . Enlist all the superior men you can who will be a credit to the regiment." And he informed Col. S. Hendrickson, who was gathering men in Boston, that "quality is more important than numbers."[8] As white officers and black enlisted men of the regiment began to gather at Fort Leavenworth, Gen. William Hoffman, the post commander, made life difficult for Grierson and his Tenth Cavalry. Scornful of black troops and those who served with them, Hoffman ordered them to set up their tents on low, swampy ground and refused to allow raised walkways to be built so the men could keep their feet dry. He even instructed one unit, encamped on the road from Fort Leavenworth to the nearby town, to "get out of sight."[9] During inspections, officers were told black troopers must be kept at a distance from white soldiers; African Americans were not to be given the honor of passing in review at parades. Grierson sent "fiery" protests to Washington, complaining about the "invidious distinctions between white and Negro troops," but they achieved little.[10] The commander struggled to get his regiment organized and away from the harassment at Fort Leavenworth as quickly as possible.

"Old Fogies" such as Hoffman had been against the action when the secretary of war authorized formation of regular army Negro regiments following the Civil War, but young blacks had been eager to enlist. The thirteen dollars per month salary was more than they could earn in civilian life, assuming they could even get a job. By the 1890s, the Tenth had many highly educated blacks who were unable to work at their professions in civilian life. The band leader was a graduate of the Boston Conservatory of Music and had studied in Vienna; the hospital sergeant was a graduate M.D. Unlike their white counterparts, morale in the black units was high, the desertion rate low, and alcoholism almost unknown. The army provided an opportunity to develop black leadership and increase African-American pride. It gave blacks a steady income, food, clothing, shelter, and a chance for schooling and status. However, despite black courage and service, only the necessity of protection against the Indians made those in the Southwest tolerate the presence of what southerners called "occupation" forces.

The Griersons were with black troops at Forts Riley, Gibson, Sill, Concho, and Davis, and in Whipple Barracks, Arizona. When Ben was away from the regiment, Alice acted, in effect, as an unofficial adjutant, sending him reports of activities and personnel. During the colonel's absence in 1869, Gen. H. N. Davis, the army assistant inspector general, visited Fort Sill, and Alice encouraged several of the "Buffalo Soldiers" to report their grievances to him. She wrote her son, Charlie, that the men's complaints would discourage white officers from abusing them.[11] When black trooper Matt Moss killed another man in self-defense that same year, Alice personally intervened with her husband on his behalf. A year earlier she had taken even more direct action when a captain's wife had a black noncommissioned officer and two enlisted men thrown in the guardhouse. Mrs. Henry Alvord felt she had been treated with disrespect when one of the men, Private Innes, had not hitched up her buggy as quickly as she wished. Alice had Innes brought to her quarters so she could hear his side of the story and expressed her interest in the case to Maj. Montgomery Bryant, apparently in command at Fort Gibson during Grierson's absence. The colonel's wife then went to see the captain's wife and "very decidedly" expressed to Mrs. Alvord that Colonel Grierson would not approve of the men being imprisoned. Since Mrs. Alvord was going to meet her husband, who was traveling with Ben, Alice warned Grierson in a letter to be "very guarded in expressing approval of her conduct until you hear the other side of the story."[12]

Alice and Ben were away from the frontier in 1881 and thus unable to help when Lt. Henry Flipper was charged with embezzlement of commissary funds at Fort Davis. The former slave, the first African American to graduate from West Point, and the only black line officer in the U.S. Army at the time, had been assigned to Capt. Nicholas Nolan's Company A in the Tenth Cavalry. There he had won the respect of the troops and praise from both Nolan and Grierson for his bravery in warfare with the Indians. The trouble apparently began when the black lieutenant became a regular riding companion of the captain's white sister-in-law, Molly Dwyer, one of the few eligible women in the garrison. Several officers were jealous, and most were offended by the relationship. When infantry officer Col. William R. Shafter arrived to take command at Fort Davis, he was not amused to discover that the post's quartermaster and acting commissary officer was a black lieutenant. He tried unsuccessfully to relieve Flipper from these duties. Soon afterward, two thousand dollars was discovered missing from the commissary funds in what the lieutenant claimed was a frame-up due to racial prejudice and his association with Molly Dwyer. Shafter had Flipper arrested and locked in a filthy cell for four days—a white officer similarly charged would have been held under house arrest. The black lieutenant was eventually found innocent but still dismissed from the service in what the army would acknowledge ninety-five years later was a serious miscarriage of justice. When they heard about the action, the Griersons agreed that racial prejudice and personal vendettas were responsible and assumed the dismissal would be overturned. The army, in fact, recommended Lieutenant Flipper's reinstatement; but, for some reason, President Chester A. Arthur, who had won an early reputation for defending the civil rights of blacks, refused to do so. Despite Flipper's dismissal, the Grierson family maintained their friendship with the former officer. Robert Grierson wrote Alice in 1885 that he had heard from "Lieut. Flipper," who asked to be remembered kindly to his parents.[13]

Ellen Biddle and Elizabeth Burt enjoyed many social events during their years at Fort Robinson in the 1880s and 1890s, but it is doubtful that the three black chaplains (Henry Plummer, George Prioleau, and William Anderson) and three black line officers (Lts. John Alexander, Charles Young, and Benjamin O. Davis) were often in their company. The white officers and their wives apparently approved that Plummer only associated with enlisted personnel at the post. Meanwhile, Alexander and Prioleau kept to themselves, and Davis departed for Wilberforce University to become an instructor of military science. None of these officers were ever mentioned in *Army Navy Journal* reports of social events at the post. The garrison did note Lieutenant Alexander's death in 1894, praising him in regimental orders for "appreciating the delicate distinction of social intercourse which the peculiar and oft-time trying position of his duties thrust upon him."[14]

When Mexican women in Texas expressed genuine esteem for Joseph Williams, the extremely talented black servant who served the Vieles "with grace and elegance," Teresa was offended. "This admiration for Negroes disgusted me . . . for, in spite of philanthropy, Christian Charity, and liberal views, I do not believe that the colored and white races can ever by any possibility amalgamate to an equality."[15]

While the women wrote absolutely nothing of a sexual nature in their diaries or letters about the black troopers, there may well have been some integration through liaisons, given the officers' extended absences on patrols or campaigns. An honor code existed in the East based on the inviolability of ladies and the forbidden nature of miscegenation; the code could have become a victim of loneliness and isolation in the West. Although such hidden relationships would not necessarily have outward manifestations, army wives were experiencing on a daily basis extensive racial interaction between black men and white women that would have been impossible anywhere else in the United States. Given the differences between black/white, officer/enlisted, and rich/poor, however, the relationships can hardly be called equal. However, when the white officers rode out on patrol or joined in a long campaign, women at many frontier posts remained under the protection of black troopers. The officers' wives then realized what it was like to be a white minority living in a black man's world. Their tolerance may not have grown with the experience, but their comprehension undoubtedly did.

While most officers' wives had difficulty accepting a shared humanity with blacks, it may have been easier for them to identify with servants, laundresses, Mexicans, and Native Americans of their own sex. A sense of "sisterhood" in the face of danger and desolation would have been necessary to cross the class barrier that society had erected between ladies and women. Laundresses, for example, labored as matrons at military hospitals; worked as cooks, maids, and seamstresses for officers' wives; and offered various "specialized services" to the troops. However, no matter what descriptive title they had, no one ever referred to the laundresses as ladies. When Teresa Viele described herself as the only lady at Ringgold Barracks, there may have been as many as five laundresses assigned there. When Lt. Andrew Canfield's wife, Sarah, arrived at Fort Berthold, North Dakota, in 1867, she also was acknowledged as the only lady at the post. Two other women were in residence—one was a laundress and the other was the Canfield's cook—but a distinction existed that both groups instinctively recognized and accepted. In 1856, a U.S. Senate document made the classification official for the military, reporting that there were one lady and four laundresses living at Fort Merrill, Texas.[16]

The harsh reality of this division reflected the fact that society regarded ladies as protectables and women as consumables. Historian Dee Brown described in his book, *Wondrous Times on the Frontier,* how the West divided its women into categories. While Wyatt Earp was assessed one dollar, the lowest fine possible under the law, for slapping a dance hall girl in Dodge City, Kansas, in 1877, a drunk who left a saloon and molested a "lady" on the streets of Alamosa, Colorado, paid a higher price. His corpse was discovered the next morning, "swinging above the sidewalk with a large placard attached: Alamosa pertecks her wimmen."[17]

As offensive as this distinction seems by modern standards, it was embraced by most at both ends of the social spectrum in the late 1800s. For example, an Irish laundress expressed to Libbie Custer her resentment of efforts to cross these class lines. A Civil War widow who had been a cook, the woman had lost her position when she became ill and had to look for a new one after she recovered. An officer who had risen from the ranks and married a former laundress needed a cook, but the Irish woman wouldn't take the job. The widow explained to Libbie, "I ken work for a leddy, but I can't go there; there was a time when Mrs. ——— and I had our toobs side by side."[18] It may have been this couple that Autie Custer had in mind when he told Libbie, "When receiving company formally, officially, treat all alike. You must not snub Mrs. So-and-So because you do not like her." When Libbie replied, "But—she is not a lady," Custer responded, "She's an officer's wife . . . one of our official family."[19] In 1866, Eveline Alexander had a similar situation with the Third Cavalry in New Mexico. One of the officers' wives was a former laundress, two were Mexican women, a fourth was a young lady from New York who was "not highly educated," and the last was a fourteen-year-old bride, "an innocent little girl."[20]

At Fort Concho the wife of Second Lt. John Conline was the daughter of an extremely wealthy man who owned a chain of hotels in the East. Every day she "dressed in her most stylish attire, would walk slowly along the front of the officers' quarters, a silk sunshade above her fashionable hat, kid gloves on her hands and a beautiful little silver-mounted pistol dangling from her wrist."[21] Mrs. Hans Gasman, the irrepressible teenager who had put taffy in General Merritt's hair, considered Mrs. Conline's actions pretentious. Deciding to mock the eastern lady, the young Texan promenaded around the post in a calico robe with a long train, wearing black gloves and a big, floppy hat such as slaves had used. She carried a green cotton umbrella and from her wrist dangled a Colt .45 service revolver. Terrified that the women would meet while so armed, officers hid in convenient quarters as each lady passed. Bloodshed was avoided between the eastern lady and the Texas tomboy when the post trader talked Mrs. Gasman into giving up her gun.

The distinction between ladies and women was not an artificial one; it was a result of different upbringings and outlooks. Officers' wives raised with education, refinement, and a strong sense of reserve considered the other women on the frontier to be brawlers—tempestuous and uncouth—but necessary for their comfort. Ellen Biddle and her children accepted cake and milk from a Dodge City hotel owner described as "a woman with a hard face, fully six feet tall and of very large frame . . . dressed in a 'bloomer' costume" and carrying a knife and pistol.[22] Teresa Viele regarded the Mexicans she associated with as "an amiable, smiling, innocent race of people, utterly unconscious of the higher emotions of civilization save the feeling of sympathy in misfortune."[23] Laundresses were described as "good, honest, industrious wives, usually well on in years, minutely familiar with their rights . . . which they dared to maintain with acrimonious volubility. . . . Yet they were kind at heart if rough in manners, always ready to assist in times of distress."[24] Many of the servants and laundresses who went west were Irish and faced life on the frontier with a sharp tongue, quick fists, and a sympathetic heart.

While the military establishment considered the cultured army wives to be civilians or camp followers, the "red-armed" laundresses were government issue. They were on the frontier because the United States had adopted the British system of hiring women to wash clothes for officers and enlisted men. From 1802 to 1876, Congress authorized the issuance of one daily ration to each laundress, supplied free medical care when they were ill, and arranged transportation for them when troops relocated. The military guaranteed them housing on what was always known as "Soapsuds Row" and fuel to warm the quarters. At a time when an enlisted man earned thirteen dollars per month, a good laundress could make forty dollars.[25] Laundresses even had the ability to strike, although their rations were stopped when they did so at Camp McDowell in 1872.

The women were so much an accepted part of the system that they were subject to army discipline. One laundress who addressed profane language to an "Officer of the Day" was court-martialed; another charged with attempted murder was drummed out of the regiment with fixed bayonets. Laundress Julia Doyle became the only woman murdered at a post on the Bozeman Trail when her gentle and popular husband shot her for abusing him continually at Fort C. F. Smith. Almost everyone at the post, including Andrew and Elizabeth Burt, thought the vicious laundress was insane. Despite his sympathy for the enlisted man, Andrew organized the court-martial where the board of officers ruled that Cpl. John Doyle killed his wife "while he was in a fit of passion engendered by severe abusive language."[26] Since the military family at the post felt extremely sorry for Doyle, no one searched for him too strenuously when he escaped from the stockade at Fort D. A. Russell a few weeks later.

In 1875 there were 1,316 women washing for the U.S. Army, and many of them were married to enlisted personnel.[27] It was a soldier's wife named Mrs. Kelly who tried to comfort Alice Baldwin during her first night at Fort Harker, Kansas. The army bride had left an elegant home in the East to travel through winter snowstorms to reach the damp and cold dugout she now occupied at the frontier post. The wife of the commissary sergeant sensed the homesickness and depression Alice was feeling and tried to reassure her, but the kindness only made the lonely girl cry.

When her husband, Jack, was ordered to the field, Mattie Summerhayes was glad to have a laundress named Mrs. Patten to stay with her at Fort D. A. Russell. The Sioux were expected to attack at any moment, and the officer's wife was nervous about being left alone. Mattie described Mrs. Patten as "an old campaigner" who made her "absolutely comfortable for those two lonely months" and expressed her gratitude for the companionship of the "dear old Irish woman."[28]

Whenever they gave a dinner party, Maria and James Kimball depended on the assistance of an Italian couple, Sergeant and Mrs. Luca. The noncommissioned officer was an Italian chief musician at Fort Wingate while his wife, Mary, was an extremely talented cook and seamstress. Searching for a diversion, the Kimballs decided to take Italian lessons from Sergeant Luca. When in uniform, the sergeant came to the back of the quarters to see his wife; but, for the lessons, he arrived in civilian clothes, knocked on the front door, and held class in the sitting room. The Kimballs grew to like the young couple and, as a doctor, the officer had more latitude to develop friendships with enlisted personnel and their families. When Luca's false teeth interfered with his ability to play the cornet, the Kimballs helped him get the money for new dentures. Their investment in the young man's mouth was rewarded soon afterward when he was hired by John Philip Sousa to play in the Marine band.

Whatever their need, officers' wives in the Seventh Cavalry could count on the expert help of a Mexican laundress named Mrs. Nash. The tall, thin wife of a noncommissioned officer was also known throughout the regiment as an extremely talented midwife, cook, and seamstress. Her long, slender fingers were in constant demand to deliver a baby, prepare intricate dishes for parties, or launder the women's delicate underwear. She decorated the McIntosh quarters for Katie Garrett's wedding; her sewing ability won praise from

Libbie Custer. The woman made delectable pies and sold them to the soldiers, earning a small fortune that her husband then absconded with. Attending the soldiers' balls in a filmy, low-necked gown, she soon found another husband, who did the same thing as the first. Without benefit of divorce from the mates who had deserted her, Mrs. Nash captured yet a third husband, the handsomest soldier in his unit. However, while he was away on patrol, Mrs. Nash died suddenly, apparently of appendicitis. She had left instructions that she was to be buried as she was, with no special preparation of her body, but the women of the regiment, who had received her gentle attention in the most intimate circumstances, wanted to honor her memory by preparing her for the grave. In doing so, they were appalled to discover that the woman who had delivered their babies, fitted their clothes, and handled their lacy unmentionables was a man! Honor quickly turned to hysterics, and Katie Gibson wrote that an article detailing the revelation made the front page of the local newspaper.[29]

Emily FitzGerald had two laundresses to help when her son, Herbert, was born in Alaska in 1874. One did the family wash, and the other took care of the baby and his older sister, Bess. Emily called them "gems." Three years later at Fort Lapwai, the FitzGeralds reciprocated by taking the family of a laundress named Mrs. Hurlbut into their home during a period of danger from Indian attacks. The woman's husband had recently been killed in a battle with the Nez Percé, and her quarters were outside the garrison. Since the laundress was near the end of her pregnancy, she was afraid she would not quickly get her family to safety in case of an Indian raid. Emily wrote, "She is a nice little woman and her children are as nice as I know. She is left destitute. After her sickness [delivery], we will all help her. A purse will be raised to take her back [east] to her friends."[30]

When the alert sounded for a possible Indian attack on the post, all the women at Fort Lapwai were gathered together in one house surrounded by fortifications. The officers' wives worked continually to reassure the excited laundresses, and Mrs. Theller, the widow of a lieutenant who had recently been killed by Indians, "put on her dead husband's gun and cartridge belt and looked as if she were ready to avenge [him]."[31] The only woman not in the shelter was the Fitz-Gerald's Eskimo servant, Jennie. Emily was concerned and sent a soldier to get her, but when he awakened Jennie and said that an attack was imminent, the Eskimo woman responded, "Me no fraid Indians. Me injun too."[32]

Three officers' wives who were relocating by train to Fort Bridger in 1876 tried to calm a young enlisted man's wife traveling with them. Rachel Lobach Brown, wife of Sgt. Henry Brown, was terrified because of Custer's annihilation by the Sioux the previous June. She described how the officers' wives encouraged her and how they frequently volunteered during the journey to help take care of her seven-month-old baby.[33]

In addition to associating with women of a different class, many officers' wives also had the opportunity to interact with women from different cultures. Following the Mexican War, Helen Chapman roomed in Matamoros with a rich widow named Dona Juanita Perello in "the finest house I have ever had the honor to live in."[34] Teresa Viele learned how to smoke from a young Mexican woman named Dolores, who described the army wife as an "apt scholar." The American and Mexican discussed sex, and Teresa "quite agreed with her that the most absurd thing a young and charming widow could do, was to barter a self-created chain of roses for the iron links of Hymen."[35] (Hymen, the Greek god of marriage, was synonymous for the act of union.) Teresa explored the countryside near Ringgold Barracks, stopping at Mexican huts to see if they had any food to sell. Visiting with the men and women, she eventually came to look upon them "as a new circle of friends and acquaintances."[36] Mattie Summerhayes apparently absorbed some of the culture when she held hands with Mexican women as they all bathed together at daybreak in the swift current of the Colorado River. Mattie envied the simplicity of their lives at Ehrenberg, found tortillas delicious, and longed to adopt their manner of dress.

Officers' wives who were forced by circumstance to interact with women of a different culture or class also found it impossible to ignore the issues of morality and prostitution. At some locations, the post sutler supplied prostitutes, and a visit to the store exposed officers' wives to these "working women," who posed as servants or clerks. In 1866 the murder of an enlisted man by an officer over a girl at the sutler's store at Fort McRae prompted an order from headquarters that all women, except laundresses, leave the post. Presumably this command included any officers' wives present. The sutler was also ordered to stop selling whiskey, which meant that officers and enlisted men had to seek their "refreshments" elsewhere.

Ladies could not disregard sexual dynamics at frontier posts, especially when some of their own servants and many of the laundresses who washed their clothes provided this important service to the troops. It was in fact this outlet of available women that helped enlisted men adhere to the code that decreed officers' wives as untouchable. Emily FitzGerald took a fifteen-year-old nursemaid named Mary with her to Sitka, Alaska, in 1874 and worked constantly to keep her separated from the enlisted men. Less than two months after arriving at the post, Mary began to dress up and fix her hair before going to the carpenter's shop because, the girl explained, there were "so many soldiers over there."[37] A few weeks later Emily docked her pay when the family caught the teenager sneaking out at night. The officer's wife wrote to her mother, "I am always in terror for fear she will do something that will ruin her. . . . Not one of all these men here is too good to get her into trouble."[38] Mary's forays continued, and within a few months she had contracted a venereal disease. Dr. FitzGerald was furious, concerned that she would spread the contagion to his wife and children. Emily wrote, "If she had seemed the least disturbed or sorry, we would both have felt so differently, but she continued her impudence."[39] A few weeks later Mary left the army family in Sitka, headed by steamer for a place in Portland where she had been told she could get "big wages."

As for the laundresses, Soapsuds Row was usually located conveniently near the barracks. A survey at Fort D. A. Russell in 1870 showed twenty-four laundresses at the post, seventeen of whom were single with children fathered by military personnel.[40] At Fort Mason, Texas, in 1856, First Lt. Charles Field lived openly as man and wife with a laundress who had a husband in St. Louis. Despite this behavior that would have gotten him ostracized in the East, Eliza Johnston, wife of the commanding officer, Albert Sidney Johnston, still associated with the lieutenant. When Lydia Lane needed washing done on a Sunday, the laundresses refused. Lane remarked that it might speak well for the women's piety, but "I am inclined to think they had something more "entertaining" on hand for the day."[41] Fort Phil Kearny had "Colored Susan," who sold whiskey, fruit pies, and women to the troops stationed there. A special order issued in November 1866 reported that, "The same woman is disorderly, breeding mischief in the garrison by inciting officers' servants to abandon their situations, and as an inducement setting forth the large sums of money she realizes and accumulates by the methods above referred to [prostitution]. This woman, profane, abusive, and of bad repute before her arrival must observe better behavior or she will not be tolerated in the garrison."[42]

Despite such threats, it was usually the danger of contagion from syphilis that forced a woman off post. Regulations stated that a laundress "infected by the venereal disease shall in no case . . . be allowed to remain with the army or draw rations."[43] Such infections were pervasive—Gen. Tasker H. Bliss quoted the military proverb "that [post surgeons] had nothing to do but confine laundresses and treat clap."[44] In one year at Fort Robinson venereal disease cost the army 2,963 days of duty; during the same period alcoholism and injuries only resulted in the loss of 321.[45] In January 1877 Mrs. Maria Straw, the wife of a Ninth Cavalry band member, was quarantined with venereal disease at Fort Union in order "to prevent contagion among the troops."[46] If the laundress had not been quarantined, Mrs. Straw could have taken advantage of some hot springs about five miles away from the post, which Army Surgeon D. C. Peters noted for their "efficacy in relieving . . . chronic syphilitic complaints."[47]

Given the labor shortage, the wives seem to have been willing to overlook the additional "roles" played by their servants and laundresses as long as the women proved capable and dependable at their more socially acceptable domestic tasks. Alice Grierson acknowledged that her maid, "drank, smoked, and chewed, and was accused of continually treating the soldiers," but nonetheless employed her.[48] Thus, servants and laundresses of questionable morals entered the officers' homes and, under certain conditions, became accepted members of the households. The wives seemed to make a small but significant moral distinction between, on the one hand, the women who labored honestly and succumbed to the temptation of needed money and, on the other, the professionals who profited immeasurably.

That the women's eastern view of prostitution itself did not change is reflected by their condemnation of the local "hog ranches" near military posts. These establishments provided prostitutes and liquor in a profitable combination and attracted both officers and enlisted men, especially after President Rutherford B. Hayes banned the sale of alcohol at army posts in 1881. The ruling had been inspired by the Women's Christian Temperance Union, but Mattie Summerhayes believed the action did the soldiers "incalculable harm."[49] Far better for them to seek the milder entertainment available on post than go to nearby establishments that cheated them at gambling and served weak whiskey and sick women.

Communities were pleased to profit from the soldiers' demand for relaxation and feminine companionship. If no towns existed near the post, enterprising individuals set up whorehouses in wagons. Such establishments hired mostly Irish, blacks, and Mexicans with names like Poker Alice, Tit Bit, and Big Nose Kate.[50] Near Fort Fauntleroy, New Mexico, Navajo Indian women filled the need; at Fort Randall, it was Sioux. If their tribe went on the warpath, these women were considered traitors by both sides. For poor women, the profits to be made from the soldiers were irresistible. Some of the women received five dollars for a "quick date" and might make up to thirty dollars per night.[51] In comparison, laundresses scrubbed for a month to earn the same amount. One entertaining lady, whose will was probated in California, left jewelry, an extensive wardrobe, and $1,520 in cash.[52] More women could identify with a "soiled dove" in Texas who confessed, "I've laid it in all of 'em, Borger, Kilgore. . . . I threw my fannie 21 times a night, 5 bucks a throw and time old red-eye come up I was eatin' breakfast drunker'n an Indian."[53] Such prostitutes lived in caves overlooking Fort Union, then moved into the old post ruins when a new fort was constructed. Two miles west of Fort Stephen Kearny in Nebraska were a half-dozen sod huts where the soldiers could share a beverage called "tanglefoot" with an obliging companion. After imbibing it, all their feet undoubtedly were. Hog ranches named "Dew Drop Inn" and "My Lady's Bower" were located on the banks of the Missouri River near Fort Abraham Lincoln. The officers' wives at the post watched with some sympathy as a spring flood in 1875 suddenly carried off the hovels and their inhabitants.

Business became so lucrative in communities near army posts that in many places city fathers decided to augment the town treasury by charging a special "whore tax." At one location where women had to pay a yearly fee of $150.00 apiece, there were so many prostitutes that the town's profit was more than $4,000.[54] Not surprisingly, the "big money" carried commensurate risks. In 1880, 8 percent of the servicemen in the U.S. Army were infected with venereal diseases.[55] Doctors at Crawford, Nebraska, near Fort Robinson, examined the women regularly but passed on the cost of doing so to brothel proprietors. By accompanying their husbands to the more promiscuous West, some army wives greatly increased their odds of contracting a sexually transmitted disease from their spouses. Whatever their class, culture, or race, it was a risk all women shared.

The dangers from disease, the months of loneliness, and the agony of childbirth so far from friends and family were among the experiences that helped form bridges between the groups of women at western outposts. If it was a toll bridge for the "inferior orders," paid for with the proper amount of deference and service, it was a drawbridge for officers' wives, who had to lower their prejudices and expectations. When Teresa Viele departed from Ringgold Barracks to return to New York, she realized that she took with her from the frontier "new and enlarged views of life as it really is, robbed of conventionalities. The people by whom I had been surrounded, though bold, reckless, and perhaps rough in their exterior, had exhibited a . . . true refinement more elevated than that generally acknowledged by the world."[56] Despite differences of class and culture, the existence these ladies and women shared in a world of men inspired a certain degree of cohesiveness and even empathy.

This breakdown of barriers was made possible by women like Mattie Summerhayes, who clambered up on a stagecoach box because she "liked these stage drivers." She "liked to have them talk to me, and I liked to look out upon the world through their eyes."[57] In the East, Mattie might have envisioned the army lifestyle through rose-colored glasses; in the West, her view of life and people became sharper through what Summerhayes acknowledged was an "evolutionary" process. Helen Chapman's mother wrote that she (Helen) had become indifferent to things she once considered important, and Chapman agreed. The officer's wife decided that a brush with death had changed her outlook and launched her on a "new phase of society."[58] Katie Gibson described the unified frontier army as "a handful of people . . . afloat upon an unchartered sea of desolation, miles and miles from civilization—and the shared hardships of a bleak climate with its privations, and the daily perils they faced together. These were the factors that brought these army pioneers closer to each other in some instances than many brothers and sisters, and forged ties of friendship that neither time nor circumstances could sever."[59]

Apaches on the Porch

WHILE SOME EASTERNERS were sympathetic to the plight of the "noble savage" and thought the Indians were mistreated by the federal government, others moving west coveted the Indians' lands and demanded their extinction. Even some who viewed the Indians as human considered them inferior and believed the white man could better exploit the great potential of the West. The military stood between these exponents of compassion and commerce and, as a result, was attacked from all sides. Humanitarians asserted that officers like Sherman, Sheridan, and Custer were exterminators who provoked the Indians' violent responses; expansionists objected to the military protection of Indian rights, especially after gold was discovered in the Black Hills. Meanwhile Native Americans resented the loss of their lands and the army enforcement of a life limited to reservations. Officer's wife Almira Hancock railed at northern philanthropists and their "ignorance of a class of human beings, whom they know little about."[1] Emily FitzGerald complained that army men pursuing Chief Joseph and the Nez Percé got "no pay, and abuse from the country that they risk their lives to protect."[2]

As a group officers' wives were ambivalent about Native Americans, depending on whether or not their husbands or families were in danger. A survey of one hundred diaries and reminiscences kept by settlers' wives shows that 16 percent were strongly positive in their view of Indians, 18 percent strongly negative, and 66 percent were of mixed reactions.[3] Most women went west terrified of the natives, thanks primarily to literary images that depicted them as consummate villains, devoid of humanity. Many of the women had read dime novels about the ferocious "red man" or attended lectures such as those presented in New York by Autie Custer concerning his campaign against the Cheyenne chief, Black Kettle. As a result, most army wives, and many officers, approached the frontier with trepidation.

The women certainly weren't reassured by the fact that "any military detail escorting white women on the plains in those days had one standing order: the leader was to shoot the women in his charge sooner than let them fall captive to the Indians."[4] Mrs. D. B. Dyer, traveling to Fort Reno, imagined her "corpse as it lay blackening in the sun, with the glossy ravens perched on my scalpless head, plucking my eyes."[5] Lydia Lane described her fears in a letter to her family back east: "Woe to the helpless party that fell into the devilish hands of a band of Indians. Men were generally put to death by slow torture, but they were allowed to live long enough to witness the atrocities practiced on their wives and children."[6] Margaret Carrington was walking along the Platte River when Maj. Jim Bridger advised her, "Better not go fur. There is Injuns enough lying under wolf skins, or skulking on them cliffs, I warrant! They follow ye always. They've seen ye, every day, and when ye don't see any of 'em about, is just the time to look out for their devilment."[7] The Sioux put a pole sporting red flags and locks of hair in the path of the Seventh Cavalry when it was relocating to Dakota Territory in 1873. It was a warning to the soldiers that the Indians would fight if the advance continued. Although officers and men paid little attention, Libbie Custer reported that her "heart was like lead for days afterward."[8] Helen Chapman went west determined to be brave and "not to die a thousand deaths in fearing one."[9] Teresa Viele felt brave enough in daylight but with nightfall and the sound of the howling wolves, "terror . . . was such as to destroy all claims of ever being looked upon as anything approaching a heroine."[10] Ada Vogdes felt the same way when she moved to the frontier in 1868: "I am frightened nearly to death every evening, when the sun goes down, until it comes up the next A.M."[11] Two months later Vogdes had developed into a fearless frontier hostess. She entertained Indian chiefs at the sutler's dining room, shook hands with them, and said a few words in their language. She reported that one had "a good fatherly countenance" and another "the most splendid chest and shoulders I ever laid eyes upon."[12] Although the "fatherly" Red Cloud was considered a fearsome warrior, over the next two years he became Ada's close friend. When she showed him her picture in a photograph album he kissed it "in the most affectionate manner."[13]

Experience in the West taught the women to mix their fear of the Indians with a combination of admiration, revulsion, curiosity, amusement, sympathy, and condescension. Their response depended largely on the actions of the warriors and their wives—judged, of course, from a white easterner's perspective. Ellen Boyd became interested in the Paiutes and Shoshones near Camp Halleck and "soon regarded red men as fearlessly as if I had been accustomed to them all my life."[14] At Fort Lapwai, Emily FitzGerald was not interested when a group passed her post because "Indians are no novelty to us now."[15] Katie Gibson saw her first Native American in Chicago: "A war bonnet capped his straight black hair and zigzagged down his lean, bare back. Shabby buckskin trousers encased his thin, long legs, and his agile feet, moccasin clad, were executing rhythmic, pounding steps interspersed by sudden leaps into the air, accompanied by occasional whoops and droning minor sounds supplied by a bareheaded squaw. A huge basket of beadwork stood beside her, evidently for sale, and the side show had been staged for advertising purposes."[16]

It was the "genuine article" that military wives experienced each day at frontier outposts. Ellen Biddle discovered eight to ten natives sitting in a circle on her kitchen floor at Fort Grant, playing with her children. Mattie Summerhayes found two naked squaws concealed in her kitchen closet at Ehrenberg. As she opened the door, the women darted out and leaped through a nearby window "like two frightened fawns." Hearing the commotion, Charley came in and explained that a "bad man go to kill 'em; I hide 'em." Mattie later discovered that one of the women was Charley's sister.[17] Mescalero Apaches sat on Lydia Lane's front porch at Fort Stanton and watched her through the window, their painted noses "flattened against the glass." When a sudden noise attracted her attention, Lydia found that some had wandered into the house, and she "did not use much ceremony in putting them out."[18] Mrs. R. H. McKay had the only sewing machine at Fort Sill and was making it hum one summer day when the Kiowa war chief, Satanta, entered through an open door to investigate the sound. The warrior was fascinated by the machine and returned to the house several times just to watch the woman making clothes for her family. An organ attracted a Navajo to Alice Baldwin's quarters—he loved to listen to her play. One day he offered to dance to her accompaniment. After going away, he came back to the living room ready to perform, his dancing costume a freshly killed beef hide still dripping blood. Sally Upham had a whole group of Indians drinking and quarreling near her house at Camp Apache in 1872. Shooting erupted, and some of them hid behind the Upham's quarters. Realizing that the bullets could easily penetrate the thin walls of the military housing, endangering her life and that of her child, she grabbed a riding crop and charged outside. Swinging the whip and beating everyone she could reach, Upham chased the stumbling Indians away from the house.

Although army wives were not always pleased with such close contact with Native American men, it did give the women an opportunity to notice and comment on the strong torsos, muscular legs, and broad shoulders of the warriors that they met. Even Frances Roe, who did not like black men, admired the physique of a red one. Indian men wore little clothing, and wives like Sarah Canfield had ample opportunity to appreciate these "magnificent specimens of manhood."[19] When the chiefs attending a council at Fort Berthold shook hands with her, their robes had "a way of slipping down and displaying their splendid brown shoulders." Another wife observed that while some natives were clumsy at draping the cloth, others looked like Roman senators.[20] One warrior who visited the women at Fort Davis wore an officer's coat, enlisted man's cap, moccasins, and a sword dangling from a leather belt around his waist, but no pants. Ione Bradley at Fort Wingate admired the Navajo men "stripped to a breach-cloth, moccasins, and a gay head band, their matchless figures shining in the sun like pieces of bronze statuary."[21] Mrs. D. B. Dyer, raised in a governor's home and educated in a convent school, praised the natives near Fort Reno as being "splendid specimens of physical strength and symmetry," but decided that she "would as soon think of contracting a fondness for a tornado."[22]

There was often a certain amount of sexual tension between Indian men and officers' wives, as reflected by Mattie Summerhayes' sensual description of "my Charley," the Cocopah Indian in scant attire she employed at Ehrenberg. This included praise of "the supple muscles of his clean-cut thighs."[23] Ellen Biddle had an opportunity to admire Charley when her family stayed with the Summerhayes on their way up the Colorado River but made no mention of his lack of clothes. On the trip she had seen natives in loincloths every day "and got accustomed to their nakedness."[24] She did, however, comment on the fact that he came into the room and placed a tray on a nearby table while she was taking a bath. Charley's casual attitude about intruding on a naked white woman suggests it may have been accepted practice in the household.

Biddle had her own Charlie, a young Apache boy at Fort Whipple. Raised until he was fourteen by soldiers who had found him on a battlefield, the native boy had served as valet for various officers. When he was nineteen or twenty, the officers returned east and the Biddles hired the "tall, attractive young man" as a houseboy. The morning after he arrived, Ellen was in the living room sewing when Charlie came in and sat down facing her. His only response to her order to leave was, "I like you much."[25] Knowing she must not show her fright, Ellen rose, took his arms, and escorted him from the room. She then ran to her husband's office for protection. After that, Biddle always felt ill at ease when alone with the young Apache. She did teach him to read, and he later enlisted as a scout. However, Charlie eventually returned to his tribe and, despite what Ellen called a "civilising" influence for several years, reverted to the Apache lifestyle. Biddle decided that it was a waste of time and money to send native children to institutions such as the Carlisle Indian School in Pennsylvania if they later returned to life on the reservations.

Rachel Lobach Brown was getting a bucket of water from the creek when a young Indian expressed his "admiration" for her. He tried to tempt Rachel to go away with him by offering her various things, but the woman adamantly refused. The next morning the warrior arrived at their quarters with a pony, saddle, beads, buffalo robes, blankets, moccasins, and other items to offer in trade for her. Brown's husband refused the bargain "in good old fashioned Army language."[26]

When a bachelor, Maj. William Worth, gave a dance at Camp Apache, "all the officers and their wives, and the chiefs with their harems, came to this novel fete."[27] Entranced by the beautiful young wife of one of the officers, a chief named Diablo, noticed by Summerhayes for his "great good looks," offered the husband a string of ponies for her. At a northern post, the Sioux chief Spotted Tail felt an attraction to Nannie Mills, wife of Capt. Anson Mills, and painted a picture of his war exploits to give her. One of them included a scene of the warrior killing an army captain. Some natives visiting Capt. Randolph Marcy greatly admired his wife's embroidery skill. One chief was so impressed with the woman's talent that he sent for one of his own wives to trade for Mrs. Marcy. The only way the army wife could persuade him to change his mind was by taking out her false teeth and demonstrating that she would not be able to chew his buckskin to the "flexibility and silken smoothness required." The chief "relinquished her with many gestures of regret and good will."[28] Elizabeth Burt formed a friendship with the Shoshone chief Washakie and said he was "born to command."[29] His word was law to the tribe. When the warrior departed on a hunting trip, he left instructions for his wife to move their village to a new location. He arrived at the new campsite to find it empty and traveled on to the old locale. When he asked his wife why she had not obeyed his instructions, she responded that her mother would not permit her to move the camp. Washakie promptly shot his mother-in-law. Officials later gave this chief, who was the "great good friend" of the frontier army, a military funeral.

While many white women admired the red man, even the more liberal society of the West would not allow army wives the intimacy with warriors that their husbands sometimes experienced with Indian women. The Seventh Cavalry's Capt. Miles Keogh wrote from Fort Hays, "We have here about ninety squaws—from our last fight [the Battle of the Washita]—some of them are very pretty. I have one that is quite intelligent. It is usual for officers to have two or three lounging around."[30] Some military personnel formed liaisons with these "spoils of war," but army wives preferred to ignore the adultery, much as southern women had refused to acknowledge their husbands' relationships with slaves. Frederick Benteen charged that Custer had an affair with a Cheyenne woman named Mo-nah-see-teah; if so, Libbie Custer was careful not to mention it in any of her writings. Officers' wives called handsome Indian women who might attract their husbands' attention "princesses," but also considered them rare exceptions in the tribes. Teresa Viele described one as the "most beautiful specimen of humanity" she ever saw.[31] The Indian maiden was wearing a wolfskin blouse embroidered with beads and had large, dreamy eyes with heavy lashes.

Capt. Randolph Marcy was extremely embarrassed when a Comanche acquaintance named Is-sa-keep offered him such a "temporary wife" in front of five hundred soldiers and emigrants. Whether he was more chagrined at the offer or the audience is not known. When the officer refused, the warrior told Marcy that he was the strangest man he had ever met. Officers described Indian women in letters to their wives but were quick to add that they had no personal interest in the natives. While located near Cheyenne and Arapaho villages, Capt. Albert Barnitz promised his wife, Jenny, that he would not "fall in love with any of their dirty little squaws."[32] Capt. E.O.C. Ord wrote to his wife, "Tell Mrs. Hardie the capt. is looking extremely youthful & when any good looking squaws come along he looks toward them & sighs—for home. . . . Remember if Mrs. H. takes this too hard—tell her Hardie is as anxious to get home—home, home! as your affectionate and devoted husband."[33] When Captain Marcy jokingly asked a Comanche woman to leave her husband and go home with him, he showed her a picture of his wife. The woman pointed at the photo and made a slashing motion across her throat, suggesting that his house "would be anything but a safe place for her." Marcy said he was of rather the same opinion.[34]

When a civilian clerk at Fort Sill named Hauser married Molly Curtis, the daughter of an Indian woman and an army scout, Flora Cooper assisted with arrangements for the ceremony. The army wife provided white kid gloves and a lace collar for the wedding dress; her daughter loaned the bride a sash to wear with the outfit. All the officers and their wives at the post attended the event, which was held at the Kiowa Agency. Afterward the guests discovered that Molly had gone through with the marriage only to honor an agreement her father had made with the clerk. She refused to live with Hauser, returned to her tribe, and later married again—to an Indian.

Although officers' wives had opportunities to interact with native women, most tended to see the majority of squaws as drudges dominated by the males of the tribe. Further study would have shown the eastern women that the wives of Navajo chiefs spoke up at council meetings and that Hopi husbands were not allowed to sell any household goods without their wives' permission. Among the Shawnees and the Delawares, divorce by either spouse was common, and in most tribes there was no shame to a woman bearing a child out of wedlock. During periods of war, Indian women sometimes followed their men into battle, holding fresh horses or bringing water to them in the midst of a fight. Despite the fact that most white women didn't have the freedom to exercise any of these options without being censured, many still considered Indian women "inferior." When the Summerhayes visited a rancher near Camp McDowell who had two Indian wives, Mattie wrote, "Now this was too awful. . . . I had a difficult time, in those days, reconciling what I saw with what I had been taught was right, and I had to sort over my ideas and deep rooted prejudices a good many times."[35]

The ladies at Fort Davis discovered that the fifty-year-old widowed sister of Cochise was the "presiding genius" of an Indian outpost near the fort.[36] Although it was unusual for a native woman to lead in this way, the great Apache chief trusted her judgment. Lt. John Van Deusen Du Bois agreed that her "independence and force seemed to justify this faith in her ability."[37] When a group of soldiers from another post was fired on by a sharpshooter, they charged the position and found that the sniper was a wounded Indian woman with an infant. As the men approached, the woman, who had a shattered leg from a bullet wound, drew a knife and fought until their numbers overwhelmed and disarmed her. The "drudge" with such courage uttered not a single sound as her leg was amputated without anesthesia. Dr. R. H. McKay told how a white man had attempted to explain the story of Adam and Eve to some chiefs attending a dinner. At the end, one of the Indians mused, "That is just like a white woman. Now if that had been a squaw, she would have taken a stick and killed that snake, and saved all the trouble."[38]

If times were peaceful, military wives traded with the natives, interacted with Indian women, attended peace councils, and visited camps. When two hundred warriors arrived to attend a council at Fort Laramie in 1869, Ada Vogdes traded a jet button off her coat for some arrows. She also exchanged a bag of flour, twenty pounds of bacon, some coffee, and a little sugar for a beautiful blanket handworked with beads.[39] John FitzGerald bought Emily "a fine beaded squaw robe, so you need not go to the expense of a new dress to go East in." He informed his wife that the outfit had belonged to a "Piute high society lady."[40] When Ellen Biddle asked a Native American at Fort Robinson if he had any beadwork to trade, he indicated that he would bring her some the next day. He arrived as promised at her quarters with a bag full of items, asking only for some trousers in return. Ellen gave him a pair of Colonel Biddle's old pants with a set of suspenders that so pleased the native that he immediately stripped to put on his new garment. Before the army wife fled the room, she noticed that the huge native had surprisingly small, skinny legs for his size.

It was Indian women who were intrigued by Alice Baldwin's clothes and hair. The officer's wife had agreed to undress to demonstrate the various layers, but the natives didn't care for the restrictive crinolines or corset and thought that so many clothes would make them hot. However, the Indian women at Fort Wingate were fascinated with her hair. When Alice took it down in response to their request, the natives were amazed at how long and thick it was. They were sure she had another scalp attached to it. The Indian women were also enthralled by the way in which Baldwin's hair was crimped. Showing one squaw how she pinned it up, Alice told the woman to come the next morning to see the result. Eager to do so, the native arrived before Alice was even out of bed. The Indian watched as Alice's hair was combed out and was so pleased with the result that she asked to have her hair done the same way. Alice agreed, and the squaw spent that night in hairpins. When the native's hair was arranged the next morning, the Indian woman was delighted and so were the rest of the women in the tribe. They all came to Alice for similar styling. During the remainder of Alice's stay at Fort Wingate, Indian women exchanged many favors for the assistance of this frontier beauty shop.

It was an army wife's hat that intrigued an Indian warrior at Fort Lapwai in 1876. As Emily FitzGerald and Mrs. Perry, the wife of the post's commanding officer, watched the proceedings at a peace conference, an elderly warrior sitting on the floor nearby was amused by the little dotted veil on Mrs. Perry's hat. Apparently it reminded him of a piece of black cotton net in the odd assortment of items that made up his own unusual headdress. Removing the headgear, he rummaged through it until he discovered the netting, then emulated the officer's wife by affixing it over his own face. Pleased with the re-sult, the Indian wore the veil the rest of the day.

Sarah Canfield knew that she was the curiosity when Andrew took her to an encampment of about two thousand Indians near Fort Berthold. A crowd of approximately one hundred natives soon gath-ered around her. "They often ran in front of us and peering into my face which was somewhat hidden by my sunbonnet, then dodge back laughing and chattering as though it was great fun."[41] Autie Custer took Libbie and their black cook, Eliza, to visit a stockade near Fort Hays where three chiefs and several women who had been captured at the Battle of the Washita were being held. The Indian women were mesmerized by Eliza's coloring and pulled up her sleeve to see if her skin was still black beneath the dress. They tugged on Libbie's curls and were amazed when the hair bounced back. They rubbed their cheeks against her's in the Indian form of a kiss. A few days later these same Indian women at Fort Hays, so friendly and so curious with the army wife and black servant, attacked the soldiers guarding them and stabbed the officer in charge when they thought the troop-ers were taking their chiefs away to be hanged.

Custer took his wife to the stockade because he wanted her to be-come acquainted with Native Americans and their culture. At the same time, he encouraged Libbie to listen to stories of reported In-dian atrocities as a warning not to take foolish risks. Custer had a woman and her three daughters, who had been held by Indians, show Libbie their scars and describe their treatment. The events at the stockade and the stories she heard undoubtedly inspired the letter she wrote to her aunt from Fort Hays: "Surely you do not believe the current rumors that Autie and others are cruel in their treatment of the Indians. Autie and others only do what they are ordered to do. And if those who criticize these orders could only see for themselves . . . as we see . . . the brutalities of the men, the venom of the squaws. . . . People in civilized conditions cannot imagine it. But we who have seen it know. Death would be merciful in comparison."[42] Lt. G. A. Hesselberger and two sisters he had ransomed from the Kiowas for twenty-eight hundred dollars worth of supplies visited with Alice and Frank Baldwin at Fort Harker. The older sister, who was seventeen, had been beaten, starved, and abused until she had lost her mind; the fourteen-year-old was still sane. Alice reported that the military wives at the post received the sisters with great kindness.

Fannie Boyd traveled twenty miles to watch an Indian war dance and commented that it was picturesque at night, lit by the huge fires. However, as the chant and movement increased in volume and wildness, she felt the dance graphically depicted its savage origins and was glad for the large escort accompanying her on the trip. Mattie Summerhayes watched a similar dance, sitting on the trunk of a fallen tree in an Apache camp. The performers were naked except for loin cloths; their bodies were painted and bunches of feathers were attached at their elbows and knees. Each wore a headdress that resembled the horns of an elk, and ornaments jingled around their neck and arms. Two of the dancers brandished knives. As the tom-toms sounded a "dreadful din," Mattie "saw uneasiness in the faces of the other women, and by mutual consent we got up and slowly took our departure."[43] Three months later the group of Indians who had performed so realistically for the officers and their wives fired into the garrison at Camp Apache and fled the reservation.

Army wives at Fort Sill received permission to visit the nearby Washita Agency to trade with the Indians. On the way back, renegades attacked the group at Cache Creek. The driver deserted the women and some officers' wives were taken, held for two weeks, and later ransomed. Flora Cooper almost had a similar experience at the post when she was one of a party that went eight miles away to a picnic at Mount Scott. Prevented from returning to Fort Sill until after dark by heavy fog, their carriage was stopped by a group of Indians from a nearby camp. The officer's wife and her friends managed to get away, but only after the natives pelted them with rocks.

Caroline Frey Winne was not frightened by the Indians at Sidney Barracks but was annoyed when they continually peeked in her windows. She decided that "it would be a great mercy to them if they could all freeze to death, as many of them have this winter."[44] Winne's reaction was during a time of peace. When a state of war existed and family members were in danger, army wives expressed even stronger sentiments. Teresa Viele asserted that the Comanche had the instincts and intelligence of a brute. They were "bloody, brutal, licentious," with an innate hatred of white men. She decided that "actual extermination seems to suggest itself as the only remedy against this scourge."[45] When the Modocs went on the warpath, Ada Vogdes "hoped they kill the whole tribe."[46] When the Nez Percé threatened Fort Lapwai, Emily FitzGerald wished the renegades "could be exterminated."[47] Fighting them, she said, was "like fighting to exterminate wild animals, horrible beasts."[48] The officer's wife sat on her back porch at the post, churning butter, and "kept one eye and one ear up the ravine watching for Indians all the time. It is a horrible feeling, this constantly expecting sounds that you dread to hear."[49] Libbie Custer and the Seventh Cavalry wives at Fort Abraham Lincoln felt safer, despite the fact that the regiment was away on the Black Hills Expedition. The women knew that an infantry unit with a Gatling gun was situated on a bluff overlooking the post. When the complacent wives later thanked the infantry officer profusely for his protection, the elderly bachelor informed the women that he did not believe in marriage for army officers. He had been there to protect government property—defense of the women would have been his last priority.[50]

Ellen Biddle was sick in San Francisco when the Modoc War began. James Biddle, who had asked to be attached to General Schofield's staff so he could be near his wife, immediately requested to return to his unit. Knowing that his wife was ill and believing that the peace commissioners would settle the dispute before fighting erupted, Biddle decided to take his six-year-old son, David, with him on what the officer thought would be field maneuvers. There was no peace, and the Biddles' little boy came under fire and struggled for twelve days through snow so heavy that three men froze to death.

Alice Baldwin sat in her quarter's window at Fort Harker and watched the fire as Indians burned a nearby ranch and killed the men living there. Eveline Alexander was residing in tents at Fort Stevens when warriors attacked that outpost. She buckled on a gun, then took refuge behind flour sacks and boxes of food in the nearby supply tent. After the attack was over, the officer's wife provided medical care for the wounded because the doctor was away on patrol with her husband, Andrew. Indian snipers lay on the cliffs above Fort

Davis, killing those who ventured out to the post garden or nearby creek. Two days after a sixteen-year-old boy at the fort was taken prisoner, the troopers found his remains. His captors had tortured him to death by sticking pine needles into his body until he looked like a porcupine, then setting them on fire. The wives at Fort Phil Kearny watched as an enlisted man who had been badly wounded by arrows and partially scalped dragged himself back to a camp in the nearby woods. He had broken off the arrows so they wouldn't impede his crawling through the brush. In response to such sights, Helen Chapman wrote to her mother, "Fancying what I should do in case of attack, I often realize that I have not that shrinking horror of the shedding of blood I once possessed."[51]

The Baldwins were already in bed when the "long roll," a signal of danger for the infantry troops, sounded at Fort Wingate. The post resounded in a cacophony of yells, whoops, oaths, and orders. Frank brought the two family dogs into the quarters to stand guard and ordered his wife to extinguish the fire. After her husband departed, Alice did not comply with his orders because she could not bear to wait alone in the dark. Sitting beside her sleeping child, Baldwin was amazed at her own composure. Only after the Indian raid was over did Alice experience strong hysterics and periods of insomnia. Dr. R. H. McKay said that when the long roll sounded, officers scurried to their command, and wives and children were left, scantily dressed, to hasten to a place of safety. All were agreed, "What did it [lack of clothes] signify in such an emergency."[52] The doctor may have heard the danger warning many times. During his eighteen months of service at Fort Sill, seventeen men were killed and scalped by Indians.[53]

When warriors drove off a herd of mules at Fort Abraham Lincoln, almost all of the regiment gave chase. Only a few men remained at the post, and the wives began to fear that stealing the animals had been a diversion for an attack on the fort. Gathering at the Custers' house, the women took turns standing on the porch railing with a pair of field glasses, watching eagerly for their husbands' return. Having listened to stories from white women in Kansas who had been captured by Indians, the wives agreed that they would kill themselves rather than be taken. The men did not return until nightfall— the women waited in suspense and fear all day.

Indian prisoners were being held at Fort Union in 1881 when the troops were ordered out to pursue renegades. Guarded by only a few men, two of the prisoners escaped during a heavy fog, and army wives and children from the twenty-five families on post searched all the buildings at the fort. Army daughter Genevieve LaTourrette was fearful but also thrilled: "I'm quite sure some of us were almost disappointed that we were not able to prove ourselves a heroine by finding those two young renegades without the assistance of a man. . . . That evening was spent in telling of our experiences in the day's excitement. We were all sitting on the end of the porch near the side gate of our yard, when we heard the shuffling of some kind of noise coming toward the gate. All was silent, when a poor little innocent burro poked his head through."[54] The army families later discovered that the warriors had quickly left the area to return to the reservation.

Because of the ever-present threat of danger from Indians, officers' wives often found their freedom of movement severely curtailed. Sioux attacks in 1866 near Forts Reno and Phil Kearny took place on August 12, 14, and 17, and September 8, 10, 13, 14, 16, 17, 20, 21, 23, and 27. During this period, Fort Phil Kearny had only forty-five rounds of ammunition per man, Fort Reno had thirty.[55] The constant confinement at Fort Kearny under periods of tremendous stress finally proved unbearable to three officers' wives, and they went for a stroll near the post. Only minutes after the women returned, Indians appeared on the path that they had taken. After troops at Fort Abraham Lincoln found a white man staked out and disemboweled, they warned their wives not to wander outside the picket line near the post. Chafing at the restrictions, Libbie Custer and other wives finally convinced Burkeman, the trooper who cared for the Custers' horses, to take them for a ride. The wives returned safely but perhaps were in greater danger when their husbands discovered the expedition. The women were given a severe lecture, but what Burkeman received was undoubtedly considerably worse.

Mrs. George Downey was sitting outside a fort on the banks of a stream, playing a guitar and singing, when she looked up to find herself surrounded by an audience of Indians. Continuing her song, she got up, nodded to the natives, sauntered slowly back to the fort, and was amazed to reach it alive. Elizabeth Burt, her sister, Kate, the

Burts' four-year-old son, Andrew, and another officer's wife were visiting a beautiful spring near Fort C. F. Smith when they heard the sentinel's warning shot and a cry of "Indians." Elizabeth and Kate each took one of Andrew's hands and ran back to the stockade, dragging the child with them. Sioux warriors, who were trying to carry off a herd of mules, had passed near the stream where the women sat picking flowers. After that, the Indians made regular forays near the post until the wives began to watch the action from the fort's ramparts, rather like a stage play.

In 1867, newspapers in the East informed their readers that the commanding officer and eighty men at Fort Buford, Dakota Territory, had held off three thousand Indians during two days of pitched battle.[56] Articles reported that when it appeared the garrison was about to be overrun, Lieutenant Colonel Rankin shot himself and his wife, the only woman on post. Because of escalating warfare and winter weather in the area, it was months before the families of military personnel assigned to Fort Buford discovered that the story was a complete fabrication.

Army wives in the West had learned the truth about Indians, but it was a truth that varied depending on the risk factor that the women perceived. Wives who discovered that natives had a sense of humor, enjoyed music, and were innately curious also saw mangled bodies and heard stories of torture from victims. The warriors who seemed so handsome and friendly to the women were capable of extreme cruelty; the same squaws who wanted their own hair crimped hung scalps from their lodgepoles. Officers' wives discovered that the Indians, like the blacks and "women of lower classes," were much more complex and compelling figures in person than had been suggested by eastern stereotypes.

Most army wives also came to a new understanding of the Indians' determination to fight for their land and lifestyle. Army wife Marian Russell wrote, "I like to think about the sound of their war drums, the cry of a lost race calling."[57] In 1873, 1,200 Comanches, Kiowas, and Cheyennes revolted in Texas; the Apaches later joined them.[58] By 1879 the situation was so severe that Col. Benjamin Grierson led a full campaign against Victorio and his Apache band. When the warrior was finally defeated and killed, Alice Grierson's sister-in-law,

Louise Semple, wrote from New York that she was glad that Ben had not been present at the "butchery."[59] She was among those who believed that dealings with the natives had been shameful.

Alice and other frontier army wives who faced the daily reality of life and death with the Indians were unable to adopt Semple's detached viewpoint. From January 1, 1866, to January 7, 1891, 932 military personnel were killed in 1,065 actions on the frontier, and another 1,060 were wounded.[60] Fathers, brothers, husbands, and sons were included in those statistics. Personal experience, periods of peace, and contact with Native Americans had enabled officers and their wives to see the human face, both good and bad, of the enemy. It had not diminished their anxiety about Indians but neither had it dulled their shared sense of humanity. In 1878 when an official at the Kiowa Agency near Fort Sill issued rancid supplies to local natives, army families purchased food from the commissary to feed them. The soldiers might have to shoot the Indians in times of war, but officers and their wives at frontier posts were not willing to let Native Americans starve in times of peace. The action also served a political purpose since it lessened the threat of an Indian uprising that the military would have to quell.

Lt. George H. Morgan of the Third Cavalry met an Indian who proudly presented a piece of paper from the valuables he carried in a bag around his neck. The paper, written by Capt. John Bourke, an aide to Gen. George Crook, stated that "the bearer was about the most unmitigated rascal in the Arapaho nation and that anyone reading this trusted him at his own peril."[61] Morgan decided that the statement might be true, but the "trusting" way in which it was handed out made it "very impressive." This episode dramatizes the complexity of the relationship between white men and Native Americans on the frontier. It was not the first time that an Indian had misplaced his trust in the incomprehensible written words of a white man; nor was it the first time a white man had been tempted to accept the superficially benign image of a "noble savage," despite good counsel to the contrary. Mattie Summerhayes called the Indians "children of Nature, after all, living close to the earth."[62] Frances Roe referred to them as "simply, and only, painted, dirty, and nauseous-smelling savages."[63] The truth was an amalgam that was strongly affected by circumstance.

Western historian Robert Utley once described legends as "far more influential in shaping our attitudes and beliefs than the complex, contradictory, and ambiguous truth."[64] Army wives came west knowing what they believed about Indians—they had read the "truth" in books and had heard experts lecture on the subject. It was only when the women assimilated daily experience on the frontier that a convoluted reality challenged the legends and made officers' wives reexamine their view of Native Americans.

A Drink of Dirty Water

ON DECEMBER 29, 1890, more than two hundred men, women, and children of the Teton Sioux were killed in the engagement at Wounded Knee. Many historians consider this event and its aftermath the end of more than forty years of warfare with Native Americans on the frontier. However, military personnel continued to have small skirmishes with Indians until 1896, only seven years before the Wright brothers' flight at Kill Devil Hills, North Carolina, in 1903. That was also the same year that Henry Ford and his partners formed the Ford Motor Company.

When Libbie and Autie Custer moved west with the Seventh Cavalry after the end of the Civil War in 1865, there were approximately two million people on the frontier. Less than twenty-five years later, the population had grown to more than four times that many.[1] In 1866 officers and their families saw great herds of the estimated thirteen million buffalo that provided food and clothing for the Indians; by the time of Wounded Knee, most of the animals had been slaughtered by white men. No transcontinental railroad crossed the United States when north and south were reunited; in 1890 there were four. Women who wanted to experience a few months of civilization no longer had to travel east—it was coming west to meet them on the wheels of industrialization.

Army wives who had eagerly awaited two-month-old mail were able to hear within hours, via the telegraph, of the assassination attempt on President James A. Garfield in 1881. Officers who had once been away on campaigns for so long that their children did not recognize them could, by the end of the Indian Wars, communicate with their families by telephone. Grace Maxon wrote Alice Grierson about the ultimate evidence that Victorian society had arrived in San Antonio—the trains were running on time. Before, they had not departed the station until the cars were full of passengers. Fannie Boyd had cried when she arrived at Fort Halleck in 1868 because of the crudities of life on the frontier. When the Summerhayes were assigned there fourteen years later, the railroad had brought so many eastern luxuries that Mattie could exclaim, "Oh! What a lovely post!"[2] Alice Grierson had "invested little in furnishings" during the years at Fort Concho so that packing would be easier and moving less costly.[3] When the family was reassigned to Fort Davis in the 1880s, she realized that the railroad was "making further inroads each year, bringing with it an array of conveniences and amenities."[4] The nearest railroad stop to Fort Davis was at Marfa Station, only twenty-two miles from the post. Alice was able to decorate the commanding officer's quarters with a new sofa, four upholstered chairs, and a Chickering grand piano. By 1894, when Ellen Biddle returned to the West after several years of living in the East, she found a new formality and lifestyle. Officers left calling cards, and the railroad delivered supplies, books, and ample food from markets that were only hours away. Biddle decided that this interaction with the outside world had decreased the residents' dependence on each other. She felt that the frontier post had lost much of its simple charm and was now just like the city she had left in the East.

As Teresa Viele returned east after her husband's tour of duty in Texas, she had witnessed the increased traffic on the Mississippi River: "The rush of commerce of these western waters seems almost a miracle, so short a time ago the skiff of the aborigines or the breath of Heaven alone disturbed their repose. . . . Enterprise— avarice—adventure—so are our human passions ordained to fulfill the destiny of the universe."[5] Fannie Boyd loved the West and felt that there was "a rare and nameless charm in the contemplation of those extended prairies, with their soft gray tints, dreary to Eastern people, but so dearly loved" by westerners. She could "never become reconciled to localities where the eye cannot look for miles and miles beyond the spot where one stands" and disliked "to think that the day will surely come when it will teem with human life and all its warring elements!"[6]

Women who had grown up in eastern cities became accustomed to the West's clean air and open spaces and had to balance the return to eastern "dirt and congestion" with the excitement of visiting families and friends. Arriving in St. Louis on a trip from New Mexico to New York in 1871, Fannie Boyd's "heart sank at the prospect of again breathing air too heavy and dense to be anything but suffocating."[7] When preparing for the trip, she had "looked forward with intense longing to that moment, supposing ineffable happiness would be my portion when again there [New York]." However, after she arrived in the East, "no longing had ever equaled in intensity the one which then took possession of me—to be back again in my dear Western home, surrounded by all the lonely grandeur of its lovely scenery. . . . Besides missing my own home . . . I missed the quiet and freedom from that mad rush which seems an inevitable part of life in a great city."[8] Even the thought of being in the western metropolis of Omaha appalled Frances Roe. When Faye was assigned there in 1888 to serve as an aide-de-camp to Gen. John R. Brooke, commander of the Department of the Platte, Frances "was almost heartbroken over it, as it will be a wretched life for me—cooped up in a noisy city."[9]

Frances especially felt out of place when she discovered that "all the women here have such white skins, and by comparison I must look like a Mexican, my face is so brown from years of exposure to dry, burning winds."[10] After years of shopping at the sutler's store and out of catalogs, Frances found it confusing to deal with shop girls over the counter. She also forgot how to carry a parasol, continually leaving it in stores or neglecting to open it to protect her complexion from the sun. Since it was the "first summer I have been East [Omaha] in nine years," Frances decided that it was "not surprising that parasols and things mix me up at times."[11]

Women and their children who traveled east were often viewed by friends and relatives as eccentrics or "waybacks from wayback."[12] There was no way that an upper-class eastern boy with his regular school schedule, religious instruction, and structured Victorian behavior could comprehend the cold and dangerous life the Biddles' six-year-old son had endured while on an Indian campaign with his father. Fanny Corbusier's two-year-old did not know what a tree was and so defined lampposts, telegraph poles, oaks, maples, and evergreens all by that title. An army child who was teased by eastern children retaliated with the threat, "I'll put you in the guardhouse, I will." Libbie Custer said the phrase was "Choctaw" to the civilian children, who did not know what a guardhouse was.[13] Army daughter Forrestine Cooper described how military children were "born in the regiment and, guided by the officers and Negro soldiers, we learned to walk and talk. From the offspring of the colonel down to the brood on 'Suds Row,' we were all children of the Tenth Cavalry. We felt that we owned the regiment and the regiment felt it owned each child."[14] When families went east after years on the frontier, it was a time of adjustment for everyone. For children born and raised in the West, however, it was not just a period of adaptation—it was a completely new and often frightening lifestyle.

Caroline Winne warned her family, "When I come, be prepared to be ashamed of your backwoods sister, for I am actually shabby."[15] Elizabeth Burt and her sister, Kate, were offended when a group of young girls in Chicago giggled at their weather-beaten faces and out-of-date clothes. Their mother responded that it wasn't strange they were stared at since they presented such an odd appearance. Ellen Biddle's sisters informed her that she looked as though she had "just escaped from the Ark" when she returned East wearing an old-fashioned bonnet.[16]

When she arrived in the West, Mattie Summerhayes was condescending toward army wives in Arizona who presented a "ridiculously old-fashioned" appearance but also wondered if she would look that way when she left. Living at the isolated Ehrenberg, bathing in the Colorado River, longing to wear the looser and cooler Mexican clothing, learning to smoke cigarettes, and attracted to the sensuous Charley, Mattie changed even more. Leaving the frontier, she acknowledged that she "could not break away from my Arizona habits." Her aunt informed the army wife that she was in a state of "semi-barbarism."[17]

After seven months in the East in 1885, Frances Roe decided that the trip had been enjoyable, "but citizens and army people have so little in common [that] no matter how near and dear the relationship may be . . . one half of them . . . could not distinguish an officer of the Army from a policeman!"[18] When Mattie Summerhayes visited family in Nantucket, the lack of interest in her stories about life in the West made her feel a world apart. She was pleased when an elderly uncle who was a whaling captain asked her to show him where she had been but was frustrated in the attempt when the only map available defined all the country between the Mississippi River and California as "unexplored." On a visit to family in Monroe, Michigan, Libbie Custer felt out of place with civilians who understood few of the challenges and realities of living in the West. She saw the women in her hometown "so fagged with domestic cares, kitchen drudgery, leading a monotonous life" that she decided, "No Civil life for me, except as a visitor."[19]

After Autie Custer's death in 1876, Libbie eventually settled in New York City, "the one place in my small world where women who are rightly disposed and who know what they are about, can enjoy a great degree of the sweet freedom and independence which in other places [in the East] is accorded only to men."[20] Army wives such as Custer and Boyd had begun their westward journey with naiveté and youth, ignorant of what they would find. Experience brought changes in their lifestyles and outlooks. Fashion yielded to searing heat and prairie winds; the definition of necessity was adjusted by reality; and danger from Indians and animals overcame fear of firearms. When Eveline Alexander killed a mountain lion with her small pistol, her husband, Andrew, began to call her "Eveline, the great panther killer of the prairie."[21]

Interaction with other races and classes became a question of survival and symbiosis. The wives' association with Indians eroded their eastern stereotypes and carried a curious mix of risk and excitement. Even the women's vocabulary changed as houses became quarters, the grocer was the sutler or commissary, and the commanding officer's wife was the "KOW." Cavalry wives on the frontier did not need clocks because they lived—and sometimes died—to the sound of bugle calls defining their day. Infantry wives quickly learned to recognize the various drum beats, especially the long roll signal for danger.

Strong and successful in meeting the challenges of life on the frontier, the women returned east with self-confidence, multifaceted capabilities, and a maturity of spirit that would not always be welcome. On the frontier a confluence of human and natural factors redefined the officer's wife's role in the rugged and demanding western society. She was, in ways alien to eastern culture, her husband's full partner in business and life. She shared in the risks and successes of an existence very much on the edge of civilization; a life that demanded and esteemed her intelligence, resourcefulness, imagination, and courage.

In the East the army wife was merely part of the family, destined to be no more than a reflection of her husband's success. In the West women began to see themselves as self-reliant individuals who could succeed on their own terms and abilities. Many army wives returning east refused to revert to a social standard they had come to regard as vacuous or shallow. Historian Sandra Myres prepared a study of army wives after they returned east and found that almost all of them supported women's suffrage. Many, such as Jessie Frémont and Libbie Custer, became extremely successful authors, and some of the women formed their own businesses. Several clung to the survival skills that had become instinctive on the frontier. Almost all conserved water, and Lydia Lane continued to pick up branches whenever she found them on the ground, a holdover from the days of wood shortages. Wives surrounded by plenty in the East still planned far ahead for holidays, recalling the extensive lead time required in the West for acquiring foodstuffs and presents. Some officers' wives would use the abilities they had developed in the West on yet another frontier—in the Philippines after the Spanish-American War.

Finally, and perhaps most important, the women had been a part of something greater than themselves, and they knew it. Even if they lacked a sense of history, army wives still felt the personal pride of achievement in their dangerous, exciting, and victorious lives. Ellen Biddle wrote, "I am but a woman, but I have helped 'bear the burden and heat of the day' in the West."[22] This existence set apart the military wives on the frontier as a tough, tiny segment within the army subculture; part of a small group of men and women who, for a fleeting period, had been through the fire together and shared experiences, heartaches, and joys beyond even the strongest family ties. They had relied on each other for strength and companionship, and had grown to realize their own potential. Gen. Philippe de Trobriand, a French-born officer who served on the frontier, declared, "American women really have blood: courage in danger, constancy in sacrifice, resignation . . . seem to be virtues inherent in their character." He asserted that "these young women . . . brave all these mishaps—and for them I could even say suffering—with courage and even an heroic gaiety. If they complain, it is with a rather resigned manner that clearly indicates that they foresaw all this and do not regret that they have exposed themselves to it."[23] Helen Chapman wrote to a friend, "What I once should have called miseries, I laugh at now. . . . A mouse once put me into a very lady-like nervousness, but not much more than a year since, I slept in a weather-beaten loft where real rats held their revel all night long and now a whole regiment of them would not disturb me."[24]

Like the Native Americans whose independent lifestyle had been sacrificed to the constraints of civilization, army wives returning east sometimes felt like their foundations of freedom had been cut away. Officers' wives such as Alice Grierson had enjoyed a special status at frontier posts, with accompanying authority. Eveline Alexander rode at the head of a military column with her husband and, to give her "a warlike appearance," wore a pistol in a holster and a silver-hilted dagger.[25]

The scarcity of women in the West meant that the wives were treated as royalty. Helen Chapman lived on the Brazos "in a kind of feudal state" with a walled quartermaster's "castle" guarded by sentinels at every entrance. Her husband was the "Old Major" and her ten-year-old son, the "Little Major." Realizing that the boy faced "a great danger of his thinking the world was made for Caesar," she forced the child to wait on himself and say "will you please" whenever he needed help from the soldiers.[26] No lady was ever a wallflower at an army dance; a handsome young officer was always there to escort her. Army wives discovered that arrival in the East reminded those who were plain of their lack of beauty and forced older women to recognize their age and matronly status.

Fannie Boyd's "heart was so bound up in frontier life I had hoped until the last moment that the spring rains, which had been unusually severe would keep us storm-bound in Texas."[27] She later wrote that her fears that she "should not feel at home in civil life, where everything was so different," were justified.[28] There was a legend that anyone drinking from the Rio Grande would be compelled by some strong, subtle charm to return to the West. Apparently Fannie had drunk the dirty water filled with sediment because, during the four years the family remained in the East, "not one moment had passed in which I would not gladly have been there [the West]."[29] The Boyds returned to Fort Clark in 1885 but were there only four months when Orsemus Boyd died of pneumonia. Fannie returned east and was apparently able to maintain a freer lifestyle there due in part to family money. She died at her estate, Alancourt, in Boonton, New Jersey, in 1926.

When Caroline Winne arrived in the West, she described it to her brother as "a barren, desolate country, and we'll be two happy ones if the day ever comes when we can turn our backs upon it and never see it again." Years later she would decide that although they had been deprived of "very much that we would greatly enjoy seeing and having . . . these months and years we have spent in this happy house . . . we shall always remember as a very happy time."[30] The Winnes served six years on the frontier before Charles retired in 1902 as deputy surgeon general.

Teresa Viele described how memory of life in the West "turns the past to gold," but twenty years after the family left Texas, she divorced Gen. Egbert Viele for adultery and moved with their eight-year-old son to Paris.[31] A few years later she returned to the United States and kidnapped her daughter, Emily, from the Viele estate near Poughkeepsie, New York. The action won her a place in the *New York Police Gazette*. A woman of beauty, intelligence, and strong character, she formed a literary salon in Paris and became an expert on Islam. After traveling to Constantinople and meeting the Sultan, Viele lectured on the topic at the 1893 World's Columbian Exposition in Chicago. Historian Sandra Myres described Teresa as "an intelligent and strong minded woman struggling to express herself within the narrow bounds allowed women of her time."[32]

Another employee at the exposition was Mrs. D. B. Dyer. While her "civilized friends of the East were indulging in the many fads of the day," Dyer "was interested in the barbaric gems of my surrounding neighbors."[33] She "became a curio-fiend and no tribe in the remotest parts of space escaped me."[34] Dyer became such an expert on Native American artifacts and lifestyles that she was recommended to work in the Indian Branch of the Chicago fair.

When Lydia Lane was packing away the relics of her army days, she discovered a small battered tin box used to carry their lunch when moving from camp to camp. "As I raised the lid a faint odor seemed to rise from its depths, and in a second memory was busy with the past, traveling back to the old happy days when the little tired, hungry children with eager out-stretched hands stood by my side waiting to be served. With a sigh I closed the box, putting it aside as worthless, to be thrown away, but the tender recollections awakened by the sight of the old friend were too strong. Hurriedly seizing it, I cleared a comfortable corner in a chest and carefully replaced the worn-out box, retiring it, like an old soldier, from active service forever."[35]

Katie Garrett Gibson's memories were of dancing with Frank under the stars when she first arrived in the West. It had seemed to her that "slowly my Eastern life was receding into the background, and its comforts, crowded streets, and congested spaces were becoming less alluring to me."[36] After years on the frontier, the family had to readjust to life in Washington when Frank was retired for physical disability. The Gibsons and Katie's sister and brother-in-law, Mollie and Donald McIntosh, lie near each other in Arlington National Cemetery. They chose this resting place because they would "always be within sound of the trumpet calls we loved."[37]

Jack and Mattie Summerhayes are also buried in Arlington. The family served at several posts during their more than thirty years together in the army, but Mattie knew she had developed most as an individual while on the frontier. After a year of living there, she began to tolerate "about everything that I had been taught to think wicked or immoral" and "was willing to reserve judgement" on people's behavior and values.[38] After Jack's retirement, he was content with civilian life, but Mattie still felt ". . . that fatal spirit of unrest from which I thought to escape, and which ruled my life for so many years, sometimes asserts its power, and at those times my thoughts turn back to the days when we are all Lieutenants together, marching across the deserts and mountains of Arizona. . . . Sometimes I hear the still voices of the Desert: they seem to be calling me through the echoes of the Past . . . But how vain these fancies! Railroad and automobile have annihilated distance, the army life of those years is past and gone, and Arizona as we knew it, has vanished from the face of the earth."[39]

Notes

The Girl I Left Behind Me

1. Harvey Green, *The Light of the Home: An Intimate View of the Lives of Women in Victorian America* (New York: Pantheon Books, 1983), 27.

2. Mary Elizabeth Massey, *Bonnet Brigades* (New York: Alfred A. Knopf, 1966), 19.

3. Green, 9.

4. Shirley Anne Leckie, ed., *The Colonel's Lady on the Western Frontier: The Correspondence of Alice Kirk Grierson* (Lincoln: University of Nebraska Press, 1989), 189.

5. Red Reeder, *Born at Reveille* (New York: Duell, Sloan and Pearce, 1966), 15.

6. Massey, 14.

7. Daniel Walker Howe, ed., *Victorian America* (Philadelphia: University of Pennsylvania Press, 1976), 151.

8. Massey, 24.

9. Ibid., 359.

10. Ibid., 347.

11. Katherine Gibson Fougera, *With Custer's Cavalry* (1942; reprint, Lincoln: University of Nebraska Press, 1986), 14.

12. Ibid., 16–18.

13. Ibid., 22.

14. Ibid., 29.

15. Ibid., 44.

16. Ibid., 49.

17. Louise L. Stevenson, *The Victorian Homefront: American Thought and Culture, 1860–1880* (New York: Twayne Publishers, 1991), 122, 125.

18. Elinor Richey, *Eminent Women of the West* (Berkeley, CA: Howell-North Books, 1975), 15.

19. Ibid., 16.

20. Mary Virginia Fox, *The Story of Women Who Shaped the West* (Chicago: Childrens Press, 1991), 26.

21. Dorothy Levinson, *Women of the West* (New York: Franklin Watts, Inc., 1973), 82.

22. Frederick Jackson Turner, *The Frontier in American History* (1920; reprint, New York: Holt, Rinehart and Winston, 1962), 38.

23. Glenda Riley, *The Female Frontier: A Comparative View of Women on the Prairie and the Plains* (Lawrence: University of Kansas Press, 1988), 56.

24. Edward M. Coffman, *The Old Army: A Portrait of the American Army in Peacetime, 1784–1898* (New York: Oxford University Press, 1986), 294.

25. Shirley Anne Leckie, "The Woman Behind the Myth," *American History Illustrated* 28, no. 4 (September/October 1993); 40.

26. Catherine Coffin Phillips, *Jessie Benton Frémont: A Woman Who Made History* (San Francisco: John Henry Nash, 1935), 47.

27. Caleb Coker, ed., *The News from Brownsville: Helen Chapman's Letters from the Texas Military Frontier, 1848–1852* (Austin: Texas State Historical Association, 1992), 75.

28. Emily V. Mason letter to her sister, Catherine Mason Rowland, n.d. Emily Mason Letters, Mason (J. T.) Family, Burton Historical Collection, Detroit Public Library, Detroit. Copy obtained from the Fort Gibson National Historic Site, Fort Gibson, OK.

29. Margaret Carrington, *Ab-sa-ra-ka, Home of the Crows: Being the Experiences of an Officer's Wife on the Plains* (Philadelphia: J. B. Lippincott and Co., 1868), 174.

30. Lydia Spencer Blaney Lane, *I Married a Soldier; or, Old Days in the Army* (1893; reprint, Albuquerque: University of New Mexico Press, 1987), 101.

31. Martha Summerhayes, *Vanished Arizona, Recollections of the Army Life of a New England Woman* (1908; reprint of 1911 edition, Lincoln: University of Nebraska Press, 1979), 111.

32. Sandra L. Myres, "Romance and Reality on the American Frontier: View of Army Wives," *Western History Quarterly* 14, no. 4 (October 1983); 426.

33. Donald K. Adams, "The Journal of Ada A. Vogdes, 1868–71," *Montana, the Magazine of Western History* 13, no. 3 (Summer 1963); 12.

34. Glenda Riley, "Through Women's Eyes: Indians in the Trans-Mississippi West" (Paper presented at the Twentieth Annual Conference of the Western History Association, Kansas City, MO, October 1980), as quoted in Sandra L. Myres, "Romance and Reality," 426.

If You Have Courage, Stay

1. Teresa Griffin Viele, *Following the Drum: A Glimpse of Frontier Life* (1858; reprint, Lincoln: University of Nebraska Press, 1984), 17.

2. Mrs. Orsemus Bronson Boyd, *Cavalry Life in Tent and Field* (1894; reprint, Lincoln: University of Nebraska Press, 1982), 22.

3. Summerhayes, 20.

4. Sherry L. Smith, *The View from Officers' Row: Army Perceptions of Western Indians* (Tucson: University of Arizona Press, 1990), 17.

5. Constance Wynn Altshuler, *For Better or For Worse: Frontier Army Life* (Sedona, Arizona: The Pronto Press, 1982), 1.

6. Marguerite Merington, ed., *The Custer Story: The Life and Intimate Letters of General George A. Custer and His Wife Elizabeth* (Lincoln: University of Nebraska Press, 1950), 165.

7. Elizabeth B. Custer, *Boots and Saddles, or Life in Dakota with General Custer* (New York: Harper and Brothers Publishers, 1885), 2.

8. Merington, 119.

9. Fougera, 137–138.

10. Ibid., 139.

11. Patricia Y. Stallard, *Glittering Misery: Dependents of the Indian Fighting Army* (Fort Collins, CO: The Old Army Press, 1978), 11.

12. Carrington, 33.

13. Coffman, 291.

14. Summerhayes, xiii.

15. U.S. Congress, Senate, *Statistical Report on the Sickness and Mortality in the Army of the U.S. (1839–55)*, by Richard H. Coolidge, 1856, 34th Cong., 1st sess., Senate Executive Document no. 96, vol. 18, serial 827, 417.

16. *Army and Navy Journal* 7, no. 14 (November 20, 1869).

17. Mary Custis Lee deButts, *Growing Up in the 1850s: The Journal of Agnes Lee* (Chapel Hill: University of North Carolina Press, 1984), 124.

18. Boyd, 30.

19. Ibid., 43.

20. Ibid.

21. Emily V. Mason letter to sister Catherine Mason Rowland, n.d.

22. Maria Brace Kimball, *My Eighty Years* (N.p., 1934), 25.

23. Betty Sowers Alt and Bonnie Domrose Stone, *Campfollowing: A History of the Military Wife* (New York: Praeger Publishers, 1991), 46.

24. Summerhayes, 68.

25. Emmett M. Essin, "Army Mule." *Montana, the Magazine of Western History* 44, no. 2 (Spring 1994): 34.

26. Kimball, 23.

27. Maj. James P. Tate, ed., *The American Military on the Frontier: The Proceedings of the 7th Military History Symposium* (Washington, D.C.: Office of Air Force History, 1978), 158.

28. Custer, *Boots and Saddles*, 158.

29. S. Leckie, *Alice Grierson*, 48.

30. Melpomene Institute for Women's Health Research, *The Bodywise Woman* (New York: Prentice Hall, 1990), 12.

31. Sandra L. Myres, *Cavalry Wife: The Diary of Eveline M. Alexander, 1866–1867* (College Station: Texas A & M University Press, 1977), 71.

32. Helen Fuller Davis, Account of Tenth Cavalry March with Col. Benjamin Grierson, Davis Collection of Letters, National Historic Site Library, Fort Davis, TX.

33. Robert C. Carriker and Eleanor R. Carriker, eds., *An Army Wife on the Frontier: The Memoirs of Alice Blackwood Baldwin, 1867–1877* (Salt Lake City: Tanner Trust, 1975).

34. Oliver Knight, *Life and Manners in the Frontier Army* (Norman: University of Oklahoma Press, 1978), 44.

35. *Army and Navy Journal* 7, no. 16 (December 4, 1869).

36. Susan Miles, "Mrs. Buell's Journal, 1877," *Fort Concho and the South Plains Journal* 22, no. 4 (Autumn 1990): 117.

37. Lane, 60.

38. Alexander, 32.

39. Sandra Myres, *Eveline Alexander*, 32.

40. Custer, *Boots and Saddles*, 8.

41. Ibid., 69.

42. Knight, 41.

43. Ibid., 46.

44. Elizabeth B. Custer, *Following the Guidon* (1890; reprint, Norman: University of Oklahoma Press, 1966), 72.

45. Merington, 191.

46. R. H. McKay, *Little Pills: Being Some Experiences of a United States Army Medical Officer on the Frontier Nearly a Half Century Ago* (Pittsburg, KS: Pittsburg Headlight, 1918), 26.

47. Sandra Myres, *Eveline Alexander*, 46.

48. Col. Harold B. Simpson, *Cry Comanche: The 2nd U.S. Cavalry in Texas, 1855–1861* (Hillsboro, TN: Hill Junior College Press, 1979), 41.

49. Carrington, 21.

50. Boyd, 62.

51. Merrill J. Mattes, *Indians, Infants and Infantry: Andrew and Elizabeth Burt on the Frontier* (Lincoln: University of Nebraska Press, 1960), 40.

52. *Annual Report of the Attorney General of the United States for the Year 1885.* (Washington, D.C.: Government Printing Office, 1885).

53. Carrington, 36.

54. Glenda Riley, *Women and Indians on the Frontier, 1825–1915* (Albuquerque: University of New Mexico Press, 1984), 48.

55. Carriker, 83.

56. Sandra Myres, *Eveline Alexander*, 32.

57. Summerhayes, 36.

58. Ray H. Mattison, ed., "An Army Wife on the Upper Missouri: The Diary of Sarah E. Canfield, 1866–1868," *North Dakota History* 20, no. 4 (October 1953): 198.

59. George Frederick Howe, "Expedition to the Yellowstone River in 1873: Letters of a Young Cavalry Officer," *Mississippi Valley Historical Review* 39 (1952): 521.

60. Viele, 47.

61. Ibid., 69.

62. Ibid., 74.

63. Coker, 6.

64. Viele, 81.

65. Carriker, 86.

66. Myres, "Romance and Reality," 416.

67. Ellen McGowan Biddle, *Reminiscences of a Soldier's Wife* (Philadelphia: Press of J.B. Lippincott Company, 1907), 107.

68. Custer, *Following the Guidon*, 171.

69. Custer, *Boots and Saddles*, 37.

70. Custer, *Following the Guidon*, 117.

71. Boyd, 82.

72. Myres, *Eveline Alexander*, 101.

73. McKay, 39.

74. Turner, 37.

75. Coker, 26.

A Cannon in the Dining Room

1. William F. Rae, *Westward by Rail: The New Route to the East* (1870; reprint, New York: Indian Head Books, 1993), 78.

2. Col. Forrest R. Blackburn, "Army Families in Frontier Forts," *Military Review* 49 (October 1969): 18.

3. Senate Executive Document no. 96, 413.

4. Report of the Secretary of War, 1867. Pentagon Library (Washington, D.C.: Government Printing Office), 28.

5. Robert G. Athearn, *Forts of the Upper Missouri* (Lincoln: University of Nebraska Press, 1967), 231.

6. Tate, 8.

7. Carrington, 106.

8. Ibid., 146.

9. Ibid., 123.

10. U.S. Senate, "Disposition and Conduct of the Indians About Fort Phil Kearny and the Causes of the Same" (1867), 40th Cong., 1st sess., Senate Document no. 13, 28. Regarding the investigation of the Fetterman Massacre of December 21, 1866.

11. Carrington, 180.

12. Ibid., 153.

13. Summerhayes, 104.

14. Roe, 222.

15. Alexander B. Adams, *Sunlight and Storm: The Great American Plains* (New York: G.P. Putnam's Sons, 1977), 357.

16. Carrington, 231.

17. Roe, 314–317.

18. Ibid., 30.

19. Boyd, 266.

20. Ibid., 124.

21. *Army and Navy Journal* 12, no. 20 (December 26, 1874).

22. Robert M. Utley, ed., *Life in Custer's Cavalry: Diaries and Letters of Albert and Jennie Barnitz, 1867–1868* (Lincoln: University of Nebraska Press, 1977), 125.

23. David Nevin, ed., *The Old West: The Soldiers* (Alexandria, VA: Time-Life Books, 1973), 57.

24. Carriker, 34.

25. Tate, 90.

26. Summerhayes, 19.

27. Darlis A. Miller, *Soldiers and Settlers: Military Supply in the Southwest, 1861–1885* (Albuquerque: University of New Mexico Press, 1989), 377.

28. Thomas R. Buecker, ed., "Letters of Caroline Frey Winne from Sidney Barracks and Fort McPherson, Nebraska, 1874–1878," *Nebraska History* 62, no. 1 (Spring 1981): 45.

29. Altshuler, 1.

30. Kimball, 73.

31. Carriker, 71.

32. Custer, *Following the Guidon*, 228.

33. Merington, 269.

34. Barbara E. Fisher, ed., "Forrestine Cooper Hooker's Notes and Memoirs on Army Life in the West, 1871–1876" (Master's thesis, University of Arizona, 1963), 36.

35. Fisher, 44.

36. Fougera, 229.

37. Biddle, 123.

38. Stallard, 37.

39. Buecker, 12.

40. Viele, 105.

41. Abe Laufe, ed., *An Army Doctor's Wife on the Frontier: The Letters of Emily McCorkle FitzGerald from Alaska and the Far West, 1874–78* (Lincoln: University of Nebraska Press, 1962), 207.

42. Fougera, 128.

43. Ibid., 68.

44. Ibid., 134.

45. Myres, "Romance and Reality," 421.

46. Interview with Mrs. Morris Thompson, December 11, 1982. National Historic Site Library, Fort Davis, TX.

47. Summerhayes, 10.

48. Sandra Myres, *Eveline Alexander*, 123.

49. Summerhayes, 169.

50. Viele, 174.

51. Helen Fuller Davis letter to Alice Kirk Grierson, September 2, 1883.

Servants, Shortages, and the Sutler

1. Green, 87.

2. Biddle, 16.

3. Green, 59.

4. Mary Swanson letter to her grandmother, 1890. Mary Swanson Collection of Letters, National Historic Site Library, Fort Davis, TX.

5. Boyd, 220.

6. Luther P. Bradley letter to wife, Ione, January 4, 1871. The Luther P. Bradley Papers, Family Correspondence, 1861–85, U.S. Army Military History Institute, Carlisle Barracks, PA.

7. Merington, 61.

8. Custer, *Following the Guidon*, 238.

9. Viele, 131.

10. Ibid.

11. Custer, *Boots and Saddles*, 187.

12. Blackburn, 22.

13. Biddle, 86.

14. Buecker, 18.

15. Laufe, 230.

16. Boyd, 230.

17. Roe, 351.

18. Coffman, 302.

19. Summerhayes, 136.

20. Ibid., 159.

21. Boyd, 91.

22. Ibid., 150.

23. Coffman, 304.

24. Memoirs, William and Grace Bunce Paulding Papers, U.S. Army Military History Institute, Carlisle Barracks, PA, 12.

25. Nevin, 78.

26. Utley, *Jennie Barnitz*, 15.

27. Ibid., 246.

28. Custer, *Boots and Saddles*, 180.

29. Boyd, 47.

30. Summerhayes, 49.

31. Laufe, 218.

32. Roe, 69.

33. Viele, 138.

34. Custer, *Following the Guidon*, 245.

35. Mattes, 157.

36. Biddle, 150.

37. Mary L. Williams, ed., *An Army Wife's Cookbook: With Household Hints and Home Remedies* (Tucson, AZ: Southwest Parks and Monuments Association, 1972), 9.

38. Biddle, 173.

39. Ibid.

40. Roe, 262.

41. Ruth Ellen Patton Totten, "The Army Wife Heritage," *Armor* (November–December 1973), 41.

42. Boyd, 128.

43. Biddle, 174.

44. Mrs. D. B. Dyer, *Fort Reno or Picturesque Cheyenne and Arrapahoe Army Life Before the Opening of Oklahoma* (New York: G.W. Dillingham, 1896), 73.

45. Boyd, 174.

46. Custer, *Boots and Saddles*, 162.

47. Mattison, "Sarah E. Canfield," 28.

48. Capt. R. T. Jacob, "Blazing Trails for Civilization in Oklahoma: Memories of Early Days History as Recalled by a Former Army Officer." Tonkawa Public Library Collection, Box T-3, Western History Collections, University of Oklahoma, Norman, 5.

49. Mattison, "Sarah E. Canfield," 29.

50. Buecker, 12.

51. Helen Davis letter to Alice Grierson, September 2, 1883.

52. Mary Swanson letter to her grandmother, 1890.

53. Williams, 45.

54. Myres, "Romance and Reality," 421.

55. Senate Executive Document no. 96, 369.

56. Mattison, "Sarah E. Canfield," 27.

57. McKay, 87.

58. Roe, 74.

59. Custer, *Boots and Saddles*, 160.

60. Boyd, 128.

61. Mattes, 144.

62. Francis Paul Prucha, ed., *Army Life on the Western Frontier: Selections from the Official Reports Made Between 1826 and 1845 by Colonel George Crogham* (Norman: University of Oklahoma Press, 1958), 104.

63. Sutler's List, *Post Council Administrative Records: Fort Gibson* (Cherokee Nation, May 1845–June 1857), 1821–1920 (Fort Gibson Military Park, Fort Gibson, OK).

64. Laufe, 224.

65. Green, 79.

66. Anonymous, *Ladies Vase: or Polite Manual for Young Ladies* (Lowell, MA: N. L. Dutton, 1843), Tilghman Collection, Box 3, Folder 24, Western History Collections, University of Oklahoma, Norman, 70.

67. Mattes, 45.

68. Dyer, 51.

69. Lane, 118.

70. Robert M. Utley, *Frontier Regulars: The United States Army and the Indian, 1866–1891* (Lincoln: University of Nebraska Press), 90.

71. Leavitt Corning, Jr., *Baronial Forts of the Big Bend* (Austin, TX: Trinity University Press, 1967), 46.

72. Summerhayes, 147.

73. Totten, 44.

74. Summerhayes, 147.

75. Corning, Jr., 46.

76. Custer, *Boots and Saddles*, 18.

77. Custer, *Following the Guidon*, 231.

78. Lucile M. Kane, trans., and ed., *Military Life in Dakota: The Journal of Philippe Régis de Trobriand* (St. Paul, MN: Alvord Memorial Commission, 1951), 317.

79. Carrington, 178.

Holidays, Horse Races, and Hops

1. Barry Scobee, *Fort Davis, Texas: 1583–1960* (El Paso, TX: Hill Printing Co., 1963), 67.

2. Ibid., 64.

3. Boyd, 140.

4. Fougera, 246.

5. Roe, 218.

6. Adams, 6.

7. Roe, 221.

8. Joan Swallow Reiter, ed., *The Old West: The Women* (Alexandria, VA: Time-Life Books, 1978), 74.

9. Roe, 61.

10. Merington, 174.

11. Carriker, 112.

12. Custer, *Following the Guidon*, 124.

13. Memoirs, William and Grace Paulding Papers, 10.

14. Fougera, 88.

15. Ibid., 156.

16. Tate, 161.

17. Simpson, 76.

18. Frank N. Schubert, *Outposts of the Sioux Wars: A History of Fort Robinson* (Lincoln: University of Nebraska Press, 1993), 50.

19. Green, 173.

20. Report of the Adjutant General, attached to the Reports of the Secretary of War, 1870. Pentagon Library (Washington, D.C.: Government Printing Office 1870), 66–73.

21. Myres, *Eveline Alexander*, 40.

22. Laufe, 231.

23. Summerhayes, 209.

24. Thomas J. Schlereth, *Victorian America: Transformations in Everyday Life, 1876–1915* (New York: HarperCollins, 1991), xi.

25. Biddle, 50.

26. Roe, 145.

27. Thomas C. Railsback and John P. Langellier, *The Drums Would Roll: A Pictorial History of U.S. Army Bands on the American Frontier, 1866–1900* (Poole, England: Arms and Armour Press Ltd., 1987), 15.

28. Ibid., 17.

29. Summerhayes, 15.

30. Roe, 339.

31. Ibid., 341.

32. Mattison, "Sarah E. Canfield," 36.

33. Headquarters Records of Fort Gibson, 1830–1857, December 31, 1849, Fort Gibson Military Park, Fort Gibson, OK.

34. Larry A. Toll, "The Military Community on the Western Frontier, 1866–1898" (Ph.D. diss., Ball State University, Muncie, IN, 1990), 115.

35. Boyd, 170.

36. Mattes, 146.

37. McKay, 123.

38. Myres, *Eveline Alexander*, 88.

39. Roe, 320.

40. Biddle, 89.

41. Custer, *Boots and Saddles*, 232.

42. Ibid.

43. Custer, *Following the Guidon*, 114.

44. Ibid.

45. Schubert, 108.

46. Scobee, 107.

47. S. Leckie, *Alice Grierson*, 82.

48. Boyd, 243.

49. Mattison, "Sarah E. Canfield," 40.

50. Schubert, 113.

51. Green, 152.

52. S. Leckie, *Alice Grierson*, 79.

53. Roe, 372.

54. Ibid., 42.

Cholera and Creosote

1. Utley, *Jennie Barnitz*, 177.

2. Mattes, 202.

3. Surgeon General's Report, Reports of the Secretary of War, 1870. Pentagon Library (Washington, D.C.: Government Printing Office, 1870), 273.

4. Adjutant General's Report, 1870, 66–73.

5. Utley, *Frontier Regulars,* 87.

6. Biddle, 206.

7. McKay, 108.

8. Buecker, 6.

9. Mattes, 231–232.

10. Schubert, 45.

11. S. Leckie, *Alice Grierson*, 119.

12. William H. McNeill, *Plagues and People* (New York: Anchor Books, 1977), 231.

13. Senate Executive Document no. 96, 367.

14. "A Report on Barracks and Hospitals with Descriptions of Military Posts." Circular no. 4, War Department, Surgeon General's Office (Washington: Government Printing Office, December 5, 1870), 291.

15. Fisher, 104.

16. Senate Executive Document no. 96, 357.

17. Ibid., 359.

18. Circular no. 4, 177.

19. Ibid., 343.

20. Ibid., 326.

21. Ibid., 348.

22. Fougera, 173–177.

23. Nevin, 75.

24. Ibid., 73.

25. Knight, 39.

26. Green, 142.

27. James Reagle, Jr., Collection, Box 1147, Western History Collections, University of Oklahoma, Norman.

28. Laufe, 245.

29. Summerhayes, 11.

30. Custer, *Following the Guidon*, 211.

31. Mattes, 106.

32. Schubert, 145.

33. Dee Brown, *Wondrous Times on the Frontier* (Little Rock, AR: August House Publishers, Inc., 1991), 187.

34. Ferne Shelton, *Pioneer Comforts and Kitchen Remedies* (High Point, NC: Hutcraft, 1965), 8.

35. Green, 29.

36. Levinson, 39.

37. Green, 166.

38. Circular no. 4, 323.

39. Fougera, 168.

40. Boyd, 134.

41. Thomas P. Lowry, *The Story the Soldiers Wouldn't Tell: Sex in the Civil War* (Mechanicsburg, PA: Stackpole Books, 1994), 94.

42. Laufe, 165.

43. Ibid., 198.

44. Merington, 251.

45. Green, 30.

46. Lowry, 96.

47. Ibid., 95.

48. Poison Register, Klapps Drug Store Collection, Box K-8, Western History Collections, University of Oklahoma, Norman.

49. S. Leckie, *Alice Grierson*, 62.

50. Green, 29.

51. Melpomene, 15.

52. Green, 114.

53. Ibid., 115.

54. Biddle, 72.

55. Ibid., 70.

56. Ibid., 97.

57. Viele, 169.

58. Fougera, 248–249.

59. Ibid., 236.

60. Boyd, 130.

61. Fougera, 140.

62. Coker, 94.

An Itch for Epaulets

1. Senate Executive Document no. 96, 381.

2. Viele, 107.

3. Biddle, 50.

4. Coker, 165.

5. Roe, 28.

6. Knight, 139.

7. Ibid., 140.

8. Ibid., 139.

9. Ibid., 138.

10. S. Leckie, *Alice Grierson*, 75.

11. Merington, 258.

12. Emily V. Mason letter to Catherine Mason Rowland, April 6, 1845.

13. Emily V. Mason to Catherine Mason Rowland, February 9, 1845, portion of February 2, 1845, letter.

14. Ibid.

15. Laura Mason to sisters Catherine Mason Rowland and Julia Mason, January 24, 1845.

16. Ibid.

17. Margaret Mason postscript to Emily V. Mason letter to Catherine Mason Rowland, February 2, 1845.

18. Laura Mason to sisters Catherine Mason Rowland and Julia Mason, January 24, 1845.

19. Memoirs, William and Grace Paulding Papers, 8.

20. Custer, *Boots and Saddles*, 207.

21. S. Leckie, *Alice Grierson*, 76.

22. Fougera, 135.

23. S. Leckie, "Woman Behind the Myth," 155.

24. Totten, 43.

25. Custer, *Boots and Saddles*, 181.

26. Merington, 182.

27. Ibid., 253.

28. Ibid., 307.

29. Coffman, 295.

30. Ibid.

31. S. Leckie, *Alice Grierson*, 2.

32. Ibid., 61.

33. Custer, *Boots and Saddles*, 219.

34. Merington, 238.

35. Ibid., 194.

36. Custer, *Following the Guidon*, 161.

37. S. Leckie, *Alice Grierson*, 71.

38. Oliver Nixon Unthank letter to Emma Brandon Unthank, October 24, 1873. Collection of Letters, to Wife, Emma Brandon Unthank, 1871–1874. Fort Laramie National Historic Site, Fort Laramie, WY.

39. Stallard, 113.

40. Ibid., 114.

41. Ibid., 116.

42. Ibid., 117.

43. Ibid., 111.

44. Ibid., 105.

45. Ibid.

46. Anne M. Butler, *Daughters of Joy, Sisters of Misery: Prostitutes in the American West, 1865–90* (Urbana: University of Illinois Press, 1985), 128.

47. Helen Fuller Davis letter to her aunt, Alice Kirk Grierson, January 2, 1887.

48. Philip Katcher, *U.S. Cavalry on the Plains: 1850–1890* (London: Osprey Publishing, 1985), 22.

49. Lane, 101.

50. Carriker, 6.

51. Fougera, 251.

52. Myres, "Romance and Reality," 424.

53. McKay, 127.

54. Summerhayes, 307.

55. S. Leckie, "Woman Behind the Myth," 159.

A Touch of Class

1. Butler, 125.

2. William H. Leckie, *The Buffalo Soldiers: A Narrative of the Negro Cavalry in the West* (Norman: University of Oklahoma Press, 1967), 9.

3. Roe, 65.

4. Stallard, 38.

5. Fisher, 108.

6. David Maraniss, "Due Recognition and Reward," *The Washington Post Magazine*, January 20, 1991, 16.

7. Morris J. MacGregor and Bernard C. Nalty, eds., *Blacks in the United States Armed Forces: Basic Documents* (Wilmington, DE: Scholarly Resources, Inc., 1977), 85.

8. W. Leckie, 12.

9. Ibid., 14.

10. Ibid.

11. S. Leckie, *Alice Grierson*, 43.

12. Ibid., 23.

13. Ibid., 163.

14. Schubert, 54.

15. Viele, 158.

16. Senate Executive Document no. 96, 352.

17. Brown, 74.

18. Stallard, 63.

19. Merington, 194.

20. Myres, *Eveline Alexander*, 36.

21. Fisher, 120.

22. Myres, "Romance and Reality," 416.

23. Viele, 155.

24. Utley, *Frontier Regulars*, 89.

25. Reiter, 71.

26. Barry J. Hagan, "I Did It But Did Not Mean It," *Periodical Journal of the Council on Abandoned Military Posts*, no. 32 (Spring 1977): 22.

27. Utley, *Frontier Regulars*, 88.

28. Summerhayes, 18.

29. Fougera, 223.

30. Laufe, 262.

31. Ibid., 265.

32. Ibid., 281.

33. Alice Mathews Shields, "Army Life on the Wyoming Frontier," *Annals of Wyoming* 13, no. 4 (October 1941): 337.

34. Coker, 9.

35. Viele, 152.

36. Ibid., 155.

37. Laufe, 60.

38. Ibid., 133.

39. Ibid., 182.

40. Butler, 248.

41. Lane, 75.

42. Butler, 247.

43. Ibid., 140.

44. Stallard, 70.

45. Schubert, 143.

46. Butler, 248.

47. Senate Executive Document no. 96, 259.

48. S. Leckie, *Alice Grierson*, 81.

49. Summerhayes, 248.

50. Myres, *Westering Women and the Frontier Experience, 1800–1913* (Albuquerque: University of New Mexico Press, 1982), 254.

51. Reiter, 142.

52. Julie Roy Jeffrey, *Frontier Women: The Trans-Mississippi West, 1840–1880.* (New York: Hill & Wang, 1979), 121.

53. Myres, *Westering Women*, 255.

54. Garry D. Ryan and Timothy K. Nenninger, *Soldiers and Civilians: The U.S. Army and the American People* (Washington, D.C.: National Archives and Records Administration, 1987), 97.

55. Nevin, 75.

56. Viele, 244.

57. Summerhayes, xix.

58. Coker, 129.

59. Fougera, 74.

Apaches on the Porch

1. Sherry L. Smith, "Officers' Wives, Indians, and the Indian Wars," *Journal of the Order of the Indian Wars* (Winter 1980): 43.

2. Ibid., 44.

3. Myres, *Westering Women,* 64.

4. Merington, 284.

5. Dyer, 34.

6. Lane, 73.

7. Carrington, 83.

8. Custer, *Boots & Saddles*, 74.

9. Coker, 8.

10. Viele, 220.

11. Smith, *Officers' Row*, 28.

12. Ibid.

13. Ibid., 29.

14. Boyd, 64.

15. Laufe, 201.

16. Fougera, 19.

17. Summerhayes, 170.

18. Lane, 66.

19. Mattison, "Sarah Canfield," 203.
20. Dyer, 53.
21. Smith, *Officers' Row*, 46.
22. Dyer, 54.
23. Summerhayes, xviii.
24. Biddle, 147.
25. Ibid., 181.
26. Shields, 336.
27. Summerhayes, 95.
28. Totten, 40.
29. Mattes, 84.
30. Smith, *Officers Row*, 82.
31. Viele, 212.
32. Smith, *Officers' Row*, 83.
33. Ibid.
34. Ibid., 85.
35. Summerhayes, 106.
36. Smith, *Officers' Row*, 6.
37. Ibid., 69.
38. McKay, 53.
39. Adams, 7.
40. Laufe, 341.
41. Mattison, "Sarah Canfield," 204.
42. Merington, 284.
43. Summerhayes, 91.
44. Buecker, 8.
45. Viele, 121.
46. Coffman, 298.
47. Laufe, 249.
48. Ibid., 204.
49. Ibid., 277.
50. Custer, *Boots & Saddles*, 172.
51. Coker, 135.
52. McKay, 49.
53. Ibid., 47.
54. Genevieve LaTourrette, "Fort Union Memories," *New Mexico Historical Review* 26, no. 4 (1951): 281.
55. Carrington, 263.
56. Alt and Stone, 56.

57. Myres, "Romance and Reality," 414.

58. Department of Texas, Letters Sent by Headquarters, 1870–1894 and 1897–1898, Record Group 393, National Archives and Records Administration, Washington, D.C.

59. S. Leckie, *Alice Grierson*, 132.

60. Maurice Frank with Casey E. Barthelmess, *Photographer on an Army Mule* (Norman: University of Oklahoma Press, 1965), 13.

61. John M. Carroll, ed., *The Papers of the Order of Indian Wars* (Fort Collins, CO: The Old Army Press, 1975), 260.

62. Summerhayes, 84.

63. Roe, 10.

64. Robert M. Utley, "The Contribution of the Frontier to the American Military Tradition," Harmon Memorial Lectures in Military History, no. 19 (Colorado Springs: United States Air Force Academy, 1977), 3.

A Drink of Dirty Water

1. Utley, *Frontier Regulars*, 410.
2. Coffman, 292.
3. S. Leckie, *Alice Grierson*, 153.
4. Ibid., 150.
5. Viele, 247.
6. Boyd, 175–176.
7. Ibid., 180.
8. Ibid., 181.
9. Roe, 357.
10. Ibid., 366.
11. Ibid.
12. Custer, *Following the Guidon*, 260.
13. Ibid., 310.
14. Fisher, 146.
15. Buecker, 41.
16. Biddle, 137.
17. Summerhayes, 222.
18. Roe, 333.
19. Merington, 251.
20. S. Leckie, "Woman Behind the Myth," 215.
21. Myres, *Eveline Alexander*, 55.

22. Biddle, 209.
23. Kane, 214.
24. Coker, 166.
25. Myres, *Eveline Alexander*, 41.
26. Coker, 176.
27. Boyd, 294.
28. Ibid., 295.
29. Ibid.
30. Buecker, 27–28.
31. Viele, 8.
32. Ibid., 9.
33. Dyer, 87.
34. Ibid., 93.
35. Lane, 193.
36. Fougera, 127.
37. Ibid., 284.
38. Summerhayes, 165.
39. Ibid., 289.

Bibliography

Adams, Alexander B. *Sunlight and Storm: The Great American Plains*. New York: G. P. Putnam's Sons, 1977.

Adams, Donald K. "The Journal of Ada A. Vogdes, 1868–71." *Montana the Magazine of Western History* 13, no. 3 (Summer 1963): 2–17.

Alt, Betty Sowers, and Bonnie Domrose Stone. *Campfollowing: A History of the Military Wife*. New York: Praeger Publishers, 1991.

Altshuler, Constance Wynn. *For Better or For Worse: Frontier Army Life*. Sedona, AZ: The Pronto Press, 1982.

"Annual Report of the Adjutant General of the Army to the Secretary of War," November 1882. The Pentagon Library, Washington, D.C., 1882.

Annual Report of the Attorney General of the United States for the Year 1885. Washington D.C.: Government Printing Office, 1885.

Anonymous. *Ladies Vase; or Polite Manual for Young Ladies*. Lowell, MA: N. L. Dutton, 1843. Tilghman Collection, Box 3, Folder 24, Western History Collections, University of Oklahoma, Norman.

Army and Navy Journal 7, no. 14 (November 20, 1869).

Army and Navy Journal 7, no. 16 (December 4, 1869).

Army and Navy Journal 12, no. 20 (December 26, 1874).

Athearn, Robert G. *Forts of the Upper Missouri*. Lincoln: University of Nebraska Press, 1967.

Barlow, Maj. J. W. *Outline Description of the Military Posts in the Division of the Missouri* (originally a government document, 1876). Fort Collins, CO: The Old Army Press, 1972.

Berdan, Marshall S. "The Pestilence That Walketh in Darkness: The Cholera Epidemic of 1832." *Virginia Cavalcade* 43, no. 1 (Summer 1993): 14-23.

Biddle, Ellen McGowan. *Reminiscences of a Soldier's Wife*. Philadelphia: Press of J. B. Lippincott Company, 1907.

Billington, Ray Allen, and Martin Ridge. *Westward Expansion: A History of the American Frontier*. New York: MacMillan Publishing Company, Inc., 1982.

Blackburn, Col. Forrest R. "Army Families in Frontier Forts." *Military Review* 49 (October 1969): 17–28.

Boyd, Mrs. Orsemus Bronson (Frances). *Cavalry Life in Tent and Field*. 1894. Reprint. Lincoln: University of Nebraska Press, 1982.

Bradley, Luther P., Papers, Family Correpondence, 1861–1885, U.S. Army Military History Institute, Carlisle Barracks, PA.

Brown, Dee. *Wondrous Times on the Frontier*. Little Rock, AR: August House Publishers, Inc., 1991.

Buecker, Thomas R., ed. "Letters of Caroline Frey Winne from Sidney Barracks and Fort McPherson, Nebraska, 1874–1878." *Nebraska History* 62, no. 1 (Spring 1981): 1–46.

Butler, Anne M. *Daughters of Joy, Sisters of Misery: Prostitutes in the American West, 1865–90.* Urbana: University of Illinois Press, 1985.

Carriker, Robert C., and Eleanor R., eds. *An Army Wife on the Frontier: The Memoirs of Alice Blackwood Baldwin, 1867–1877.* Salt Lake City: Tanner Trust, 1975.

Carrington, Frances Courtney. *My Army Life and the Fort Phil Kearny Massacre.* 1910. Reprint. Freeport, NY: Books for Libraries Press, 1971.

Carrington, Margaret. *Ab-sa-ra-ka, Home of the Crows: Being the Experiences of an Officer's Wife on the Plains.* Philadelphia: J. B. Lippincott and Company, 1868.

Carroll, John M., ed. *The Papers of the Order of Indian Wars.* Fort Collins, CO: The Old Army Press, 1975.

Cochran, Mrs. M. A. *Posey or from Reveille to Retreat: An Army Story.* Cincinnati: Robert Clark Company, 1896.

Cocke, Bartlett. "Outline of the Development of Early American Architecture: The South-Western States, District Texas-3." Department of the Interior Report, 1937. Record Group 515. "Records of the Historic American Buildings Survey (HABS)/ Historic American Engineering Records (HAER) Division." National Archives and Records Administration, Washington, D.C.

Coffman, Edward M. *The Old Army: A Portrait of the American Army in Peacetime, 1784–1898.* New York: Oxford University Press, 1986.

Coker, Caleb, ed. *The News from Brownsville: Helen Chapman's Letters from the Texas Military Frontier, 1848–1852.* Austin: Texas State Historical Association, 1992.

Conlan, Roberta, ed. *The Wild West.* New York: Time Life Books, 1993.

Corning, Leavitt, Jr. *Baronial Forts of the Big Bend.* Austin, TX: Trinity University Press, 1967.

Custer, Elizabeth B. *Boots and Saddles; or Life in Dakota with General Custer.* New York: Harper and Brothers Publishers, 1885.

———. *Tenting on the Plains; or, General Custer in Kansas and Texas.* 1887. Reprint. Williamstown, ME: Corner House Publishers, 1973.

———. *Following the Guidon; or, Into the Indian Wars with General Custer and the Seventh Cavalry.* 1890. Reprint. Norman: University of Oklahoma Press, 1966.

Davis, Helen Fuller. Collection of Letters. National Historic Site Library, Fort Davis, TX.

Day, James M. *Frontier Forts of Texas: Ft. Davis.* Waco, TX: Texian Press, 1966.

deButts, Mary Custis Lee. *Growing Up in the 1850s: The Journal of Agnes Lee.* Chapel Hill: University of North Carolina Press, 1984.

Department of Texas, Letters Sent by Headquarters, 1870–1894 and 1897–1898. Record Group 393. "Records of U.S. Army Continental Commands, 1821–1920." National Archives and Records Administration, Washington, D.C.

Dyer, Mrs. D. B. *Fort Reno or Picturesque Cheyenne and Arrapahoe Army Life Before the Opening of Oklahoma.* New York: G. W. Dillingham, 1896.

Essin, Emmett M. "Army Mule." *Montana, the Magazine of Western History* 44, no. 2 (Spring 1994): 30–45.

Fisher, Barbara E., ed. "Forrestine Cooper Hooker's Notes and Memoirs on Army Life in the West, 1871–1876." Master's thesis, University of Arizona, 1963.

Flexner, Eleanor. *Century of Struggle: The Woman's Rights Movement in the United States.* New York: Atheneum, 1972.

Fougera, Katherine Gibson. *With Custer's Cavalry.* 1942. Reprint. Lincoln: University of Nebraska Press, 1986.

Fox, Mary Virginia. *The Story of Women Who Shaped the West.* Chicago: Childrens Press, 1991.

Frank, Maurice, with Casey E. Barthelmess. *Photographer on an Army Mule.* Norman: University of Oklahoma Press, 1965.

Fraser, Robert W. *Forts of the West.* Norman: University of Oklahoma Press, 1972.

Gaff, Alan, and Maureen Gaff, eds. *Adventures on the Western Frontier: Major General John Gibbon.* Bloomington and Indianapolis: Indiana University Press, 1994.

Giese, Dale F., ed. *My Life with the Army in the West: The Memoirs of James E. Farmer, 1858–1898.* Santa Fe, NM: Stagecoach Press, 1967.

Graf, Leroy P. "The Economic History of the Lower Rio Grande Valley, 1820–1875." Ph.D. diss., Harvard University, Cambridge, MA, 1942.

Green, Harvey. *The Light of the Home: An Intimate View of the Lives of Women in Victorian America.* New York: Pantheon Books, 1983.

Grierson, Benjamin. Letter to his father, December 17, 1866. Benjamin H. Grierson Papers, Illinois State Historical Library, Springfield, IL.

Haas, Irvin. *Citadels, Ramparts and Stockades: America's Historic Forts.* New York: Everest House, 1979.

Hagan, Barry J. "I Did It But Did Not Mean It." *Periodical Journal of the Council on Abandoned Military Posts* no. 31 (Spring 1977): 17–23.

Howe, Daniel Walker, ed. *Victorian America.* Philadelphia: University of Pennsylvania Press, 1976.

Howe, George Frederick. "Expedition to the Yellowstone River in 1873: Letters of a Young Cavalry Officer." *Mississippi Valley Historical Review* 39 (1952): 519–534.

Jacob, Capt. R. T. "Blazing Trails for Civilization in Oklahoma: Memories of Early Days History as Recalled by a Former Army Officer." Tonkawa Public Library Collection, Box T-3, Western History Collections, University of Oklahoma, Norman.

Jeffrey, Julie Roy. *Frontier Women: The Trans-Mississippi West, 1840–1880.* New York: Hill & Wang, 1979.

Kane, Lucile M., trans. and ed. *Military Life in Dakota: The Journal of Philippe Régis de Trobriand.* St. Paul, MN: Alvord Memorial Commission, 1951.

Katcher, Philip. *U.S. Cavalry on the Plains: 1850–1890.* London: Osprey Publishing, 1985.

Kimball, Maria Brace. *My Eighty Years.* N.p., 1934.

Knight, Oliver. *Life and Manners in the Frontier Army.* Norman: University of Oklahoma Press, 1978.

Lane, Lydia Spencer Blaney. *I Married a Soldier; or, Old Days in the Army.* 1893. Reprint. Albuquerque: University of New Mexico Press, 1987.

Langellier, John P., and Cameron Laughlin. *Soldiers at Play: Recreation and Pastimes of the Frontier Army.* Fort Leavenworth: U.S. Army Command and General Staff College, 1984.

LaTourrette, Genevieve. "Fort Union Memories." *New Mexico Historical Review* 26, no. 4 (1951): 277–286.

Laufe, Abe, ed. *An Army Doctor's Wife on the Frontier: The Letters of Emily McCorkle FitzGerald from Alaska and the Far West, 1874–78.* Lincoln: University of Nebraska Press, 1962.

Leckie, Shirley Anne, ed. *The Colonel's Lady on the Western Frontier: The Correspondence of Alice Kirk Grierson.* Lincoln: University of Nebraska Press, 1989.

_____. *Elizabeth Bacon Custer and the Making of a Myth.* Norman: University of Oklahoma Press, 1993.

_____. "The Woman Behind the Myth." *American History Illustrated* 28, no. 4 (September/October 1993): 38–45, 67–79.

Leckie, William H. *The Buffalo Soldiers: A Narrative of the Negro Cavalry in the West.* Norman: University of Oklahoma Press, 1967.

Levinson, Dorothy. *Women of the West.* New York: Franklin Watts, Inc., 1973.

Lowry, Thomas P. *The Story the Soldiers Wouldn't Tell: Sex in the Civil War.* Mechanicsburg, PA: Stackpole Books, 1994.

MacGregor, Morris J., and Bernard C. Nalty, eds. *Blacks in the United States Armed Forces: Basic Documents.* Wilmington, DE: Scholarly Resources, Inc., 1977.

McKay, R. H. *Little Pills: Being Some Experiences of a United States Army Medical Officer on the Frontier Nearly a Half Century Ago.* Pittsburg, KS: Pittsburg Headlight, 1918.

McNeill, William H. *Plagues and People.* New York: Anchor Books, 1977.

Maraniss, David. "Due Recognition and Reward." *The Washington Post Magazine* January 20, 1991, 14–36.

Martin, I. T. *Recollections of Elizabeth Benton Fremont.* New York: Frederick H. Hitchcock, 1912.

Mason, Emily V. Collection of letters. Originally part of Mason (J. T.) Family, Burton Historical Collection, Detroit Public Library, Detroit. Copies at Fort Gibson National Historic Site, Fort Gibson, OK.

Massey, Mary Elizabeth. *Bonnet Brigades.* New York: Alfred A. Knopf, 1966.

Mattes, Merrill J. *Indians, Infants and Infantry: Andrew and Elizabeth Burt on the Frontier.* Lincoln: University of Nebraska Press, 1960.

Mattison, Ray H. "The Army Post on the Northern Plains, 1865–1885." *Nebraska History* 35 (March 1954): 17–44.

_____. ed. "An Army Wife on the Upper Missouri: The Diary of Sarah E. Canfield, 1866–1868." *North Dakota History* 20, no. 4 (October 1953): 191–220.

Maxon, Grace F. Collection of letters. National Historic Site Library, Fort Davis, TX.

Medical History of the Posts. Record Group 94. "Records of the Adjutant General's Office, 1780s–1917." National Archives and Records Administration, Washington, D.C.

Melpomene Institute for Women's Health Research. *The Bodywise Woman.* New York: Prentice Hall, 1990.

Merington, Marguerite, ed. *The Custer Story: The Life and Intimate Letters of General George A. Custer and His Wife Elizabeth.* Lincoln: University of Nebraska Press, 1950.

Miles, Susan. "Mrs. Buell's Journal, 1877." *Fort Concho and the South Plains Journal* 22, no. 4 (Autumn 1990): 109–126.

Miller, Darlis A. *Soldiers and Settlers: Military Supply in the Southwest, 1861–1885.* Albuquerque: University of New Mexico Press, 1989.

Myres, Sandra L. *Cavalry Wife: The Diary of Eveline M. Alexander, 1866–1867.* College Station: Texas A & M University Press, 1977.

_____. *Westering Women and the Frontier Experience, 1800–1915.* Albuquerque: University of New Mexico Press, 1982.

_____. "Romance and Reality on the American Frontier: View of Army Wives." *Western Historical Quarterly* 14, no. 4 (October 1983): 409–427.

Nevin, David, ed. *The Old West: The Soldiers.* Alexandria, VA: Time-Life Books, 1973.

Paquin, Donald. "The Women of Fort Sill, Indian Territory and Other Western Forts, 1869–1889." Ph.D. diss., Cameron University, Lawton, OK, 1990.

Paulding, William, and Grace Bunce Paulding, Papers, Memoirs, U.S. Army Military History Institute, Carlisle Barracks, PA.

Phillips, Catherine Coffin. *Jessie Benton Frémont: A Woman Who Made History.* San Francisco: John Henry Nash, 1935.

Poison Register, Klapps Drug Store Collection, Box K-8, Western History Collections, University of Oklahoma, Norman.

Post Council Administrative Records: Fort Gibson (Cherokee Nation, May 1845–June 1857), 1821–1920. Fort Gibson Military Park, Fort Gibson, OK.

Powell, Sarah, and Randall Roots, compilers. *Preliminary Inventory of the Records of United States Regular Army Mobile Units, 1821–1942.* Expedition Records, Fourth Cavalry. NM 93. National Archives and Records Administration, Washington, D.C., 1970.

Prucha, Francis Paul, ed. *Army Life on the Western Frontier: Selections from the Official Reports Made Between 1826 and 1845 by Colonel George Crogham.* Norman: University of Oklahoma Press, 1958.

Rae, William F. *Westward by Rail: The New Route to the East.* 1870. Reprint. New York: Indian Head Books, 1993.

Railsback, Thomas C., and John P. Langellier. *The Drums Would Roll: A Pictorial History of U.S. Army Bands on the American Frontier, 1866–1900.* Poole, England: Arms and Armour Press Ltd., 1987.

Reagle, James, Jr., Collection. Box 1147, Western History Collections, University of Oklahoma, Norman.

Reeder, Red. *Born at Reveille.* New York: Duell, Sloan and Pearce, 1966.

Reiter, Joan Swallow, ed. *The Old West: The Women.* Alexandria, VA: Time-Life Books, 1978.

Report of the Adjutant General, attached to the Reports of the Secretary of War, 1870. The Pentagon Library, Washington, D.C.: Government Printing Office, 1870.

"Report on Barracks and Hospitals with Descriptions of Military Posts." Circular no. 4, War Department, Surgeon General's Office. Washington: Government Printing Office, December 5, 1870.

Reports of the Secretary of War, 1865, 1867, 1877, and 1882. Pentagon Library. Washington, D.C.: Government Printing Office.

Returns from U.S. Military Posts, 1800–1916. Fort Davis, roll 297 and 298, September 1854–June 1891. Record Group 393. "Records of U.S. Army Continental

Commands, 1821–1920," National Archives and Records Administration, Washington, D.C.

Richey, Elinor. *Eminent Women of the West*. Berkeley, CA: Howell-North Books, 1975.

Rickey, Don, Jr., and Thomas N. Crellin. "Fort Larned National Historic Site, Kansas: Historic Structures Report, Part I." Division of History, Office of Archeology and Historic Preservation, National Park Service, Department of the Interior, Washington, D.C., April 1967.

Riley, Glenda. *Women and Indians on the Frontier, 1825–1915*. Albuquerque: University of New Mexico Press, 1984.

_____. *The Female Frontier: A Comparative View of Women on the Prairie and the Plains*. Lawrence: University of Kansas Press, 1988.

Roe, Frances M. A. *Army Letters from an Officer's Wife, 1871–1888*. 1909. Reprint. Lincoln: University of Nebraska Press, 1981.

Ryan, Garry D. and Timothy K. Nenninger, eds. *Soldiers and Civilians: The U.S. Army and the American People*. Washington, D.C.: National Archives and Records Administration, 1987.

Schlereth, Thomas J. *Victorian America: Transformations in Everyday Life, 1876–1915*. New York City: HarperCollins, 1991.

Schlissel, Lillian. *Women's Diaries of the Westward Journey*. New York City: Schocken Books, 1982.

Schubert, Frank N. *Outpost of the Sioux Wars: A History of Fort Robinson*. Lincoln: University of Nebraska Press, 1993.

Scobee, Barry. *Fort Davis, Texas: 1583–1960*. El Paso, TX: Hill Printing Co., 1963.

Shelton, Ferne. *Pioneer Comforts and Kitchen Remedies*. High Point, NC: Hutcraft, 1965.

Sherman, Gen. William T. "Report to the Secretary of War, October 16, 1882." Secretary of War Report, 1882. Pentagon Library, Washington, D.C.

Shields, Alice Mathews. "Army Life on the Wyoming Frontier." *Annals of Wyoming* 13, no. 4 (October 1941): 331–344.

Sibbald, John R. "Army Women of the West: Camp Followers All." *The Retired Officer* (April 1967): 10–21.

Simpson, Col. Harold B. *Cry Comanche: The 2nd U.S. Cavalry in Texas, 1855–1861*. Hillsboro, TN: Hill Junior College Press, 1979.

Smith, Jane F., and Robert M. Kvasnicka, eds. *Indian-White Relations: A Persistent Paradox*. Papers and Proceedings of the National Archives Conference on Research in the History of Indian-White Relations. Washington, D.C.: Howard University Press, 1976.

Smith, Sherry L. "Officers' Wives, Indians, and the Indian Wars." *Journal of the Order of the Indian Wars* (Winter 1980): 35–46.

_____. *The View from Officers' Row: Army Perceptions of Western Indians*. Tucson: University of Arizona Press, 1990.

Stallard, Patricia Y. *Glittering Misery: Dependents of the Indian Fighting Army*. Fort Collins, CO: The Old Army Press, 1978.

Stevenson, Louise L. *The Victorian Homefront: American Thought and Culture, 1860–1880*. New York: Twayne Publishers, 1991.

Summerhayes, Martha. *Vanished Arizona, Recollections of the Army Life of a New England Woman.* 1908. Reprint of 1911 edition. Lincoln: University of Nebraska Press, 1979.

Swanson, Mary. Collection of Letters. National Historic Site Library, Fort Davis, TX.

Tate, Maj. James P., ed. *The American Military on the Frontier: The Proceedings of the 7th Military History Symposium.* Washington, D.C.: Office of Air Force History, 1978.

Thompson, Mrs. Morris. Interview, December 11, 1982. National Historic Site Library, Fort Davis, TX.

Toll, Larry A. "The Military Community on the Western Frontier, 1866–1898." Ph.D. diss., Ball State University, Muncie, IN, 1990.

Totten, Ruth Ellen Patton. "The Army Wife Heritage." *Armor* (November–December 1973): 39–44.

Turner, Frederick Jackson. *The Frontier in American History.* 1920. Reprint. New York: Holt, Rinehart and Winston, 1962.

Unthank, Oliver Nixon. Collection of Letters to Wife, Emma Brandon Unthank, 1871–1874. Fort Laramie National Historic Site, Fort Laramie, WY.

U.S. Congress. House. *Military Posts.* 1866. 39th Cong., 2d sess. House Executive Document no. 20, vol. 6. Serial 1288.

U.S. Congress. House. Letter from Col. I.V.D. Reeve to Cong. John Coburn, March 20, 1872. 42nd Cong., 3rd sess. House Report 74.

U.S. Congress. Senate. *Statistical Report on the Sickness and Mortality in the Army of the U.S. (1839–55),* by Richard H. Coolidge, 1856. 34th Cong., 1st sess. Senate Executive Document no. 96, vol. 18. Serial 827.

U.S. Congress. Senate. *Disposition and Conduct of the Indians About Fort Phil Kearny and the Causes of the Same.* 40th Cong., 1st sess. Senate Document no. 13.

Utley, Robert M. *Frontier Regulars: The United States Army and the Indian, 1866–1891.* New York: Macmillan Publishing Co., Inc., 1973.

_____. "The Contribution of the Frontier to the American Military Tradition." Harmon Memorial Lectures in Military History, no. 19. Colorado Springs: United States Air Force Academy, 1977.

_____, ed. *Life in Custer's Cavalry: Diaries and Letters of Albert and Jennie Barnitz, 1867–1868.* Lincoln: University of Nebraska Press, 1977.

Viele, Teresa Griffin. *Following the Drum: A Glimpse of Frontier Life.* 1858. Reprint. Lincoln: University of Nebraska Press, 1984.

Weems, John Edward. *Death Song: The Last of the Indian Wars.* Garden City, NY: Doubleday and Co., 1976.

Williams, Mary L., ed. *An Army Wife's Cookbook: With Household Hints and Home Remedies.* Tucson, AZ: Southwest Parks and Monuments Association, 1972.

Index